T
BIRTHPLACE
BOOK

ALSO BY CHRIS EPTING

Led Zeppelin Crashed Here
The Ruby Slippers, Madonna's Bra, and Einstein's Brain
Elvis Presley Passed Here
Marilyn Monroe Dyed Here
James Dean Died Here
Roadside Baseball

THE BIRTHPLACE BOOK

A Guide to
Birth Sites of Famous People,
Places, and Things

Chris Epting

STACKPOLE
BOOKS

Published by
STACKPOLE BOOKS
5067 Ritter Road
Mechanicsburg, PA 17055
www.stackpolebooks.com

Printed in the United States of America

10 9 8 7 6 5 4 3 2 1

FIRST EDITION

Cover design by Tessa Sweigert

Picture credits appear on page 277. All other pictures are by the author or from the author's collection.

Library of Congress Cataloging-in-Publication Data

Epting, Chris, 1961–
    The birthplace book : a guide to birth sites of famous people, places, and things / Chris Epting. — 1st ed.
       p.   cm.
  Includes index.
  ISBN-13: 978-0-8117-3533-9 (pbk.)
  ISBN-10: 0-8117-3533-8 (pbk.)
  1. Birthplaces—United States—Guidebooks. 2. Historic sites—United States—Guidebooks. 3. United States—Biography—Miscellanea. 4. United States—Social life and customs—Miscellanea. 5. United States—History, Local. I. Title.
CT215.E65 2009
917.304'929—dc22

                                              2009010127

Contents

Introduction

Where were you born? Have you ever been back to visit the site? I, along with my twin sister, Margaret, was born December 22, 1961, at New York Hospital in New York City. Whenever I go back and visit New York today, and I see the hospital from East River Drive, I look up near the window where we were born (my mom once pointed out the location). I'm not sure why, though it probably ties in with my interest in the past. There is a simple, whimsical feeling that I think many of us feel—"That's where I started. That's where I entered the world." Same thing goes for where our children were born in Santa Monica, California. Though part of the delivery wing was razed after the 1994 Northridge earthquake, it's still sacred ground for me and my wife, whether the building is there or not.

I have been interested in birthplaces since I can remember. For me, there's something compelling about "places of origin." When a future president of the United States is born, nobody has a clue that the infant will someday be the leader of the free world, and that goes for the many other babies who go on to change the planet. A visit to the birthplaces of people such as Mark Twain, Amelia Earhart, John Wayne, and Lucille Ball may help us see more of their lives, particularly when the home has been preserved or perhaps even turned into a museum.

Unfortunately, some birthplaces are now gone, perhaps marked only by a plaque. Society sometimes is a little too anxious to bulldoze historic structures to make room for the next mini-mall or parking lot.

But there are also birthplaces of ideas, works of art, businesses, social movements, and religions. In many cases, these places of origin can all be traced to a location, even a specific address where they began. When two tech-savvy California teens started tinkering around in a garage back in the 1970s, who knew that their project would be the first Apple computer? And back in the 1940s, two brothers, Maurice and Richard McDonald, had no idea that their little barbecue restaurant in San Bernardino, California, would become the largest fast food chain in the world.

Blue jeans, plutonium, Sinatra, Slinkys, kazoos, the blues, Oprah, the Cobb salad, feminism, Google, Superman, e-mail, rock and roll, baseball, and hundreds of other notable people and things all have birthplaces. I've tried to include as many as possible, ranging from the sublime to the serious to the ridiculous. I think the latter can help make the journey more fun, so I wasn't afraid to include things that might seem trivial, such as the birthplace of the Fried Twinkie.

Whether you visit these places in person, or simply use the book as a guide to learn about notable birthplaces, my hope is that you come away with an appreciation of how seemingly insignificant places take on a special meaning when something is realized there—the cabin in the woods where "Home on the Range" was written, the hotel in upstate New York where potato chips were first created, or the unassuming Chicago home where Walt Disney was born. These sites, along with many other birthplaces, have been brushed by history. Those brushes with destiny inspired me to complete this collection, which I hope you enjoy.

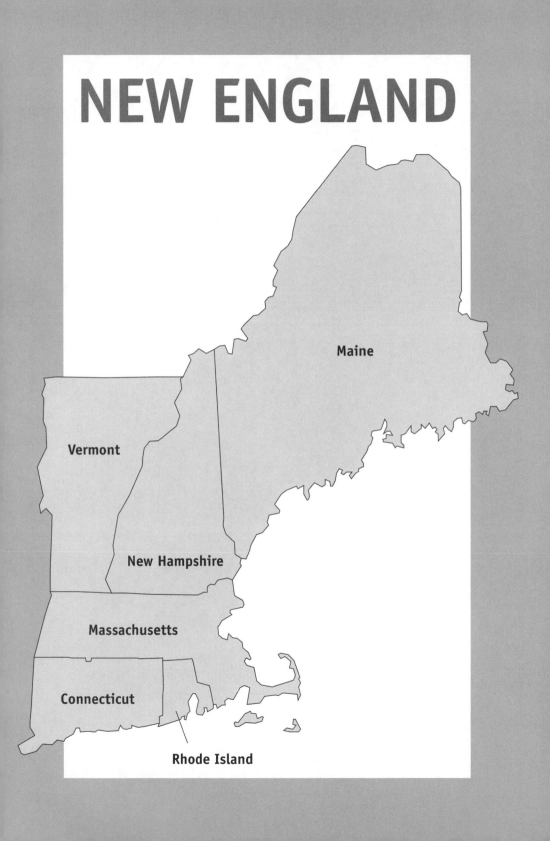

NEW ENGLAND

Maine

Vermont

New Hampshire

Massachusetts

Connecticut

Rhode Island

Connecticut

William Beaumont

1785–1853
Beaumont Homestead
16 West Town Street
Lebanon
(860) 642-6579

William Beaumont, the "Father of Gastric Physiology" and one of the most respected figures in the history of American medicine, was born here in 1785. He became one of the first doctors to explain the digestive system with his ground-breaking 1833 book *Experiments and Observations on the Gastric Juice and the Physiology of Digestion*, a classic medical study still used today. The book details his work with Alexis St. Martin, a Canadian trapper who suffered a gunshot wound that caused a permanent hole in his stomach. Through this hole, Dr. Beaumont observed the chemical process of digestion.

Beaumont's birthplace, operated by the Lebanon Historical Society, is a tribute to early nineteenth century medicine. Visitors can see period medical instruments and a re-creation of a doctor's exam room. The small farmhouse was built by Dr. Beaumont's father, Samuel. William lived here until age twenty-one, when he moved to New York to be a schoolteacher; the house was sold in 1850. In 1973, the Beaumont Homestead Preservation Trust purchased and restored the birthplace and boyhood home of Dr. Beaumont. It is open to the public from the third Saturday in May through Columbus Day weekend.

PRESIDENTIAL BIRTHPLACE
George W. Bush

43RD

1947–
Yale–New Haven Hospital (formerly
 Grace–New Haven Community Hospital)
20 York St.
New Haven

George Walker Bush, the forty-third president of the United States, was born July 6, 1946, in Grace–New Haven Community Hospital in New Haven (today known as Yale–New Haven Hospital). He was the first child of Barbara and George H. W. Bush, who was attending Yale University after returning home from World War II. George W. Bush, or "W," is only the second president to be the son of a former president (see also John Adams and John Quincy Adams, page 9).

George W. Bush grew up in Midland and Houston, Texas. He graduated from Yale University and earned an MBA from Harvard. Bush worked in the energy business, was partial owner of the Texas Rangers baseball team, and became governor of Texas in 1994.

In 2000, Bush was elected president. Less than nine months after his inauguration, the nation was faced with the terrorist attacks of September 11, 2001. This ushered in one of the most turbulent eras in American history, during which Bush would oversee controversial wars in Iraq and Afghanistan.

Business Computer

1947
33 Highland Avenue
Rowayton
(203) 838-5038

The world's first business computer was born here in 1947 in a building, formerly known as "The Barn," which now houses the Rowayton Public Library and Community Center. The computer, designed by a team of engineers from Remington Rand, was officially introduced in 1949. It was known as the Remington Rand 409 plugboard programmed punch card calculator. First sold in 1951, it came in two models, the UNIVAC 60 and the UNIVAC 120. The model number referred to the number of memory storage locations provided for data.

Hamburger

1900
Louis' Lunch
261–263 Crown Street
New Haven
www.louislunch.com

America's most famous culinary creation was born in typical American fashion—in a hurry—more than one hundred years ago in this small New Haven luncheonette. One day in 1900, a man dashed in and asked for a quick meal that he could eat on the run. Louis Lassen, the owner, quickly sandwiched a broiled beef patty between two slices of bread and sent the customer on his way with America's first hamburger. Today, Louis' grandson, Ken, carries on the family tradition, specializing in hamburgers that have changed little from their historic prototype. Using beef that's ground fresh daily, each hamburger is broiled vertically in the original cast iron grill and served between two slices of toast. Cheese, tomato, and onion are the only acceptable garnish—no true hamburger connoisseur would corrupt the classic taste with mustard, ketchup, or "secret sauce."

Pepperidge Farm

1937
Sturges Highway at Ridge Common
Fairfield

Margaret Rudkin was a Connecticut housewife and mother of three young children. In the early 1930s, she discovered that one of her sons was allergic to the preservatives and artificial ingredients found in commercial breads. So, in 1937, she started baking her own preservative-free bread for her ailing son. Eventually she developed a mouthwatering whole-wheat loaf that contained only natural ingredients. Encouraged by her family, Rudkin began selling her delicious, freshly baked bread at Mercurio's Market in Fairfield (located at 1508 Post Road). The bread caught on with locals, and as Rudkin's business grew, she felt compelled to give her bread business a name. She dubbed it Pepperidge Farm in honor of the farm on which she lived; the farm itself was named for the pepperidge tree located in the front yard. Today, you can still get a glimpse of the original Pepperidge Farm, exactly as it appears on the product packages. Much of the original property has been sold and subdivided. However, the iconic, vine-covered stone farmhouse is still there, along with the inspirational pepperidge tree.

Subway

1965
Jewett Avenue
Bridgeport

How did a teenager trying to earn money for college accidentally start a fast-food empire? It happened in 1965 in Bridgeport. Seventeen-year-old Fred DeLuca's pet project, an attempt to earn money for college tuition, would eventually grow into Subway Restaurants, the world's second largest fast-food franchise. Fred opened a sub shop called "Pete's Super Submarines" with a $1,000 loan from family friend Dr. Peter Buck. In the early days, Fred personally purchased and delivered all the produce used by the restaurant. He even removed the seats from his Volkswagen Beetle to load it up with crates of fresh vegetables, making the drive from the famous Hunts Point Market in the Bronx to his shop in Connecticut. He eventually traded in the Beetle for a Volkswagen van once the business started to expand. In 1968, DeLuca opened his fifth sandwich shop and used the name "Subway" for the first time. Today, there are more than 28,000 locations in eighty-six countries. The oldest continuously operating Subway location is at 1 River Street in Milford, Connecticut.

Maine

Paul Bunyan

Circa 1834
Paul Bunyan Statue and Birthplace
Bangor Region Chamber of Commerce
519 Main Street
Bangor
(207) 947-0307

The tall tales of Paul Bunyan are outrageous and plentiful; it's not surprising that varied tales of his origin flourish as well. Dozens of cities claim to be the birthplace of this mythical lumberjack, but two stand above the rest: Bangor, Maine, and Oscoda, Michigan (see page 172). According to Bunyan's symbolic birth certificate, he was born in Bangor, Maine, on February 13, 1834. The city's gigantic 31-foot statue, "Reputed to be the largest statue of Paul Bunyan in the world," according to the sign, stands in front of the Bangor Civic Center. The statue, made of fiberglass, was donated to the city in 1959. Author and Maine native Stephen King brought the statue to life in his 1986 novel *IT*.

Henry Wadsworth Longfellow

1807–82
Wadsworth–Longfellow House
489 Congress Street
Portland
(207) 774-1822
www.mainehistory.org/house_overview.shtml

Henry Wadsworth Longfellow was one of nineteenth-century America's premier literary figures. He penned a number of well-known poems, including *Evangeline*, *The Song of Hiawatha*, and *Paul Revere's Ride*. Henry was born on February 27, 1807, to Stephen and Zilpah Longfellow. At the time, the Longfellows were staying with Stephen's sister. A few months later, they moved into the house on Congress Street that would become Longfellow's childhood home. Four generations of the family would inhabit the dwelling, built in 1785 by the poet's grandfather, General Peleg Wadsworth. The last family member to live there was Anne Longfellow Pierce, Henry's younger sister, who lived in the house until her death in 1901. Her 1895 deed provided that the house would go to the Maine Historical Society to be preserved as a memorial to her famous brother and their family. Most of the furnishings are original, reflecting changes in style and technology over the eighteenth and nineteenth centuries. The Wadsworth–Longfellow House is also an important architectural example—it was the first entirely brick dwelling in Portland, and is now the oldest standing structure on the Portland peninsula. In 2002, the Maine Historical Society celebrated the centennial of the Wadsworth–Longfellow House as Maine's first house museum. It is open to the public from May to October.

Massachusetts

PRESIDENTIAL BIRTHPLACE

John Adams

1735–1826

John Quincy Adams

2ND

6TH

1767–1848

Adams National Historical Park
135 Adams Street
Quincy
(617) 770-1175
www.nps.gov/adam

George H. W. Bush and George W. Bush were not the first father and son to be elected president—that honor goes to John Adams and John Quincy Adams, the second and sixth presidents of the United States, respectively. Their homes at the Adams National Historical Park are the country's oldest presidential birthplaces.

In 1735, John Adams was born in the "salt box" house (above), just 75 feet away from the eventual birthplace of his son John Quincy Adams, who was born in 1767. In the home that would become known as the John Quincy Adams Birthplace, John and his wife Abigail started their family and Adams launched his career in politics and law. It was here that he, Samuel Adams, and James

John Adams   John Quincy Adams

Bowdoin wrote the Massachusetts Constitution, a document that greatly influenced the development of the United States Constitution. From 1720 to 1927, four generations of the Adams family lived at this site, which features the "Old House," (also known as Peacefield) and the Stone Library, which contains more than 14,000 historic volumes. The grounds also include a historic orchard and an eighteenth-century formal garden.

Susan B. Anthony

1820–1906
67 East Road
Adams
(585) 442-8497

Susan B. Anthony, history's most famous champion of women's rights, was born here on February 15, 1820. Anthony, whose image appeared on a U.S. dollar coin in 1979, was the founder of the National Women's Suffrage League and a fierce advocate of temperance and traditional values, likely gleaned from her family's long tradition in the Quaker Society of Friends. Her home was built in

1818, and to this day stands as an important symbol of the women's suffrage movement in the United States. Anthony lived in this rural, Federal-style home until the age of seven. Although Anthony worked tirelessly to ensure equal rights for women, she did not live to see women gain the vote. She died in 1906, thirteen years before the passage of the Nineteenth Amendment.

Over the years, several owners have failed in their attempts to turn her birthplace into a museum. In 2006, the 1,566-square-foot home was purchased by Carol Crossed, who has said the "use for the house will reflect the values and history of Susan B. Anthony." Today, a plaque at the home honors the memory of Anthony and there are still hopes of establishing a museum at the birthplace.

Basketball

1891
782 State Street
Springfield

Dr. James Naismith invented basketball on a cold autumn day in 1891. He was the physical education instructor at the International YMCA Training School (now Springfield College) in Springfield. Baseball had just finished up, and football was still a few weeks away. The athletes needed a sport to keep them in superb condition, and since it was too cold to train outside, Naismith had to think up a new indoor activity. He remembered a game he played as a child called "Duck on a Rock." Changing a few rules around, he came out with the sport "basketball." It was played with two peach baskets and a soccer ball, and twelve of the thirteen rules Naismith created are still used in the game. Today, a McDonald's near the Springfield College campus occupies the exact site of the "Naismith Gym." Inside are photos and some information describing the location's history.

Visit the nearby Naismith Memorial Basketball Hall of Fame at 1000 West Columbus Avenue. For information, call the Hall of Fame at (413) 781-6500 or visit their Web site, www.hoophall.com.

PRESIDENTIAL BIRTHPLACE

George H. W. Bush

41ST

1924–
173 Adams Street
Milton

George Herbert Walker Bush, the forty-first president of the United States, was born in this private home on June 12, 1924. Adams Street is named for the family of Presidents John Adams and John Quincy Adams, who once lived on the same street just a couple of miles down the road in Quincy.

George H. W.'s parents were Prescott Sheldon Bush and Dorothy Walker Bush. Prescott was an executive at U.S. Rubber and later a Wall Street investment banker and U.S. senator from Connecticut. George was named after his maternal grandfather, George Herbert Walker, who established golf's Walker Cup trophy.

Bush earned a Distinguished Flying Cross for his actions as a Navy pilot in World War II. He later served as a U.S. representative, director of the CIA, and as vice president under Ronald Reagan. As president, Bush enjoyed a surge in popularity during the liberation of Kuwait in the 1991 Persian Gulf War. However, an economic downturn helped lead to his defeat in the 1992 presidential election.

Emily Dickinson

1830–86
The Homestead
280 Main Street
Amherst
(413) 542-8161
www.emilydickinsonmuseum.org

Poet Emily Dickinson was born in 1830 in this brick home built by her grandparents in 1813. Although she and her family moved to another house in 1840, they returned to the Main Street residence in 1855, and the poet lived there until her death in 1886. It was after moving back here to the Homestead that Emily Dickinson began to write poetry in earnest. During her most productive years, 1858 to 1865, she compiled her poems into small packets now termed "fascicles." Only ten of her poems are known to have been published in her lifetime, all anonymously and presumably without her permission. The Dickinson Homestead is a National Historic Landmark owned by the trustees of Amherst College and is dedicated to educating the public about the life and work of one of America's greatest poets. The Homestead—as well as Dickinson's brother's home next door, the Evergreens—is open to the public.

Dunkin' Donuts

1946
534 Southern Artery
Quincy

Dunkin' Donuts, originally named the Open Kettle by founder William Rosenberg, first made a splash in 1946. Rosenberg had previously founded Industrial Luncheon Services, a company that delivered meals and coffee break snacks to customers on the outskirts of Boston. The success of this venture led Rosenberg to open his first coffee and donut shop, called the Open Kettle. In 1950, Rosenberg opted for a catchier name when he changed to Dunkin' Donuts. Today, with almost 8,000 Dunkin' Donut shops worldwide, the company is the largest chain of coffee, donut, and bagel shops. The original Dunkin' Donuts still operates at this site.

E-Mail

1971
BBN Technologies
10 Moulton Street
Cambridge

No, the first-ever e-mail was not a bad joke, a top ten list, or an advertisement for a hair-loss remedy. It is generally believed that Ray Tomlinson, a scientist at Boston-based Bolt, Beranek and Newman (BBN) Technologies, sent the first network e-mail in 1971. At the time, the company was helping to develop Arpanet, the forerunner of the modern Internet. Tomlinson sent a message between two machines sitting side-by-side in his lab in Cambridge, and then kept sending messages back and forth from one machine to the other until he was comfortable with the process. The first e-mail message he sent outside of the lab was to the rest of his work team; it announced the existence of network e-mail and explained how to use it, including the use of the @ sign to separate the user's name from the host computer name.

Benjamin Franklin

1706–90
17 Milk Street
Boston

Benjamin Franklin, one of the most important men in American history, was born here on January 17, 1706 to the family of a candlemaker. One of the Founding Fathers of our country, Franklin was also an inventor, diplomat, writer, scientist, humorist, businessman, musician, civic leader, and international celebrity. George Washington dubbed Benjamin Franklin the "father of our country," Thomas Jefferson described him as a "harmonious human multitude," and the philosopher Immanuel Kant dubbed him "a modern Prometheus" after the ancient Titan in Greek mythology who stole fire from the heavens and gave it to mankind. Franklin lived here until he was seventeen, when he left his family to find fame and fortune in Philadelphia. A bust of Franklin stands at the site, which is now occupied by an office building.

John Hancock

1737–93
Quincy Historical Society
8 Adams Street
Quincy
(617) 773-1144
www.quincyhistory.org

Legendary patriot John Hancock was born at this location in Quincy on January 12, 1737. Hancock, the first signer of the Declaration of Independence, penned a large, flamboyant signature on the document in a defiant gesture against a bounty the British had put on the heads of revolutionaries. "The British ministry can read that name without spectacles," Hancock remarked. "Let them double their reward." Hancock also led the rebellious colonies through the American Revolution as president of the Continental Congress.

The colonial house of Hancock's birth burned down in 1760. In 1872, an endowment from John Adams funded construction of the Adams Academy on the site, which operated as a preparatory school for boys until 1908. The building features a Gothic Revival style and a distinctive use of Quincy granite. In the early 1970s, the academy became the home of the Quincy Historical Society, and in 1994 was designated a National Historic Landmark, for both its connection to the legendary patriots and for its architectural significance. Today, visitors can tour the museum and enjoy a comprehensive look at the city's history from Native American times to the present day.

Nathaniel Hawthorne

1804–64
Nathaniel Hawthorne House
54 Turner Street
Salem
(978) 744-0991

The home where Nathaniel Hawthorne was born was moved and now sits adjacent to the foreboding mansion made famous in Hawthorne's 1851 novel, *The House of the Seven Gables*. Built in 1668, the House of the Seven Gables (below) is the oldest surviving wooden mansion in New England. On the grounds, visitors will also find the 1682 Hathaway House, the 1658 Reitre Beckett House, the Counting House, seaside period gardens, and a panorama of Salem Harbor. The guided tour

includes an introductory audio-visual program; six rooms and a secret staircase in the Gables; and six rooms in Hawthorne's birthplace.

Hawthorne actually wrote *The House of the Seven Gables* in a small clapboard cottage in 1850–51 on the Tappan estate, now home to the Tanglewood summer music festival in Lenox, Massachusetts. The cottage at Tanglewood is a replica of the original that burned down in 1890. Not open to the public, it contains practice rooms for Tanglewood's student musicians.

PRESIDENTIAL BIRTHPLACE
John F. Kennedy

1917–63
John F. Kennedy National Historic Site
83 Beals Street
Brookline
(617) 566-7937
www.nps.gov/jofi

35TH

This national historic site preserves the 1917 birthplace and boyhood home of John F. Kennedy, the thirty-fifth president of the United States. The modest frame house in suburban Boston was also the first home shared by the president's father and mother, Joseph P. and Rose Fitzgerald Kennedy, and represents the social and political beginnings of one of the world's most prominent families.

Kennedy served in the Navy in World War II; he was then elected to Congress and the Senate in the years following the war. He also won a Pulitzer Prize for his 1955 book *Profiles in Courage*. When he was elected president in 1960, he became the first Catholic and the youngest man to occupy the office. Kennedy was assassinated in Dallas, Texas, on November 22, 1963.

Shortly after President Kennedy's death, his family repurchased the birthplace and restored it as a memorial to him under the close supervision of Rose Kennedy. The John F. Kennedy National Historic Site was established in 1969 after the family donated the home to the National Park Service.

Jack Kerouac

1922–69
9 Lupine Road
Lowell

Jack Kerouac, born Jean-Louis Kerouac, was born and raised in Lowell. While visitors can't tour the private home where he was born on March 12, 1922, it is commemorated by a plaque placed on the house by the Lowell Historical Board. The famed author studied briefly at Columbia University in New York (1940–41), where he met Allen Ginsberg and William S. Burroughs. Together they challenged the status quo in the literary world, writing candidly about their personal lives, which were dominated by booze and wild living. Kerouac coined the phrase "Beat Generation" to represent a general feeling among young intellectuals that the American dream had gone sour somewhere along the line. He is most famous for his 1957 novel *On The Road*. Among his other notable works are *The Dharma Bums* and *Desolation Angels*. Kerouac died in St. Petersburg, Florida, in 1969.

Connie Mack

1862–1956
105 Cottage Street
East Brookfield

Cornelius Alexander McGillicuddy, better known as Connie Mack, was born on December 22, 1862, at this home in East Brookfield. Mack's Philadelphia Athletics teams won five World Series titles during his more than fifty years as manager, and the "Tall Tactician" left a huge mark in the town that he still came to visit after becoming a legend. His boyhood home is marked with a plaque, but it is now a private residence. Each year the town holds a Memorial Day parade along Connie Mack Drive, and Fourth of July celebrations end with fireworks at Connie Mack Field. Signs welcoming visitors herald the town as the birthplace of Connie Mack.

"Mary Had a Little Lamb"

Circa 1830
72 Wayside Inn Road
Sudbury

The Redstone School was used to teach the children of District Number Two, on Redstone Hill in Sterling, from 1798 to 1856. The building was moved here to Sudbury, where it sits today near Longfellow's Wayside Inn. It was used as a public school for grades one through four from 1927 to 1951. It is now a small museum and is used to demonstrate early American rural schooling traditions. But it holds an even more important place in American history. This is the building where Mary Tyler (1806–89) went to school followed by her little lamb. The famous verse is said to have been written by John Roulstone, though some accounts attribute the poem to Sarah Josepha Hale.

Edgar Allen Poe

1809–49
176 Boylston Street
Boston

"Nevermore" may be when the world will agree on the location of Edgar Allan Poe's birthplace, which remains as mysterious as some of his darkly engaging stories. Many Poe scholars believe he was born on a long-gone section of Carver Street, near the intersection of Boylston Street and Charles Street. A plaque on the side of 176 Boylston Street claims that location as his birthplace. We do know that the author of "The Raven," "The Tell-Tale Heart," and "The Pit and the Pendulum" was definitely born in Boston on January 19, 1809 to David and Elizabeth (Eliza) Poe, actors at the Boston Theatre.

Poe attended schools in England and Richmond, Virginia, before enrolling in the University of Virginia in 1826. Poe had no money to continue at the university, and so moved back to Boston. There he published his first book, *Tamerlane and Other Poems*, in 1827. After serving in the army for several years, Poe worked at a number of literary journals in Baltimore, Philadelphia, and New York, gaining a reputation for his unique style of literary criticism. Poe died in Baltimore on October 7, 1849.

Public School

1635
Tremont and School Streets
Boston

In 1635, the town of Boston established the first public school in America. Originally operating in the home of schoolmaster Philemon Pormont, it was later moved to this location on School Street. The exact location of the first public school is marked by a mosaic inlaid in the sidewalk.

Famous alumni of the school included Samuel Adams, John Hancock, and Benjamin Franklin, whose statue overlooks the site along the famous Freedom Trail. The school would later become Boston Latin School, which is still in operation in the Fenway section of Boston.

Radio

1901
Marconi Beach, Cape Cod National Seashore
Wellfleet
(508) 349-3785
www.nps.gov/caco/planyourvisit/marconi-beach.htm

In 1901, the "Father of Radio," Guglielmo Marconi, erected the first American wireless radio station on this Cape Cod beach near Wellfleet. On January 18, 1903, he transmitted a message from President Theodore Roosevelt to King Edward VII of England. The station was dismantled and the towers taken down in 1920, but in 1953 the Wellfleet Historical Society placed a bronze plaque near the original site commemorating the station. In 1974, an exhibit shelter was built to house a scale model of the wireless station and a bronze bust of Marconi, along with the earlier commemorative plaque. It's located on Main Street in the small town of Wellfleet.

The access road from South Wellfleet and U.S. 6 is clearly marked. The station site is open daily, dawn to dusk, and the historical museum is open Tuesday through Saturday. Hours vary.

Lysander Spooner

1808–87
59 Petersham Road
Athol

One of our country's first true radicals, Lysander Spooner, was born in rural Athol on his father's farm on January 19, 1808. He was the second child in a family of six sons and three daughters born to Asa and Dolly Spooner. The nineteenth-century lawyer, abolitionist, individualist, anarchist, and political radical is best known for works such as *The Unconstitutionality of Slavery* (1845), *An Essay on the Trial by Jury* (1852) and *No Treason: Constitution of No Authority* (1870), considered the most thorough and widely quoted expression of his radical views. Spooner is also known for attempting to compete with the U.S. Post Office with his American Letter Mail Company. A plaque is located near his birthplace (now a private residence) in Athol, noting that he wrote *The Unconstitutionality of Slavery* and other works in the house. Spooner died in Boston on May 11, 1887, and is buried in Forest Hills Cemetery in Jamaica Plain, Massachusetts. His monument is inscribed "Champion of Liberty."

Telephone Call

1876
Verizon Building
Post Office Square
185 Franklin Street
Boston

While trying to perfect a method for carrying multiple telegraph messages on a single wire, Alexander Graham Bell first heard the sound of a plucked spring along sixty feet of wire in a Boston electrical shop. Thomas A. Watson, one of Bell's assistants, was trying to reactivate a telegraph transmitter. Hearing the sound, Bell thought he could solve the problem of sending a human voice over a wire. He first figured out how to transmit a simple current, and he received a patent for that invention on March 7, 1876. Three days later, he transmitted actual speech. Sitting in one room, he spoke into the telephone to his assistant in another room, saying the now famous words: "Mr. Watson, come here. I need you."

The room where Alexander Graham Bell invented the telephone has been installed just off the lobby of the Verizon Building. Originally in a building at 109 Court Street, the attic was disassembled when its building was torn down in 1959.

Henry David Thoreau

1817–62
Thoreau Farm
341 Virginia Road
Concord
(978) 369-3091
www.thoreaufarm.org

The man whom many consider the father of environmentalism, Henry David Thoreau, was born July 12, 1817, in this farmhouse in rural Massachusetts. The American author, philosopher, and naturalist, who was part of the Transcendentalist movement, is best known for his two-year retreat to Walden Pond, detailed in his 1854 book, *Walden, or Life in the Woods*. He is also revered for his essay "Civil Disobedience" (a philosophy later advocated by Gandhi and Martin Luther King, Jr.), which he wrote after spending a night in jail for not paying a poll tax.

The Thoreau Farm Trust is dedicated to the restoration and reuse of the farmhouse where Thoreau was born. The "Thoreau Farm," as it is known locally, was referred to by Thoreau as the Minot House. It is listed on the National Register of Historic Places as the "Wheeler-Minot Farmhouse/Henry David Thoreau Birth House." It was built in 1730 by John Wheeler, who developed the land into a prosperous farm.

Shortly after Thoreau's death, the house took on increased significance as the place of his birth and became a destination for Thoreau disciples, tourists, scholars, and others on literary or historical pilgrimages.

Toll House Cookies

1930s
The Toll House Inn
Corner of Routes 18 and 14
Whitman

Chances are you've eaten Toll House cookies. But have you ever wondered where the name originated? The original Toll House was built in 1709 on the old Boston–New Bedford Road, now Route 18. Back then, travelers paid tolls at the house for the use of the road, but could also enjoy food and shelter while their horses were changed.

In 1930, Kenneth and Ruth Graves Wakefield purchased the property and opened the Toll House Inn. Ruth, a 1924 graduate of the Framingham State Normal School Department of Household Arts, was renowned across New England for the scrumptious desserts she created in the inn's kitchen. One day, Ruth wanted to make chocolate cookies but was out of baker's chocolate. So, she broke up a bar of Nestle's semisweet chocolate and added the pieces to the dough. Instead of melting into the dough like she expected, the morsels remained lumps of creamy, melted chocolate—and the Toll House cookie (also known as the chocolate chip cookie) was born. Ruth licensed the recipe to Nestlé, and in 1939 they began marketing Toll House Morsels, inspired by her cookie recipe.

The Toll House grew into a major restaurant, but the Wakefields sold it in 1966. It was turned into a nightclub, then back into a restaurant, and eventually the building burned down on New Year's Eve, 1984. Today, a Wendy's restaurant sits on the original site, but the classic sign from the old inn still stands nearby.

Volleyball

1895
Corner of High and Appleton
Holyoke

It's hard to believe that volleyball started out as game for middle-aged businessmen. It was invented here in Holyoke in 1895 by William G. Morgan, an instructor at the Young Men's Christian Association (YMCA). Morgan graduated from nearby Springfield College, where he met James Naismith, who had invented basketball a few years earlier in 1891.

Morgan became director of Physical Education at the YMCA in Holyoke. Influenced by his friend's invention of basketball, Morgan decided to create a game for his classes of businessmen, one which would demand less physical contact—and less running—than basketball. So, he blended the elements of basketball, baseball, tennis, and handball to create the game of volleyball, which he originally named mintonette. Morgan borrowed the idea of a net from tennis, but raised it six feet six inches above the floor, just above the average man's head. The original YMCA where the game was created burned down in the 1940s, and today a marker commemorates the game's creation (a Dollar Store sits on the actual site). The nearby Volleyball Hall of Fame is located at 444 Dwight Street. For more information, call (413) 536-0926 or visit their Web site at www.volleyhall.org.

New Hampshire

Samuel Portland Chase

1808–73
1001 Route 12A
Cornish

Samuel P. Chase, secretary of the treasury under Abraham Lincoln, and the sixth chief justice of the United States, was born here on January 13, 1808. Chase graduated from Dartmouth College in 1826, and was admitted to the bar in 1829. Chase is noted for having defended runaway blacks so often that he became known as the "attorney general for fugitive slaves." Chase also coined the slogan of the Free Soil Party: "Free Soil, Free Labor, Free Men." He devoted his enormous energies to the destruction of what he considered the abuses of slave power and the conspiracy of Southern slave owners to seize control of the federal government and block the progress of emancipation. Later in his life, Chase presided over the impeachment trial of President Andrew Johnson.

Declared a National Historic Landmark in 1975, the birthplace and childhood home of Samuel Chase today looks much the way it did when Chase lived there. A historical marker is also located at the site. The home is currently operated as a bed and breakfast.

PRESIDENTIAL BIRTHPLACE
Franklin Pierce

14TH

1804–69
The Franklin Pierce Homestead
Routes 31 and 9
Hillsboro
(603) 478-3165
http://franklinpierce.ws/homestead

Franklin Pierce, the fourteenth president of the United States, was born on November 23, 1804, to Benjamin and Anna Kendrick Pierce. Pierce graduated from Bowdoin College in Maine and entered into a life of public service. Pierce served in the U.S. House and Senate before he joined the Army. He rose from private to brigadier general during the Mexican War in 1846. In 1852, he became the youngest president ever elected. Pierce's tenure, however, was less than glorious. Just before taking office, he and his wife saw their eleven-year-old son killed when their train wrecked. Pierce entered the presidency grief-stricken and exhausted, which may have contributed to some poor decisions on the slavery issue and a lifelong bout with drinking.

Pierce's birthplace home was built in 1804 by his father, Benjamin Pierce. The home features large spacious rooms, hand-stenciled walls, and imported wallpaper. The gardens surrounding the homestead feature an artificial pond and a summer house—unusual luxuries for their day. Today, the Franklin Pierce Homestead is maintained and operated by the Hillsboro Historical Society, and is open to the public for a nominal fee.

Seventh Day Adventist Church

1842
153 King Street
Washington

In April 1842, a group of citizens in this town banded together to form "the first Christian Society." The Adventist movement of 1842–43 encouraged the observance of the original Judeo-Christian Sabbath, which fell on Saturday. In January 1844, these Washington, New Hampshire, Sabbath keepers, after meeting for many years as a loosely knit group, organized the first Seventh Day Adventist Church on this site. A New Hampshire historical marker is located on Route 31, several miles from the church.

Daniel Webster

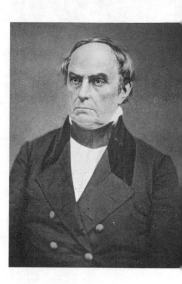

1782–1852
Daniel Webster Birthplace
Off Route 127
Franklin
(603) 934-5057
www.nhstateparks.com/danielwebster.html

The Daniel Webster Birthplace is the site of the birth and early childhood years of Daniel Webster, one of our country's most respected orators and statesmen. The home, built by his parents Ebenezer and Abigail Webster between 1779–82, replaced a log cabin on the site. The historic homestead also provides a glimpse of eighteenth-century farm life in the United States. Webster served as a U.S. congressman for New Hampshire and Massachusetts, and secretary of state under presidents William Henry Harrison, John Tyler, and Millard Fillmore. In all, Webster spent forty years in public service, helping to mold the loose collection of states into a single unified nation. One theme in particular stands out from his many impassioned speeches: "The Union, one and inseparable, now and forever."

The home, now operated by the New Hampshire Historical Society, is open to the public. From Tilton, exit 20 of Interstate 93, follow Route 3 south (west) through Franklin to Route 127. Take Route 127 south and follow the signs to the Daniel Webster Birthplace.

Rhode Island

George M. Cohan

1878–1942
90 Ives Street
Providence

George M. Cohan, world-famous composer of such standards as "Over There," "You're a Grand Old Flag," "I'm a Yankee Doodle Dandy," and "Give My Regards to Broadway," was born at this site on July 3, 1878. The multitalented Cohan was also a theatrical director, singer, actor, and playwright (*Seven Keys to Baldpate, The Song and Dance Man*). He is considered the father of American musical comedy. A plaque marks the spot where his birthplace once stood. The Fox Point Boys and Girls Club now occupies the site.

Extreme Sports

1995
Fort Adams State Park
Newport

Extreme sports did a triple back flip onto the American scene in 1995, when ESPN staged the first X-Games at Fort Adams State Park in Newport. The event was created to be the largest-ever gathering of extreme athletes and the biggest production event in ESPN history. The network used 115 cameras to capture groundbreaking (and bone-breaking) angles, including dirt jump cams, cameras positioned on top of the climbing wall and the half pipe, and even point-of-view cameras mounted on helmets, skateboard wheels, and street luge sleds. This is considered by most to be the pivotal moment in the launching of extreme sports as a national phenomenon.

Industrial Revolution

1793
Slater Mill
67 Roosevelt Avenue
Pawtucket
(401) 725-8638
www.slatermill.org

America's Industrial Revolution had its origins here at the old Slater Mill. Built in 1793, the mill was the first factory in America to success-fully produce cotton yarn with water-powered machines. Many consider it to be the "Birthplace of American Industry." Today, Slater Mill houses operating machinery used to illustrate the process of converting raw cotton to finished cloth. It is also a living history museum where you can immerse yourself in the lives of the New England villagers, inventors, artisans, and entrepreneurs who forged the American Industrial Revolution. In the authentic eighteenth- and nineteenth-century buildings, costumed interpreters demonstrate what life was like as America began moving from the farm to the factory back in the 1830s.

Rhode Island Red Chicken

1854
Main Street (by the baseball field)
Adamsville (part of Little Compton)

The beloved Rhode Island Red chicken, the official state bird of Rhode Island, was first bred here in 1854 by John Macomber and Captain William Tripp of Lit-tle Compton. The duo often experimented with poultry and developed the strik-ingly handsome breed by combining Malaysian, Javanese, and Chinese stock. The red fowls were bred extensively by farmers in this district for the produc-tion of eggs, but were brought into national prominence by poultry fanciers. First advertised in poultry journals in 1896, their extraordinary deep brown and red feathers earned them fan clubs in England and Scotland. In 1925, a monument was placed on a corner in Adamsville, funded by the Rhode Island Red Club of America and Rhode Island Red breeders throughout the world.

Gilbert Stuart

1755–1828
Gilbert Stuart Birthplace and Museum
815 Gilbert Stuart Road
Saunderstown
(401) 294-3001
www.gilbertstuartmuseum.com

You probably look at Gilbert Stuart's portrait of George Washington every day on the one-dollar bill. Stuart was born here in Rhode Island on December 3, 1755. His tremendous natural talent made him the most successful portrait painter of early America. Today, the Gilbert Stuart Birthplace and Museum takes visitors back in time. It features reproductions of Stuart's works in an authentically restored and furnished home. Situated on the banks of the Mattatuxet Brook, the homestead also features a partially restored 1662 gristmill and a fish ladder, periodically packed with migrating herring. Beneath the window of Gilbert's room, the stream pushes a huge wooden water wheel that once drove his father's snuff mill. For the restoration, a snuff mill used in the late 1700s was sent from England and installed in the original basement.

Vermont

PRESIDENTIAL BIRTHPLACE

Chester A. Arthur

21ST

1829–86
President Chester A. Arthur Historic Site
Route 36
Fairfield
(802) 828-3051
www.historicvermont.com/sites/html/arthur.html

Chester Alan Arthur, the twenty-first president of the United States, was born in Fairfield on October 5, 1829, the son of a Baptist preacher. This small frame house was reconstructed by the state of Vermont in 1953 on the location where the Arthur family moved shortly after his birth. The building houses an interpretive exhibit on Arthur's life and career. Nearby, and also open to the public, is the brick church where his father served as minister.

Arthur was a member of the Republican Party and worked as a lawyer before becoming the twentieth vice president under James Garfield. Charles Guiteau mortally wounded Garfield on July 2, 1881, but he did not die until September 19, at which time Arthur was sworn in as president, serving until March 4, 1885. Publisher Alexander K. McClure wrote, "No man ever entered the Presidency so profoundly and widely distrusted, and no one ever retired . . . more generally respected." Author Mark Twain, deeply cynical about politicians, conceded, "It would be hard indeed to better President Arthur's administration."

Ben & Jerry's

1978
Southwest corner of St. Paul and College Streets
Burlington

Childhood aspirations don't always come true, but in the case of Ben & Jerry's, their plans never melted away. They opened their first store here in Burlington in May of 1978. Their sweet dreams started in 1963, when Bennett Cohen and Jerry Greenfield met in their seventh grade gym class at Merrick Avenue Junior High School in New York. Later, while attending Calhoun High School in Merrick, Cohen hawked ice cream from a truck. Greenfield worked as an ice cream scooper when he was a student at Oberlin College in Ohio. Finally, in 1978, the pals embarked on their ice cream plans by opening Ben & Jerry's Homemade Ice Cream Parlor in a renovated gas station. Word spread rapidly of the unique ice cream place with the wildly creative flavors and community-minded business style. By 1985, Ben & Jerry's annual sales exceeded $9 million—and in 1998, they topped over $200 million worldwide. The company was acquired by Unilever in 2000. A plaque in the sidewalk marks the spot of the first store, which is now a vacant lot.

PRESIDENTIAL BIRTHPLACE
Calvin Coolidge

30TH

1872–1933
President Calvin Coolidge
   State Historic Site
3780 Route 100A
Plymouth
(802) 672-3773
www.historicvermont.com/coolidge

This historic district called Plymouth Notch was the birthplace, boyhood home, inaugural site, and also the Summer White House of Calvin Coolidge, the thir-

tieth president of the United States. In 1923, while vacationing at his boyhood home, Vice President Coolidge received notification from Washington, D.C., of the death of President Warren Harding. By the light of a kerosene lamp in the old family homestead on August 3, 1923, at 2:47 A.M., Coolidge was immediately sworn in as president by his father, a notary public. The rural Vermont village of Plymouth Notch remains much the same as it was at the time.

The homes of Calvin Coolidge's family, the community church, cheese factory, one-room schoolhouse, and general store have been carefully preserved, along with many of their original furnishings. Coolidge is buried in the town cemetery.

Plymouth Notch is six miles south of U.S. Route 4 on VT 100A, roughly midway across the state. The Coolidge State Forest is nearby.

Electric Motor

1834
Smalley-Davenport Shop
Forestdale

Thomas Davenport (1802–51) was an American blacksmith who invented the first direct-current (DC) electrical motor in 1834 with Orange Smalley (1812–93). The workshop where they developed the motor still stands today in Forestdale, though it is not open to the public. Their motor design involved mounting one magnet of the motor on a wheel while the other magnet was fixed to a stationary frame. The interaction between the two magnets caused the rotor to turn one-half of a revolution. They learned that by reversing the wires to one of the magnets, he could get the rotor to complete another half-turn.

Davenport subsequently devised what we now call a brush and commutator. The electricity source for the magnets was a battery that used a bucket of a weak acid for an electrolyte. Davenport patented a device for "Improvements in propelling machinery by magnetism and electromagnetism" in 1837, which led to the first electric railway. Davenport later started a workshop in New York City and published a journal on electromagnetism, which was printed on a press powered by motors that he devised.

Joseph Smith

1805–44
Joseph Smith Birthplace Memorial
357 LDS Lane
South Royalton
(802) 763-7742
www.lds.org/placestovisit/location/
 0,10634,1813-1-1-1,000.html

The Joseph Smith Birthplace Memorial is a granite obelisk on a hill in the White River Valley near Sharon and South Royalton. It marks the spot where Joseph Smith Jr. was born on December 23, 1805. The monument was erected by The

Church of Jesus Christ of Latter-day Saints (LDS Church), which recognizes Smith as its first president and founding prophet. The LDS Church continues to own and operate the site as a historic site. The memorial was dedicated by LDS church president Joseph F. Smith on the one hundredth anniversary of Joseph Smith Jr.'s birth, on December 23, 1905. The monument stands fifty feet tall. The shaft of the obelisk is 38 1/2 feet long, one for each year of Smith's life. The forty-ton obelisk was quarried in Barre, Vermont. There is a visitors center, and tours of the memorial site are available.

Brigham Young

1801–77
Tower Hill Common
Whitingham

Brigham Young, second president and prophet of The Church of Jesus Christ of Latter-day Saints, was born in Whitingham on June 1, 1801, the ninth child of John and Abigail Young. Young spent much of his childhood and early adult life in upstate New York, where he worked as a carpenter. He joined the LDS Church in 1832 and almost immediately began delivering sermons and performing missionary work. After he was revealed as a prophet, Young rapidly rose to a position of leadership in the church. He is famed for leading thousands of Mormon settlers across the country to found Salt Lake City.

In 1950, a memorial was erected to commemorate his birthplace. At the unveiling, Judge Harriet B. Chase of the U.S. Circuit Court, representing Whitingham Township, remarked, "The name Brigham Young has become accepted as a symbol of perseverance, courage to bear difficulties, and capacity to surmount them. This monument is a fitting tribute to a great American, Whitingham's famous son."

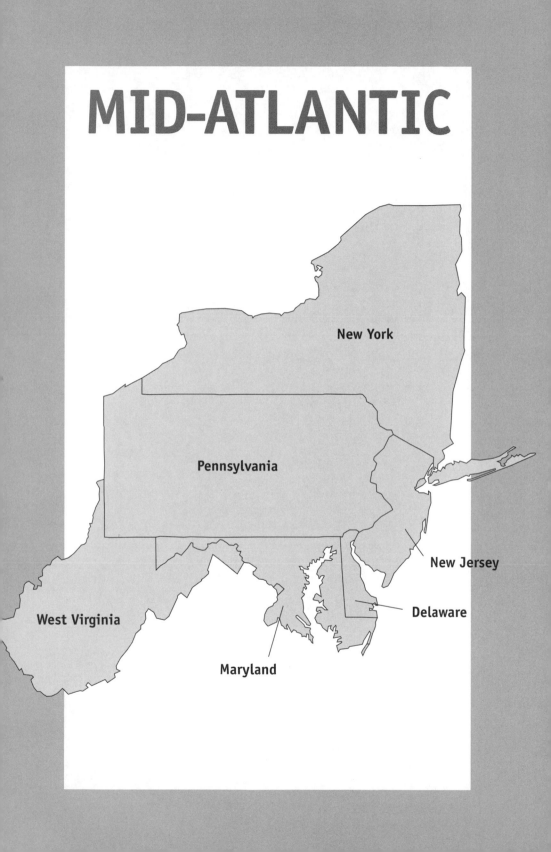

MID-ATLANTIC

New York

Pennsylvania

New Jersey

West Virginia

Delaware

Maryland

Delaware

Methodist Church of America

1784
Barratt's Chapel
6362 Bay Road
Frederica
(302) 335-5544
www.barrattschapel.org

A group of preachers met in this chapel in 1784
to organize the Methodist Church of America,
electing Francis Asbury as their first bishop. Rural Delaware seemed an apt setting to establish a new life and faith, free of the Church of England. Today, the chapel on the Delmarva Peninsula is a museum that focuses on Methodism, displaying numerous books, records, letters, and memorabilia. An 11-acre cemetery houses graves dating from 1785 to the present, including Barratt family graves. The chapel exterior remains faithful to its 1784 appearance, except for a gable window added onto the west end and the conversion of two large first-floor windows into doors. A metal star on the floor inside marks the site of a meeting between John Wesley's emissary Thomas Coke and Francis Asbury on November 14, 1784. That conference marked the official beginning of the Methodist Church in America.

Nylon

1935
400 Woodland Road
Seaford

Today, this building is known as the Invista Seaford Plant—but back in the 1930s it was the plant where DuPont Laboratories first mass-produced nylon. The synthetic material was discovered in 1935 at DuPont's Wilmington lab by a team led by chemist Wallace Carothers (the same team also developed neoprene in 1930). Following the discovery, the company went quickly to work in getting the new product to the consumer market. The Seaford plant was built in seven months and went into production on December 12, 1939. The six-story plant ran twenty-four hours a day, producing in its first year of operation enough yarn for 64 million pairs of nylon stockings. When World War II broke out, the plant shifted its focus from stockings to bomber tires and parachutes.

After the war, Seaford remained central to the company's textile fibers production program, and the fiber Dacron was developed at the plant. At its peak in the 1960s and early 1970s, the Seaford plant employed more than 4,600 people, and the town was known as "The Nylon Capital of the World."

DuPont, headquartered in Wilmington, was founded in 1802 by French immigrant E. I. du Pont. The company is responsible for developing hundreds of products, including Freon, Teflon, lycra, and Kevlar.

George Alfred Townsend

1841–1914
Route 9 near Georgetown Circle
Georgetown

This is where famed Civil War newspaper correspondent George Alfred Townsend was born on January 20, 1841. Townsend was also a novelist and poet, and all his works are imbued with a rich sense of the love he felt for the region where he was born. Townsend's historical novel *The Entailed Hat* (1884) is perhaps his best-known work. It recounts the legend of Patty Cannon, the notorious slave runner from the nearby Eastern Shore. In the late 1880s, Townsend designed and constructed Gathland, his architecturally spectacular estate in the mountains west of Frederick, Maryland. Today, Gathland is part of a state park and is a much-visited landmark. In Georgetown, a historical marker was placed by the Delaware Public Archives to honor Townsend.

District
of Columbia

GI Bill

1943–44
Room 570
Mayflower Hotel
1127 Connecticut Avenue
Washington

The GI Bill—providing educational, housing, and other benefits to GIs returning from World War II—was first written on December 15, 1943. Originally
known as the Servicemen's Readjustment Act of 1944, the bill was penned in
Room 570 of the Mayflower Hotel by Harry W. Colmery, a World War I veteran
and American Legion past national commander. The legislation, which nearly
stalled in Congress as members of the House and Senate debated its provisions,
proved to be one that greatly affected the United States socially, economically
and politically. On June 22, 1944, President Franklin D. Roosevelt officially
signed the Servicemen's Readjustment Act of 1944. The penciled outline of the
GI Bill is contained in a glass display case at American Legion National Headquarters at Indianapolis. On June 17, 2002, a plaque was dedicated to Colmery's
work at the Mayflower Hotel.

NASA

1958
1520 H Street NW
Washington

The National Aeronautics and Space Administration (NASA), was born here in 1958 at the "Little White House," which served as its headquarters until 1961. The structure was built in 1820 by Richard Cutts, and it became the home of Mrs. Dolley Payne Madison, wife of President James Madison, in 1837. She lived in the house until her death in 1849. In 1886, the house temporarily became the private Cosmos Club. The site was occupied by NASA from 1958–1961, when the agency moved its headquarters to the Federal Building located at 400 Maryland Avenue. Since 1992, NASA Headquarters has been located at 300 E Street SW. Today, NASA's original headquarters is still known as the Dolley Madison House or the Little White House. The house was restored in 1968.

John Philip Sousa

1854–1932
636 G Street SE
Washington

John Philip Sousa, the conductor and composer who wrote "Stars and Stripes Forever," was born on November 6, 1854. Also known as the "March King," Sousa was the most famous bandleader in the United States during his lifetime. The former U.S. Marine Band leader composed some of the best known marches in the world, including "The Gladiator March," "The Liberty Bell," and "Hands Across the Sea." He began as a violinist in traveling orchestras, but won fame as the leader of the U.S. Marine Band from 1880 until 1892, composing the official song of the Marine Corps, "Semper Fidelis," at the request of President Chester A. Arthur; the president was allegedly looking for a song to replace "Hail to the Chief." In 1892 Sousa started a civilian band that became internationally famous and popular, and in 1910 they toured the world. "Stars and Stripes Forever" was designated in 1987 as the national march of the United States. Today, Sousa's birthplace is a private residence.

Maryland

John Archer

1741–1810
Medical Hall house
Medical Hall Road
Churchville

John Archer, the first man to receive a medical degree in America, was born in this house on May 5, 1741. Archer was first in the first class to receive degrees in medicine in 1768 from the Philadelphia College, the earliest chartered medical school in the colonies. Devoting much of his time to the needy, he treated many patients from his office, taught medicine to dozens of students, and initiated inoculations for whooping cough. Archer founded the Harford County (Md.) Medical Society and was a charter member of the Medical and Chirurgical Faculty of Maryland. Archer served as a member of the Revolutionary committee, a member of the first state constitutional convention, and as a major in the Continental Army during the Revolutionary War, and was elected as a Republican to the Seventh, Eighth, and Ninth Congresses. Today, his birthplace is a private residence, but a marker at the intersection of Churchville Road (Route 22) and Thomas Run Road commemorates his life and work.

Samuel Chase

1741–1811
Intersection of U.S. 13 and MD 362
Princess Anne

Samuel Chase, one of the signers of the Declaration of Independence, was born in Princess Anne, Maryland, on April 17, 1741. He was a member of the colonial Sons of Liberty, the General Assembly of Maryland, the Continental Congress, and the U.S. Supreme Court (appointed by George Washington). Chase was sent on at least two "special missions" in his life. In 1776, he traveled to Canada to induce the Canadians to join in the revolution against Great Britain; and in 1783, he went to England to recover stock in the Bank of England, which the State of Maryland had purchased when it was a colony of Great Britain. He was impeached from the Supreme Court in 1804 by Thomas Jefferson but acquitted by Aaron Burr in 1805, when he resumed his seat on the bench and retained it until his death in Washington, D.C., in 1811. Today, a historical marker stands near his birthplace at the intersection of U.S. 13 and MD 362.

Tench Francis Jr.

1730–1800
11 N. Washington Street
Easton

Revolutionary patriot Tench Francis Jr. was born near here at Faulsey in 1730. A successful merchant in the decades before independence, Francis contributed heavily from his personal fortune to support the revolutionary cause. He was subsequently appointed first cashier of the Bank of North America and later headed the commission which laid out the city of Pittsburgh. He was appointed the first head of the Navy Supply Corps by George Washington in 1795. Years before, he wrote an important pamphlet on the issue of the lack of paper money in the colonies, *Considerations on a Paper Currency*. He was also treasurer of the Philadelphia and Lancaster Turnpike, one of the earliest major transportation projects in the country. This historical marker commemorates his life and is located near the site of his birthplace.

John Hanson

1715–83
Chapel Point Road
Port Tobacco

So, you think George Washington was our first president? Some argue that it was John Hanson, who served as the first president of the United States in Congress Assembled (Washington was the first president under the Constitution). Hanson was born in Port Tobacco on April 3, 1715, at Mulberry Grove. The house still stands, and is a private residence. Hanson was the first to assume the role of president after the conclusion of the Revolutionary War. Hanson ordered all foreign troops off American soil, as well as the removal of all foreign flags—quite a feat, considering that so many European countries had a stake in the new nation. He also established the Great Seal of the United States, the first treasury department, the first secretary of war, the first foreign affairs department, and the official holiday of Thanksgiving Day. Hanson died at Oxon Hill, Maryland, on November 22, 1783. A historical marker is located near his birthplace.

Johns Hopkins

1795–1873
Intersection of Reidel Road and Johns Hopkins Road
Crofton

The marker at this intersection commemorates Johns Hopkins, who was born nearby at Whitehall plantation on May 19, 1795. He became a wealthy entrepreneur, philanthropist, and abolitionist of nineteenth-century Baltimore. Hopkins made much of his fortune investing in the fledgling Baltimore and Ohio Railroad. He also financially supported the Union cause in the Civil War and used his influence to transport Union troops on the railroad.

Johns Hopkins is remembered for his philanthropy, which created the prestigious institutions that still bear his name—such as the Johns Hopkins University, Johns Hopkins Hospital, and Johns Hopkins School of Medicine.

William Tyler Page

1868–1942
121 Record Street
Frederick

A plaque on this house indicates that William Tyler Page was born here on October 19, 1868. Page was a descendant of Carter Braxton, a signer of the Declaration of Independence, and President John Tyler. In 1881, at the age of thirteen, he traveled to Washington D.C. to serve as a page at the U.S. Capitol, thus beginning a sixty-one-year-long career as a public servant. In 1917 at age forty-nine, Page wrote the *American's Creed*, the winning submission to a nationwide patriotic contest to craft a concise but complete statement of American political faith. He drew on a wide variety of historic documents and speeches, including the Declaration of Independence, the preamble to the U.S. Constitution, and Lincoln's Gettysburg Address. Page crafted a simple yet profoundly moving expression of American patriotism. On April 3, 1918, it was adopted by the U.S. House of Representatives. Today, it often comprises part of the naturalization ceremony for new Americans.

Babe Ruth

1895–1948
216 Emory Street
Baltimore
(410) 727-1539
www.baberuthmuseum.com

George Herman "Babe" Ruth Jr. was born here February 6, 1895. From humble beginnings he would become the most famous athlete of all time, baseball's greatest star, and his power and charisma would forever change the game. Babe, also dubbed "The Sultan of Swat," set home run and batting records which stood for decades. In 1936, he became one of the first five players inducted into the Baseball Hall of Fame.

The Babe Ruth Museum at his birthplace features hundreds of artifacts and treasures from Ruth's days at St. Mary's Industrial School for Boys, including his hymnal, baseball bat, the scorebook from his first professional game, and items from his father's saloons. Rare photos show Babe as a toddler with his parents and as a boy with his St. Mary's team. Three blocks east, a statue of Ruth stands outside the Eutaw Street entrance of Oriole Park at Camden Yards. Ruth's father operated a saloon in what is now centerfield at Oriole Park.

Star-Spangled Banner (Flag)

1813
The Star-Spangled Banner House
844 East Pratt Street
Baltimore
(410) 837-1793
www.flaghouse.org

The flag that inspired our national anthem was made here in 1813 in the home of Mary Young Pickersgill, who stitched the enormous 30-x-42-foot flag that flew over Fort McHenry during the War of 1812. That very flag inspired Francis Scott Key to write his famous poem, which was later set to music. To make the flag, Mary, her daughter Caroline, and their assistants hand-stitched sections of the flag. The women then assembled the pieces on the floor of Clagett's Brewery at Lombard and Granby Streets in east Baltimore. The flag required 400 yards of woolen bunting and more than a million stitches. Each of its fifteen stripes measured two feet wide, and its fifteen stars were two feet across. Here at the Star-Spangled Banner House, visitors can tour the preserved 1793 home of Mary Pickersgill, which is furnished with period antiques, as well as the War of 1812 museum with its displays of military and domestic artifacts. Pickersgill's flag now hangs at the Smithsonian Institution's National Museum of American History in Washington, D.C.

"Star-Spangled Banner" (National Anthem)

1814
Fort McHenry National Monument
 and Historic Shrine
2600 E. Fort Avenue
Baltimore
(410) 962-429
www.nps.gov/fomc

This star-shaped fort is the birthplace of the United States' national anthem. Watching the British bombardment of the fort on September 13–14, 1814, thirty-five-year-old poet and lawyer Francis Scott Key (1779–1843) was inspired to write the poem that provided the words for "The Star-Spangled Banner." The poem, later set to music, was adopted as our national anthem in 1931.

Fort McHenry is a wonderful place to visit on the Fourth of July, when you hear the national anthem set to fireworks.

New Jersey

Grover Cleveland

1837–1908
Grover Cleveland Birthplace
207 Bloomfield Ave.
Caldwell
(973) 226-0001
www.state.nj.us/dep/parksandforests/historic/
    grover_cleveland/gc_home.htm

22ND

24TH

Stephen Grover Cleveland, the twenty-second and twenty-fourth president of the United States, was born here on March 18, 1837, to Reverend Richard Cleveland and his wife Ann. He was named for the first ordained pastor of the First Presbyterian Church at Caldwell, but would eventually become known by his middle name, Grover. He is famous for being the only president to serve two non-consecutive terms and also the first to admit that he had an illegitimate son. Today, his birthplace is a New Jersey state historic site. The residence features an impressive collection of Cleveland artifacts, including the president's cradle, clothing, fishing gear, and his White House chair. Visitors can get a feel for Cleveland's life on the 2.5-acre grounds. The home features a kitchen, rear parlor, birth room, and galleries that chronicle Cleveland's political career in the height of the Victorian era.

College Football

1869
Rutgers University
130 College Avenue
New Brunswick

New Brunswick was the site for the first inter-
collegiate football game on November 6, 1869.
Rutgers University beat Princeton by a score of
6-4. The stadium where the game was played
was called College Field, which is now the site
of the College Avenue Gym and its parking lot.

Drive-in Movies

1933
Camden Drive-In
Crescent Boulevard
Camden

The phenomenon of drive-in movies was born with a less-than-glamorous debut
here in New Jersey on June 6, 1933. The first-ever outdoor movie showing took
place at the Camden Drive-In, which screened the British comedy *Wives Beware*
starring Adolphe Menjou. On May 16 of that year, Richard Hollingshead received
the first patent for the drive-in theater. With an investment of $30,000 (a tidy
sum for that era) Hollingshead opened this first drive-in theater, setting the
price of admission at 25 cents per car and another 25 cents per person. The
setup did not include the in-car speaker system we use today. Instead, three
main speakers mounted next to the screen boomed the sound across the lot.
Obviously, the sound quality was less than optimal for cars in the rear of the
theater, and probably a bit too optimal for surrounding homes. The theater has
since been demolished.

Electromagnetic Telegraph

1838
Historic Speedwell
333 Speedwell Avenue
Morristown
(973) 285-6550
http://morrisparks.com/speedwell/home.html

The electromagnetic telegraph was born on January 11, 1838, at this Historic Speedwell factory. This National Historic Landmark is where Alfred Vail worked with Samuel F. B. Morse to perfect the telegraph. It was here where the electromagnetic telegraph was first publicly demonstrated. The original structure was a one-story building with a garret and cellar dating back to the late eighteenth century. Around 1830, a second story was added for cotton looms, and in 1850 a grist mill was set up in the first floor and basement, run by a twenty-four-foot waterwheel. During the winter of 1837, Stephen Vail lent the vacant second floor to his son Alfred and Morse for their work on the telegraph.

"Jeannie with the Light Brown Hair"

1854
Corner of Sixth and Bloomfield Streets
Hoboken

One of our country's most well-known songs was born in this building in Hoboken while legendary American composer Stephen Foster lived here in 1854. A plaque on the private home marks the location. Foster's wife Jane had gone away on a trip, and he missed her so much that he wrote "Jeannie with the Light Brown Hair" in her honor. Foster would write and publish hundreds of other songs, including staples like "Camptown Races" (see page 74), "Oh! Susanna," and "Beautiful Dreamer." Sadly, Foster died penniless (due largely to the poor provisions for music copyright and composer royalties at the time) in 1864 at Bellevue Hospital in New York. He was just thirty-seven.

Lightbulb

1879
Thomas Edison Center at Menlo Park
37 Christie Street
Edison
(732) 549-3299
www.menloparkmuseum.com

Edison National Historic Site
Intersection of Main Street and
**   Lakeside Avenue**
West Orange
(973) 324-9973
www.nps.gove/edis

Extending 131 feet, 4 inches above Menlo Park, the Edison Memorial Tower at the museum marks the spot where Thomas Alva Edison conceived the first practical incandescent lightbulb. For ten years, Edison worked here on some four hundred patented ideas before eventually moving his "Invention Factory" to West Orange. The tower, which was erected in 1937, is topped by the world's largest working light bulb. The bulb is constructed of 153 individual pieces of 2-inch thick, amber-tinted Pyrex glass, weighing a total of 3 tons.

Jack Nicholson

1937–
Fitkin Hospital
1945 Route 33
Neptune

John Joseph Nicholson, aka Jack Nicholson, was born on April 22, 1937, at Fitkin Hospital in Neptune, New Jersey (today known as Jersey Shore University Medical Center). The three-time Academy Award-winning actor and beloved Hollywood "bad boy" is best known for his roles in films such as *Easy Rider* (1969), *Chinatown* (1974), *One Flew Over the Cuckoo's Nest* (1975), *The Shining* (1980), and *The Departed* (2006). Nicholson was the son of a showgirl, June Frances Nicholson, and either Donald Furcillo or Eddie King—nobody is sure about the identity of his father, and Nicholson has chosen not to pursue it. Strangely, he was raised believing his grandparents were his parents, and that his mother was his older sister. He only learned the truth after a *Time* magazine reporter uncovered the facts while researching a story on Nicholson.

Organized Baseball

1846
Elysian Fields (former site)
Corner of 11th and Washington Streets
Hoboken

In 1842 several men, including Alexander Cartwright and Daniel "Doc" Adams, began drafting rules for a game called "baseball." On June 19, 1846, the Knickerbocker Baseball Club played the first-ever organized game under the new rules against the New York Nine. With Cartwright as the umpire, the Knickerbockers lost the four-inning game, 23–1. Soon after, the sport caught on. In 1869, the first professional team, the Cincinnati Red Stockings, was formed and in 1871, the first nationwide professional league was founded. A plaque marks the exact spot where the field used to be.

Dorothy Parker

1893–1967
732 Ocean Avenue
Long Branch

Acclaimed writer and social activist Dorothy Parker was born at her family's beach cottage on August 22, 1893, in West End, a village in Long Branch in Monmouth County. The best-selling poet and short story writer gained immortal fame as a member of the Algonquin Round Table, a collection of writers, playwrights, and actors who met regularly at the Algonquin Hotel in the 1920s. Parker, an Oscar-nominated screenwriter, playwright, and the first female drama critic on Broadway, was also a vigorous champion of social justice, civil rights and left-wing causes. Among her works are a collection of poems, *Death and Taxes*, the short story collection *Laments for the Living*, and

her columns in the *New Yorker* under the byline "Constant Reader." In 2005, the birthplace of Dorothy Parker was designated a Literary Landmark by the Friends of Libraries U.S.A. A plaque was dedicated at the site on August 25, 2005. The site of her birthplace is now an apartment complex.

Frank Sinatra

1915–98
415 Monroe Street
Hoboken

"The Lady is a Tramp." "Fly Me to the Moon." "My Way." The hundreds of songs he sang resonate with the American consciousness. Frank Sinatra was born here on December 12, 1915. Sadly, the original wooden building burned down in 1967 and all that remains today is a small archway. In the sidewalk, a star-shaped plaque marks the spot in front of his birthplace. Although there are no formal Sinatra memorials in town, you can see where the Sinatra family lived in 1939 at 841 Garden Street, as well as the site where Sinatra got his first singing gig in 1935 at 600 Hudson Street, the former site of the Union Club.

Bruce Springsteen

1949–
Monmouth Medical Center (formerly
   Monmouth Memorial Hospital)
300 Second Avenue
Long Branch

On September 23, 1949, musician Bruce Frederick Springsteen was born here, at what was then called Monmouth Memorial Hospital. His parents, Douglas and Adele Springsteen, lived at 87 Randolph Street in Freehold at the time. Bruce Springsteen and the E Street Band released their first album in 1973, but it was their second disc, *The Wild, The Innocent & The E Street Shuffle* in 1974 that led a rock critic to call Springsteen "the future of rock'n'roll." A year later Springsteen released the now classic *Born to Run* to critical and popular success, and he was a bona fide rock star, nicknamed "The Boss." The 1980s saw the release of other hit albums including *The River* and *Born in the U.S.A.* His song, "My Hometown," on the latter album refers to Freehold. In the 1990s Springsteen left his backup band and did a number of solo recordings, but by the end of the decade was touring with the band again. He continues to tour and record today, both with the band and as a solo artist.

New York

Air Conditioning

1902
490 Broadway Street
Buffalo

It's wasn't the heat, it was the humidity that provided the impetus for the invention of the first air conditioner. Air conditioning was first used on July 17, 1902, at a Brooklyn printing company called Sackett-Wilhelms—but it was invented here in Buffalo by Willis Carrier. He conceived of it one year after he went to work at the Buffalo Forge Company, a manufacturer of heaters, blowers, and air exhaust systems. He was charged with solving a problem for Sackett-Wilhelms, which was having trouble trying to print a four-color magazine. Paper would shrink and expand as humidity changed; colored inks, applied in layers, failed to register properly; and printed pictures looked fuzzy. Realizing the problem was the humidity inside the building, Carrier created a device that moved air over cold coils, sucking out moisture much as an iced drink collects dew on the outside of a glass. Although the old Buffalo Forge plant is no longer in use, the building still stands—and the invention produced there has impacted lives around the world.

ATM

1969
10 North Village Avenue
Rockville Centre

Anyone who has ever needed fast cash (who hasn't?) owes a debt to Chemical Bank. It revolutionized banking by installing the first modern Automatic Teller Machine (ATM) at this Rockville Centre branch in 1969. Don Wetzel, vice president of product planning at Docutel, a company that made automated baggage-handling equipment, first got the idea in 1968 to develop a machine that dispensed cash (he and his partners also created the first ATM card with a magnetic strip). Today, the bank is the Long Island regional headquarters for JPMorgan Chase.

Baked Alaska

See Lobster Newburgh.

Lucille Ball

1911–89
69 Stewart Avenue
Jamestown

We all love Lucy. Lucille Ball was born here on the west side of Jamestown on August 6, 1911. Ball, remembered for her blazing red hair, sharp comedic instincts, and slapstick situation comedy gags, is best known for the show *I Love Lucy* (1951–57), which became one of the great television landmarks of the 1950s. The show was consistently number one in the ratings and continued in reruns for decades. *I Love Lucy* also starred Ball's real-life husband, Cuban bandleader Desi Arnaz. Jamestown is a treasure trove for Ball aficionados; there is also the Desilu Playhouse, the Lucy–Desi Museum (212 Pine Street), her high school, and The Lucille Ball Little Theater of Jamestown, New York state's largest community theatre where Lucy's movies and shows are often screened. The Lucille Ball birthplace historical marker is to the left of the front entrance of this private home. Visitors can also see her childhood home at 59 Lucy Lane in Celoron (just south of Jamestown), which is also a private residence.

Bebop

Circa 1940
Minton's Playhouse
Cecil Hotel
210 W. 118th Street
Harlem

Bebop music, a style of jazz focused on solo opportunities and complex melodies for a smaller group, is believed to have been born here in this jazz club in the early 1940s. It emerged when jazz greats like Thelonious Monk, Fats Waller, Charlie Parker, Dizzy Gillespie, Lester Young, Benny Goodman, Kenny Clarke, and others were allowed to improvise by the club owner. Impromptu sessions often began after other gigs in the late hours, so they quickly become a favorite of top jazz musicians. Legend has it that Fats Waller coined the musical term "bop" when describing improvisational rifts by the younger musicians. The playhouse now includes a housing unit for the elderly.

Buffalo Wings

1964
Anchor Bar
1047 Main Street
Buffalo
(716) 884-4083
www.anchorbar.com

Necessity is the mother of invention . . . and so it follows that a bartender's mother invented buffalo wings out of the necessity for a late-night snack. It all started in 1964 here in Buffalo at the Anchor Bar Restaurant. Bartender Dominic Bellissimo was working a late shift when a group of his friends arrived at the bar with ravenous appetites. Dominic's mother, Teressa, came to the rescue with a midnight snack that would not be soon forgotten. She brought out two plates of the dish and placed them on the bar. Intrigued by the aroma but confused by the sight, Dom and his friends asked, "What are these?" They looked like chicken wings, a part of the bird that usually went into the stockpot for soup. Teressa had deep-fried the wings and flavored them with a homemade sauce. They were an instant hit, and soon customers flocked to the bar to experience this new culinary sensation. From that point, buffalo wings became a popular part of the Anchor Bar menu.

Today, the original restaurant is an internationally famous tourist destination that serves more than a thousand pounds of wings each day, drawing famous movie stars, professional athletes, political leaders, and more who want to experience truly original Buffalo Wings.

Cell Phone Call

1973
57th Street and Fifth Avenue (approximate location)
New York City

On April 3, 1973, the first public telephone call was placed on a portable cellular phone by a gentleman named Martin Cooper, then the general manager of Motorola's Communications Systems Division. It was the incarnation of his vision for personal wireless communications, distinct from cellular car phones, that initially pushed this technology. That first call, placed to Cooper's rival at AT&T's Bell Labs, caused a fundamental technology and communications market shift toward the person and away from the place.

Glenn Curtiss

1878–1930
Glenn Curtiss Museum
8419 State Route 54
Hammondsport
(607) 569-2160
www.glenncurtissmuseum.org

Glenn Hammond Curtiss, pioneering motorcyclist and aviator who is known as the "Father of Naval Aviation," was born in Hammondsport on May 21, 1878. He is known for developing the first practical amphibious aircraft, launching the era of U.S. Naval aviation; as well as the Curtiss Jenny, the primary military training plane in the U.S. for years. After starting a career as a bicycle racer, Curtiss built an eight-cycle motorcycle and in 1907 set a world speed record of 136.3 mph. Curtiss went on to prove the practical use of the airplane, as his aircraft designs and advanced performance engines led him to establish many speed and distance records. In 1907, in collaboration with Alexander Graham Bell and others, he helped form the Aerial Experiment Association. In July of 1908, he piloted the first official public flight in the U.S., flying one kilometer and winning the 1908 Scientific American Trophy. During World War I, his Curtiss Airplane and Motor Company was deluged with orders for his "flying boat" and famed JN-4 "Jenny." Curtiss's old home was called Castle Hill. Once nearly surrounded by vineyards and fruit trees, it was later the location of the Curtiss factories.

Eggs Benedict

See Lobster Newburgh

Feminism

1848
Wesleyan Methodist Church
Women's Rights National Historical Park
136 Fall Street
Seneca Falls
(315) 568-2991
www.nps.gov/wori

Feminism is an ever-evolving movement with a complex heritage, but most historians agree that it was born at the Wesleyan Methodist Church in Seneca Falls in 1848. On July 19–20 of that year, the chapel hosted the first Women's Rights Convention, also known as the Seneca Falls Convention. An estimated three hundred women and men attended the convention, including leading reformers such as Elizabeth Cady Stanton, Lucretia Mott, and Frederick Douglass. Having fought vigorously in the antislavery movement, they were well prepared to discuss the legal limitations imposed on women. They used the language and structure of the Declaration of Independence to create the new Declaration of Sentiments, which outlined the goals and defined the new women's rights movement. The original red brick Wesleyan Methodist Church was sold by the congregation in 1871. After being altered by subsequent owners, the site was purchased by the National Park Service in 1985. The site today, part of Women's Rights National Historical Park, displays the portion that remains of the original building.

PRESIDENTIAL BIRTHPLACE
Millard Fillmore

1800–74
Fillmore Glen State Park
1686 Route 38
Moravia
(315) 497-0130

Millard Fillmore, the thirteenth president of the United States, was born into an impoverished family in Locke Township on January 7, 1800. His father apprenticed him to a clothmaker, a brutal arrangement that bordered on slavery. Fillmore eventually borrowed thirty dollars to pay off his obligation to the clothmaker and trekked the one hundred miles back home. He went on to become a lawyer, New York State assemblyman, and a U.S. congressman. Fillmore was elected vice president in 1848, and when Zachary Taylor died in 1850, he became president. He is remembered for signing the Compromise of 1850, which included a stricter fugitive slave law—a controversial legislation that undermined his re-election.

Visitors can see the site of Fillmore's actual birthplace in the town of Summerhill. Fillmore described his wilderness home as "shut out from the enterprises of civilization and advancement." The cabin was torn down in 1852, but a New York historical marker was erected near the site in 1932. In 1965, the Millard Fillmore Memorial Association constructed a replica in nearby Fillmore Glen State Park.

Fried Twinkie

2002
The Atlantic ChipShop
129 Atlantic Avenue
Brooklyn
(888)-FRYCHIP
www.chipshopnyc.com

One of the all-time decadent guilty pleasures, the deep-fried Twinkie is a relatively recent invention, born here in this English fish-and-chips shop in Brooklyn. Owner Christopher Sell got the brilliant idea of taking the popular Hostess Twinkie cake, freezing it, dipping it into batter and deep-frying it. Although variations exist in the form, the deep-fried Twinkie is usually prepared with a batter consisting of flour, egg, and vinegar. Prior to dipping, a wooden or plastic stick is inserted through one end. Conventional cooking oil is typically used, although beef suet or tallow is sometimes used to give a meaty flavor. Chris Mullen adopted the treat in 2002, and it was a runaway success after he and his brother started selling it at county fairs.

Lou Gehrig

1903–41
1994 Second Avenue
New York City

Henry Louis "Lou" Gehrig, legendary New York Yankees baseball player and American cultural hero, was born to German immigrant parents in upper Manhattan on June 19, 1903. Gehrig was famously known as "The Iron Horse" after playing in a record 2,130 consecutive games, a record which stood nearly six decades before it was broken by Cal Ripken Jr. in 1995. Gehrig was part of the Yankees glory years of the 1920s and 1930s, playing alongside greats like Babe Ruth and Joe DiMaggio. Sadly, Gehrig is also known for his tragic demise. In 1939 he was diagnosed with the degenerative disease amyotrophic lateral sclerosis (ALS), also known as Lou Gehrig's Disease. On July 4, 1939, Gehrig spoke his eternally inspiring words at Yankee Stadium: "Today I consider myself the luckiest man on the face of this earth." He died two years later. Gehrig's birthplace, an apartment building that later became a laundromat, was adorned with a memorial plaque in 1953 in a ceremony attended by Christina Gehrig, Lou's mother. The building and memorial are since gone, but a non-profit organization called Ride for Life, dedicated to helping people living with ALS, recently placed a new monument at the site (now occupied by Dimitri's Garden Center).

"The Gift of the Magi"

1902
Pete's Tavern
129 E. 18th Street
New York City

Pete's has been open since 1864 and still looks much as it did when literary history was made here in 1902. That year, the tavern's most celebrated regular, the writer O. Henry (the pen name of William Sydney Porter) wrote the Christmas classic "The Gift of The Magi" in his favorite booth at the tavern. The story features Jim and Della Dillingham, a young couple who are very much in love with each other but can barely afford their one-room apartment. For Christmas, Della buys Jim a chain for his prized pocket watch given to him by his father. To raise the funds, she cut her prized long hair and sold it. Meanwhile, Jim sells his watch to buy Della a beautiful set of combs for her lovely, knee-length hair. The moral of the story is that although their gifts proved to be useless, the thought behind them was invaluable. Today at the booth, a framed copy of the story is mounted on the wall.

Grain Elevator

1842
Commercial Street
Buffalo

We may take elevators for granted today, but elevators weren't even invented for people—they were initially created to move massive amounts of grain. In 1842, Buffalo merchant Joseph Dart and machinist Robert Dunbar, following precedents set by Oliver Evans, built the world's first steam-powered elevator. It was located at the foot of Commercial Street on Buffalo Creek. Dart came up with the idea of unloading grain ships by means of an endless belt of buckets, a system already used inside mills for moving grain and flour. Dart innovated the concept of placing the belt inside a "marine leg," which would project out of a grain warehouse and be lowered into a ship's hold to scoop up the grain. Thus, the term "elevator" originated, as the contraption elevated grain from the ship and stored it in bins until it was lowered for shipment or milling. This highly successful innovation paved the way for modern elevator technology.

Hip-Hop

1973
1520 Sedgwick Avenue
The Bronx

Hip-Hop was born here in the Bronx in the 1970s, where DJ Kool Herc (Clive Campbell) would throw massive parties, pioneering the musical style and culture that would become a way of life for generations to come. Herc used snippets of reggae and funk records to string together the breaks, or the most danceable parts, of different songs to keep a crowd on its feet all night. The site, however, eventually closed for renovations, prompting hip-hop fans and community organizers to make a bid to have the location honored as a landmark. In 2007, state officials determined that the West Bronx apartment building should be eligible to be recognized on the state and national registers of historic places as the birthplace of hip-hop.

IBM

1911
1701 North Street
Endicott

International Business Machines (IBM) was born here on June 16, 1911, as the Computing-Tabulating-Recording Company (CTR). Its origins can be traced to late nineteenth century innovations, including Dr. Alexander Dey's first dial recorder and Herman Hollerith's historic punch-card tabulating machines that streamlined the 1890 U.S. census. This location in Endicott was first used in 1906, when Harlow Bundy moved his International Time Recording Company into a three-story brick building. In 1911, he merged with the Computing Scale Company and Hollerith's Tabulating Machine Company to form CTR. At that time, CTR manufactured and sold machinery ranging from commercial scales and industrial time recorders to meat and cheese slicers, along with tabulators and punched cards. In 1924, under the guidance of president Thomas J. Watson, CTR changed its name to IBM. The Endicott facility would later be known as IBM Plant No. 1. In 1933, the original building was joined by a laboratory and a school, and in 1941 a new manufacturing building was constructed. IBM still uses the Endicott facility today.

Ice Cream Sundae

1891
216 East State Street
Ithaca

Was it divine inspiration that brought about the ice cream sundae? Perhaps. The story goes that one hot Sunday afternoon in 1891, John M. Scott, the pastor of the local Unitarian church, accompanied one of his faithful parishioners, Chester Platt, to the latter's drug store for a cool refreshment. Here, Platt supposedly got two dishes of ice cream from Miss DeForest Christiance, who was tending the soda fountain. He plopped a candied cherry on top of each dish of ice cream and covered the whole thing with cherry syrup, instinctively inventing what many Ithaca folks think was the first real ice cream sundae. Two Rivers, Wisconsin, also claims to be the birthplace of the ice cream sundae (see page 195).

Information Superhighway

1837
Cherry Valley
www.cooperstown.net/cherryvalley/index.html

The "Information Superhighway" traces its origins back to 1837, with the development of the first telegraph. In that year, Samuel F. B. Morse visited his cousin, Judge James Otis Morse, in Cherry Valley. With the assistance of Amos L. Swan, a local manufacturer, Morse introduced the first working telegraphic machine. That same year, he filed a caveat with the U.S. Patent Office. Morse returned to Cherry Valley in 1844 to establish the first telegraph office along the Albany–Syracuse telegraph run. Morse's invention had a huge impact on future technology. His use of an electric current and electromagnet to communicate digitally over long distances led to innovations such as radio speakers, telephones, and eventually, the Internet. Even microprocessors can be described as tiny telegraph operators, storing and relaying binary-encoded messages at high speeds.

Jell-O

1897
23 East Main Street
LeRoy
(585) 768-7433
www.jellogallery.org

Jell-O, one of America's most famous desserts and a pioneering force in marketing, was born here in LeRoy. It almost got its start in 1845, when Peter Cooper patented a product, which was "set" with gelatin—however, it never caught on with the public. Jell-O was officially born in 1897 at the hands of Pearle Wait, a carpenter in LeRoy. While concocting a cough remedy and laxative tea in his home, he experimented with gelatin and came up with a fruit-flavored dessert. His wife, May, named it "Jell-O." Wait tried to market his new product, but he lacked the capital and business experience. So, in 1899, he sold his formula for just $450 to Frank Woodward, one of the best-known manufacturers of medicines in the area. Initially, slow sales frustrated Woodward, who gave his plant superintendent the chance to buy the Jell-O rights for $35. But before they could complete their deal, sales took off, reaching $1 million by 1906. The company's brilliant marketing efforts included teams of well-attired salesmen trained to demonstrate Jell-O. They also distributed 15 million copies of a Jell-O recipe book containing celebrity recipes and more. In 1923, Woodward's Genesee Pure Food Company was renamed Jell-O Company, later merging with Postum Cereal to become the General Foods Corporation. In 1997, the Jell-O Museum opened its doors in LeRoy. It displays Jell-O artwork by famous artists such as Max Parrish and Norman Rockwell, and showcases more than a hundred years of memorabilia from the brand's illustrious history.

Lobster Newburgh

1876
Delmonico's
56 Beaver Street
New York City
(212) 509-1144

Delmonico's restaurant in New York is known for more than just fine dining; it is also revered as the birthplace of world-famous dishes, including Lobster Newburgh, Baked Alaska, and eggs Benedict. Opened in 1836 by brothers Giovanni and Pietro Delmonico, the restaurant's foray into culinary creativity began with an 1876 visit from shipping magnate Ben Wenberg. He asked chef Charles Ranhofer to prepare a meal he had discovered in South America—chunks of lobster sautéed in butter, served in a sauce of cream and egg, and flavored with paprika and sherry. It was such a success that "Lobster Wenberg" was permanently added to the Delmonico's menu. Wenberg eventually was banned from Delmonico's after he got into a fight at the restaurant due to consuming too much wine from Delmonico's renowned cellars. His name was taken off the menu, but the beloved dish would stay, and the renamed "Lobster Newburgh" was born.

Baked Alaska was also born at Delmonico's, created in 1876 in honor of the newly acquired territory of Alaska. An Englishman (George Sala) who visited Delmonico's in the 1880s commented: "The 'Alaska' is a baked ice . . . The nucleus or core of the entremets is an ice cream. This is surrounded by an envelope of carefully whipped cream, which, just before the dainty dish is served, is popped into the oven, or is brought under the scorching influence of a red hot salamander."

Delmonico's gave birth to a third dish—eggs Benedict. Back in the 1860s, two regulars at the upscale restaurant—a couple named Mr. and Mrs. LeGrand Benedict—complained that the restaurant's menu never changed. In response, the chef created eggs on ham served on a muffin and covered in hollandaise sauce. Of course, they loved it, and eggs Benedict was born.

The Marx Brothers

1887–1979
179 E. 93rd Street
New York City

The Marx brothers were born in this Manhattan apartment in the late 1800s, where they would spend their formative years before becoming international stars. These sibling comedians of vaudeville, stage plays, and film would forever change the world of comedy and influence generations of performers with their surreal humor and innovative gags. The brothers were Groucho (Julius Henry Marx, 1890–1977), Chico (Leonard Marx, 1887–1961), Harpo (Adolph Arthur Marx, 1888–1964), Zeppo (Herbert Marx, 1901–1979) and Gummo (Milton Marx, 1892–1977). Their careers peaked with an array of hit films, including *Duck Soup*, *Horse Feathers*, and *A Night At The Opera*. After their movie work ended in the 1940s, Groucho enjoyed a solo career as a film actor, host of the 1950s television game show *You Bet Your Life*, and superb raconteur both in concerts and on talk shows.

Memorial Day

1866
Waterloo

One of our country's most poignant and important holidays, Memorial Day was born here immediately after the Civil War. In the summer of 1865, Henry C. Welles, a local druggist in Waterloo, suggested the nation remember the patriotic dead by placing flowers on their graves. His idea did not take hold until he advanced it again the following spring to General John B. Murray. A Civil War hero, Murray jumped on the concept and recruited the help of other influential citizens. On May 5, 1866, patriotic citizens decorated Waterloo with flags flown at half-mast. Draped with evergreen and mourning black, veterans, civic society members and residents marched dramatically to the three village cemeteries, led by General Murray. One year later, on May 5, 1867, they repeated the ceremonies. In 1868, Waterloo joined with other communities in holding their observance on May 30, in accordance with General John Logan's orders, and Memorial Day has been held on that day ever since.

On March 7, 1966, the state of New York recognized Waterloo as the birthplace of Memorial Day in a proclamation signed by Governor Nelson A. Rockefeller. Congress followed when the House of Representatives and the Senate unanimously passed a resolution in May 1966. It also recognized Waterloo as the birthplace of Memorial Day. On May 26, 1966, President Lyndon B. Johnson signed a presidential proclamation naming Waterloo as the birthplace of Memorial Day. To this day, at least twenty-four communities around the country claim to be the birthplace of Memorial Day. However, Waterloo remains the "official" birthplace because that community's observance in 1866, the earliest on record, was considered so well planned and complete.

Other communities that had the foresight and good moral sense to conduct similar remembrances were Boalsburg, Pennsylvania; Mobile, Alabama; Montgomery, Alabama; Camden, Alaska; Atlanta, Georgia; Milledgeville, Georgia; New Orleans, Louisiana; Columbus, Mississippi; Jackson, Mississippi; Vicksburg, Mississippi; Raleigh, North Carolina; Cincinnati, Ohio; Charleston, South Carolina; Fredericksburg, Virginia; Portsmouth, Virginia; Warrenton, Virginia; and Washington, D.C.

Mickey Mouse

1928
Broadway Theater (formerly Colony Theater)
1681 Broadway
New York City

The world's most popular animated character, Mickey Mouse, was born here on November 18, 1928, during a premiere at the Colony Theater on Broadway and 53rd Street in Manhattan. Of course, the origins of Mickey Mouse must be traced to the imagination of twenty-six-year-old cartoonist Walt Disney, who dreamed up the character on a cross-county train ride earlier that year. Initially, Disney developed two silent films featuring Mickey, but success would come with a version featuring synchronized sound. He came back to New York to record the soundtrack to the film *Steamboat Willie*, and it premiered right here at this theater. Because of the public recognition at this event, this date is considered to be the birthday of the beloved mouse. In fact, the public response was so overwhelmingly positive that two weeks later, *Steamboat Willie* was re-released at the world's largest theater, New York's Roxy. In 1932, Walt Disney won a special Academy Award for creating Mickey Mouse.

National League

1876
673 Broadway, just south of W. 3rd Street
New York City

It was at this site in 1876 that a small group of men led by Chicago business-man William A. Hulbert and pitching star Albert G. Spalding met at the Grand Central Hotel to form the National League. As a result of the formation, eight teams were created to start the 1876 season. In 1952, a plaque was placed on the hotel stating that it was the birthplace of Major League Baseball. In 1973 the hotel collapsed after years of deterioration and the plaque was lost. Today, a New York University dormitory is located on the site.

Eugene O'Neill

1888–1953
1500 Broadway
New York City

Nobel and Pulitzer Prize–winning playwright Eugene O'Neill was born in Room 226 at the Barrett House Hotel on October 16, 1888, while his father was in town playing in *The Count of Monte Cristo*. The author of forty-two published plays, O'Neill was the only American to win a Nobel Prize for playwriting and the only dramatist to win four Pulitzer Prizes. His most memorable works include *Beyond the Horizon* (1920), *Anna Christie* (1921), *Strange Interlude* (1928) and *Long Day's Journey Into Night* (1956).

Around 1900, the hotel merged with an adjoining structure and was renamed the Cadillac Hotel. Apparently, O'Neill once took a friend up to the third floor, knocked on the door of the room in which he had been born, and explained his mission to the startled occupants. In 1957, his birthplace was commemorated by the dedication of a bronze plaque at the northeast corner of Broadway and 43rd Street, the former site of the hotel. It was situated in what was then Long-acre Square, a quiet residential area. Today, a coffee shop sits on the site of the historic hotel.

Oreos

1912
Chelsea Market
88 10th Avenue
New York City

Whether you eat the middle first or dunk it all in milk, if you love Oreo cookies, then this historic building is sacred ground. The iconic cookie was first put together in 1912 here at the Nabisco headquarters, which occupied this building from 1898 to 1958. Today, this funky, cobblestone-floored old structure contains unbelievably appetizing outlets such as Manhattan Fruit Exchange, The Lobster Place, the bakery for Sarabeth's Bakery, Fat Witch Brownies and more—including some offices for Major League Baseball, where parts of the original Nabisco red brick ovens are still visible.

Pizza, American

1905
Lombardi's
32 Spring Street
New York City

The invention of pizza arguably dates back to the ancient Greeks or the Persian Empire, and modern pizza can be traced back to the late 1800s in Naples, Italy. However, American-style pizza was born in New York City in 1905. That year, Gennaro Lombardi opened the first licensed pizzeria in Little Italy at $53^{1}/_{2}$ Spring Street. Originally opened as a grocery store in 1897, Lombardi's soon became a popular stop for workers looking for a convenient lunch to take to work. Gennaro started selling tomato pies wrapped in paper and tied with a string. Most workers could not afford the entire pie, so it was often sold by the piece. There was no set price or size, so customers were given whatever portion they could afford—often as little as two cents' worth. It wasn't until the early 1930s that Lombardi added tables and chairs and sold spaghetti as well. After passing the business on to his son and grandson, Lombardi's closed in 1984. Gennaro's grandson Jerry re-opened the shop in 1994 a block away at 32 Spring Street. Today, Lombardi's claims to still use the same recipe Gennaro Lombardi brought from Naples in 1897 to make their legendary pizza pies in coal-fired ovens.

Potato Chips

1853
700 Crescent Avenue (approximate location)
Saratoga Lake
Saratoga

How did a chef's hot temper cause him to accidentally invent potato chips? In the summer of 1853, George Crum worked as a chef at Moon's Lake House, an elegant resort in Saratoga Springs along Saratoga Lake. The restaurant menu featured french-fried potatoes, prepared by Crum in the standard, thick-cut style popularized in eighteenth-century France. One cantankerous guest complained that Crum's french fries were too thick, and asked if he could cut and fry a thinner batch. Crum complied, but the customer rejected those, too. Frustrated, Crum decided to deliberately annoy the guest by cutting fries that were excessively thin and crisp, and heavily salted. But the plan backfired. The difficult guest loved the crispy, paper-thin potatoes, and other customers began to request Crum's thin potatoes originally called "Saratoga Chips." The potato chip had been born. Moon's Lake House is long gone, and its approximate site at this upstate New York lake is now occupied by a private lakeside house.

Punk Rock

1970s
315 Bowery at Bleeker Street
New York City

In the 1970s, this seminal club was the American ground zero for some of the most influential rock and roll ever spawned, featuring such acts as the Ramones, Blondie, Patti Smith, Group, Television, and the Talking Heads. Founded by Hilly Kristal in 1973, the club was named CBGB for musical styles (country, bluegrass and blues), but soon became a forum for American punk (named OMFUG, Other Music for Uplifting Gormandizers). The storefront and large space next door to the club served as the CBGB Record Store for many years. Eventually, in the late 1980s, the record store was closed and replaced with a second performance space and art gallery, named CB's 313 Gallery. The gallery went on to showcase many popular bands and singer/songwriters who played in a musical style more akin to rock, folk, jazz, or experimental music, while the original club continued to present the best in harder, louder post-punk, metal, and alternative rock acts. The club closed in October 2006. The final concert was performed by Patti Smith on Sunday, October 15.

PRESIDENTIAL BIRTHPLACE
Franklin D. Roosevelt

1882–1945
Home of Franklin D. Roosevelt
National Historic Site
4079 Albany Post Road (U.S. Route 9)
Hyde Park
(845) 229-9115
www.nps.gov/hofr

32ND

Franklin D. Roosevelt, the thirty-second president of the United States, was born here at Springwood on January 20, 1882. His father, James Roosevelt, bought the 300-acre estate in 1867.

Franklin is notable as the only U.S. president elected to four terms. His New Deal administration provided economic relief for millions during the Great Depression and his leadership inspired America during World War II. He is responsible for the FDIC, the Civilian Conservation Corps, and the Social Security system.

Today, the Home of Franklin D. Roosevelt National Historic Site is administered by the National Park Service, and is open to the public. Inside, the home features numerous family heirlooms that provide a picture of what life at Springwood was like over the generations. FDR's corner desk reveals his many passions, including his vast collections of stamps, model ships, rare books, naval paintings, bird specimens, and coins. He donated his home to the American people in 1943, and it was transferred to the Department of the Interior in 1945, after the family relinquished their rights. Roosevelt's presidential library and his tomb are also on the grounds.

PRESIDENTIAL BIRTHPLACE
Theodore Roosevelt

26TH

1858–1919
28 E. 20th Street
New York City
(212) 260-1616
www.nps.gov/thrb

Theodore Roosevelt, perhaps the most colorful president in American history, was born in a brownstone building on this site on October 27, 1858. Roosevelt gained fame for his exploits as an outdoorsman and a colonel of the Rough Riders regiment during the Spanish-American War. He won the Nobel Peace Prize, completed construction of the Panama Canal, and established the U.S. Forest Service. He pushed for the conservation of 42 million acres of forests, more than fifty wildlife refuges, and eighteen areas of "special interest," including the Grand Canyon.

Roosevelt was born a frail and sickly child who suffered from severe asthma and other ailments. At twelve, however, his health improved and he eventually became the strapping young man that would power his persona. The original brownstone birthplace of Roosevelt was replaced by a commercial building in 1916, but in 1919 the Women's Roosevelt Memorial Association purchased the site, razed the commercial building, and reconstructed his home as a memorial. Visitors today can see about 40 percent of the original furnishings in the house, reconstructed with five period rooms, two museum galleries, and a bookstore. It is operated by the National Park Service.

Sports Television

1939
Columbia University
Andy Coakley Field
Broadway and West 218th Street
New York City

The first athletic event ever televised was broadcast from here on NBC on May 17, 1939. The second game of a college doubleheader played between the Princeton Tigers and the Columbia Lions, the contest was shot with one camera standing on a platform behind home plate. There were only four hundred television sets which could receive the signal. Three months later, on August 26, NBC broadcast its first major league game—a doubleheader between the Brooklyn Dodgers and the Cincinnati

Reds played at Brooklyn's Ebbets Field. The teams split the two games. On that day, radio legend Red Barber, the voice of the Dodgers, became the first television announcer in sports history.

Test Tube Twins

1983
North Shore University Hospital
300 Community Drive
Manhasset

America's first "test tube" twins, Heather Jean Tilton and Todd MacDonald Tilton II, were born here on Long Island on March 24, 1983. The babies were delivered by cesarean section to their parents, Nancy and Todd MacDonald Tilton, who lived in nearby Sea Cliff.

Uncle Sam

Circa 1812
Troy

Uncle Sam wants you to know that he was born here—and that he may not be who you think he is. Like many Americans, you may think Uncle Sam is merely a nickname for the U.S. government—but residents of Troy know that Uncle Sam is based on an actual person named Samuel Wilson. He worked as a meatpacker in Troy during the War of 1812, providing large shipments of meat to the U.S. Army in barrels that were stamped with the initials "U.S." Supposedly, someone commented—perhaps facetiously—that the "U.S." initials stood for "Uncle Sam" Wilson. This suggestion that the meat shipments came from "Uncle Sam" took hold, and led to the notion that Uncle Sam symbolized the federal government. To this day, it's generally accepted that Wilson's personal nickname, "Uncle Sam," was the original inspiration for the red, white and blue character that now symbolizes the U.S. government.

Samuel Wilson died in 1854, and is buried in the Oakwood Cemetery in Troy. However, the image of Uncle Sam with a white goatee and star-spangled suit is merely an invention of artists and political cartoonists. (In reality, Samuel Wilson was clean-shaven.) That iconic "Uncle Sam" image used on World War I recruiting posters was the work of artist James Montgomery Flagg. Today, the town of Troy prides itself in Uncle Sam's true heritage, displaying several monuments to the patriot. One of the more impressive monuments to Uncle Sam Wilson is a statue at the corner of River and 3rd Streets in downtown Troy.

If you want to see where the real Sam Wilson was truly born, visit the small town of Mason, New Hampshire, where his boyhood home has also become a landmark. It's located on Route 123, about one-half mile south of Mason village.

PRESIDENTIAL BIRTHPLACE
Martin Van Buren

8TH

1782–1862
46 Hudson Street
Kinderhook

Martin Van Buren National Historic Site
Route 9H, 2 miles south of Kinderhook
(518) 758-9689
www.nps.gov/mava

Martin Van Buren, the eighth president of the United States, was born in Kinderhook on December 5, 1782. He would be the first president born under the flag of the United States. His birthplace was his father's tavern; in addition to the tavern, the family had a small farm.

After graduating from the village school, Van Buren became a law clerk, entered practice, and became active in state politics as state senator and attorney general. In 1820, he was elected to the U.S. Senate. He served briefly as governor of New York (1828–1829) before he resigned to become Andrew Jackson's secretary of state. He was soon on close personal terms with Jackson and played an important part in the rise of the Democratic Party. In 1832, Van Buren became vice president; in 1836, president.

Due in part to fallout from the Panic of 1837, Van Buren lost the presidential nomination to William Henry Harrison in 1840. He was the leading contender for the Democratic nomination in 1844 until he publicly opposed immediate annexation of Texas; he was subsequently defeated by the Southern delegations at the Baltimore convention. Van Buren later joined in the movement that led to the Free Soil Party and became its unsuccessful candidate for president in 1848.

Van Buren died in Kinderhook on July 24, 1862. He is buried in the the Kinderhook Reformed Cemetery on Albany Avenue. There is a historical marker near the site of his father's tavern at 46 Hudson Street in the quaint village of Kinderhook. The National Park Service maintains Lindenwald, Van Buren's home in Kinderhook, as Martin Van Buren National Historic Site. The president lived at the home from 1841 to 62.

Walt Whitman

1819–92
246 Old Walt Whitman Road
Huntington Station
(516) 427-5240
www.waltwhitman.org

Built around 1816 by Walt Whitman Sr., this weathered farmhouse and the surrounding West Hills served as inspiration for Walt Whitman, journalist and one of America's greatest poets, perhaps best known for his collection, *Leaves of Grass*, first published in 1855. Born on May 31, 1819, Whitman remained in the New York City area throughout his early life, and worked as a writer and editor for a number of local newspapers until 1859. The beginning of the Civil War led to a new calling for Whitman. He ventured to Virginia after his brother, George, was listed as missing in action following the 1862 Battle of Fredericksburg. Whitman found his brother in a hospital suffering from a minor wound; his experiences there inspired Walt to devote the remainder of the war years working as a nurse in Washington, D.C.'s military hospitals. The war and its aftermath inspired Whitman's collection *Drum Taps* and "O Captain, My Captain," his tribute to the assassinated Abraham Lincoln.

Though he left the birthplace at an early age, Whitman returned here often. There are maps available for auto or walking tours of Whitman-related sites in historic and beautiful West Hills, including the highest point on Long Island, Jayne's Hills. Tours of the home are also available.

Pennsylvania

American Flag

1777
Betsy Ross House
239 Arch Street
Philadelphia
(215) 686-1252
www.betsyrosshouse.org

In May 1776, according to legend, widowed seam-
stress Betsy Ross received a visit from three
representatives of a secret committee from the
Continental Congress: General George Washing-
ton, Robert Morris, and George Ross (uncle of Betsy's late husband). Needing a
flag to unify the country, Washington showed Ross a rough design that included
thirteen red and white stripes and thirteen stars. Betsy impressed the men and
won the job by immediately cutting a five-pointed star in a single snip. Ross created the flag in her house, which was also her workshop. She spent her days
making curtains, tablecloths, bed coverings, and furniture upholstery. She also
earned income to support her daughters by making musket balls and cartridges
for the Continental Army. On June 14, 1777, the Continental Congress adopted
Betsy's flag in an attempt to promote national pride and unity.

Ross rented the famous house from 1773 to 1786. It was built about 1740,
with 2½ floors and nine rooms. Other businesses occupied the house after
Betsy moved, until the Betsy Ross Memorial Association acquired it in 1898 and
converted the house from a timeworn building into a national shrine.

Banana Split

1904
805 Ligonier Street
Latrobe

In the early 1900s, many pharmacists were inventing sweet remedies to treat various ailments. But David Evans Strickler, a pharmacist at Tassell's Drug Store, seemed intent on treating the whole human spirit when he invented the banana split in 1904. At this writing, the original building in Latrobe still stands, but is unoccupied. Strickler's recipe for a banana split started off with a banana sliced lengthwise, topped with three scoops of ice cream—one vanilla, one chocolate, and one strawberry. Those were topped with pineapple chunks, chocolate sauce, and strawberry sauce. The *pièce de résistance* was the tufts of whipped cream, chopped nuts, and three maraschino cherries. Purportedly, Strickler also invented the first specialty dish to hold his new creation.

Big Mac

1967
Uniontown Shopping Center
942 Morgantown Street
Uniontown

In 1967, M. J. "Jim" Delligatti, a McDonald's owner/operator here in Fayette County, invented the Big Mac as a way to revive slumping sales. His instinct to expand the menu was embraced by McDonald's, which agreed to let him test a large sandwich that featured two patties, which he called the Big Mac. Obviously, it was a hit, and so he introduced them at three of his other McDonald's locations in the Pittsburgh area. The Big Mac was rolled out nationwide the following year, and you probably know the rest, including the famous slogan "Two all beef patties special sauce lettuce cheese pickles onions on a sesame seed bun."

Daniel Boone

1734–1820
Daniel Boone Homestead
500 Daniel Boone Road
Birdsboro
(610) 582-4900
www.danielboonehomestead.org

Daniel Boone, legendary American frontiersman who explored and settled present-day Kentucky, was born here in 1734. He is famous for blazing the Wilderness Road into Kentucky through the Cumberland Gap in 1775, facing fierce resistance from American Indians trying to defend their hunting ground. More than 200,000 people entered the state by Boone's route before the end of the eighteenth century. In Kentucky, Boone founded the town of Boonesborough, one of the first English-speaking settlements beyond the Appalachian Mountains. Boone gained worldwide fame in his lifetime after a book of his adventures by John Filson was published in 1784. His legend continued to grow even after his death, as his exploits—both real and embellished—helped create the archetypal American folk hero. Visitors today can tour the Daniel Boone Homestead, which includes the Boone House, a blacksmith shop, a sawmill, and an immersive experience detailing the life of early settlers.

PRESIDENTIAL BIRTHPLACE
James Buchanan

15TH

1791–1868
Buchanan's Birthplace State Park
Route 16
Cove Gap
www.dcnr.state.pa.us/stateparks/buchanansbirthplace.aspx

Mercersburg Academy
300 E. Seminary Street
Mercersburg
(717) 485-3948

James Buchanan, the fifteenth president of the United States, was born here on April 23, 1791, in a log cabin complex known as Stoney Batter, a center of frontier commerce. During those days, anyone seeking a route west passed through Cove Gap. Buchanan served as president in the years leading up to the Civil War, overseeing events such as the Dred Scott case, which increased national tension over the issue of slavery. He was the only bachelor president, and as such, his niece Harriet Lane Johnston served as First Lady. In 1865, the owner of the site invited the former president to visit his birthplace. Buchanan wrote in reply, "It is a rugged but romantic spot, and the mountain and mountain stream under the scenery captivating. I have warm attachments for it."

Today, Buchanan's Birthplace State Park is a Pennsylvania state park on 18.5 acres, created from land donated to the state by Harriet Lane. She tried but was unable to create a memorial to her uncle and to purchase his birthplace. Finally, in 1907, Lawrason and Francis Riggs purchased the birthplace site. Today, a stone pyramid monument surrounded by majestic conifers stands on the site of the original cabin birthplace. The log cabin itself is now located on the grounds of the nearby Mercersburg Academy.

Cable Television

1948
1501 E. Center Street
Mahanoy City

A state historical marker notes that the first cable television system in the United States was established at this location in June 1948 by John Walson. This Community Antenna Television (CATV) system, operated by Walson's Service Electric Company, initially connected only three channels to his Main and Pine Street store and a few homes. In the following decade, Service Electric grew to serve many thousands of cable subscribers. In 1967, Walson was inducted into the Cable Television Hall of Fame.

"Camptown Races"

1850
Junction of U.S. 706 & PA 409
Camptown

At one time or another, you've heard the lyric "Camptown ladies sing this song, doo-dah, doo-dah." One of the most popular songs in American history originated here in Camptown, a little town in Bradford County. Apparently, Stephen Foster wrote the tune after being inspired by the horse races that ran from this village to nearby Wyalusing. A state historical marker acknowledging Camptown and its famous race-inspired song is located at the junction of Routes 706 and 409 in Camptown, 4.2 miles north of Wyalusing.

Commercial Radio

1920
KDKA
1 Gateway Center
Pittsburgh

The world's first commercial radio station, KDKA, began broadcasting on November 2, 1920. This small radio station in Pittsburgh took to the airwaves at 8 P.M. and continued until midnight with reports of the Harding–Cox presidential election returns. The news that Warren Harding had won the presidency marked a dramatic end to an historic day in politics and in American broadcasting. Although this is not the exact site where the broadcast took place (KDKA moved here in the 1950s), a state historical marker does acknowledge the station's illustrious past. The location of the first broadcast was a radio shack atop the K Building at the Westinghouse facility.

Declaration of Independence & The Constitution

1776 and 1787
Independence Hall
Independence National Historical Park
Philadelphia
(877) 444-6777
www.nps.gov/inde

Independence Hall has been called the birthplace of the United States for many relevant reasons. Constructed between 1732 and 1756, Independence Hall was originally the Pennsylvania colony's capitol building. Within its walls the Second Continental Congress met in 1775. The Congress adopted the Declaration of Independence on July 4, 1776. The document was first read in public in Independence Square four days later, an event celebrated by the ringing of the Liberty Bell, now on display in a pavilion across Independence Mall.

By 1787 the United States had outgrown the limitations of its first system of governance, the Articles of Confederation, so a Constitutional Convention met at Independence Hall and in September formally adopted the new Constitution.

Today, Independence Hall is part of the larger Independence National Park, located in the center of Philadelphia. At the park visitors can see the Liberty Bell, Independence Hall, Congress Hall, the First and Second Banks of the United States, and the site where Benjamin Franklin's home once stood. The park spans approximately 45 acres and has about twenty buildings open to the public.

ENIAC Computer

1946
S. 33rd Street, south of Walnut Street
Philadelphia

The first all-purpose electronic digital computer, ENIAC, was invented here. ENIAC, the Electronic Numerical Integrator and Computer, was invented by J. Presper Eckert and John Mauchly, and built here at the University of Pennsylvania in 1946. The invention of this first all-purpose digital computer signaled the birth of the Information Age. ENIAC, which used thousands of vacuum tubes, became in 1951 the first computer to handle both numeric and alphabetic data with equal facility and was the first commercially available computer.

Filling Station

1913
Baum and St. Clair Streets
Pittsburgh

They didn't offer steak knife sets or collectible cups, but the phenomenon of the American gas station started here at the East Liberty Station, opened in December 1913 by the Gulf Refining Co. It was the first drive-in facility designed and built to provide gasoline, oils, and lubricants to the motoring public. It was also the first to offer free road maps (produced by Gulf as a marketing tool). It also provided a restroom for customers—saving many a desperate traveler. A state historical marker commemorates the site.

Girl Scout Cookies

1934
1401 Arch Street
Philadelphia

Anyone who has ever bought a few boxes of trefoils, do-si-dos, samoas, or thin mints owes a debt of gratitude to the Girl Scouts of the Greater Philadelphia Council. On November 11, 1933, Philadelphia Girl Scouts were baking cookies for day nurseries as a community service project. As luck would have it, they were demonstrating their baking skills near the windows here at the Philadelphia Gas Works headquarters. People walking by were enchanted by the aroma of freshly baked cookies, and asked if they could buy them. The girls agreed to sell the extras, and they used the money to support troop activities and buy camping equipment. The troop held another sale the next year, attracting public interest and the attention of the press. In 1934, they approached then-Philadelphia-based Keebler Baking Company about baking and packaging a vanilla cookie in the shape of the Girl Scout emblem, the trefoil. They reached an agreement, and the first sale of commercially baked Girl Scout Cookies took place from December 8 to 15, 1934. Cookies sold for 23 cents per box or six boxes for $1.35. Girl Scouts of the U.S.A. took notice of the Philadelphia Girl Scouts' successful enterprise. In 1936, the cookie idea went national when the Girl Scouts of the U.S.A. contracted with Keebler as the national supplier for the trefoil cookie. They held their first national sale from October 24 to November 7, 1936. Today, there is a state historical marker at the site of the first sale.

Lager Beer, American

1840
800 block, N. American Street
Philadelphia

American lager beer was born here in 1840 when a Bavarian brewmaster named John Wagner brought lager beer yeast, and its innovative brewing process, with him to start a new life in America. Wagner risked punishment by taking the new and highly valued beer technology to a new country. At 455 St. John Street (now N. American Street) near Poplar, he brewed the Americas' first lager in what he described as a "home brewery"—a shed behind the house which contained a cellar for aging the beer. The visionary brewer produced batches of eight 31-gallon barrels, rivaling the scale of modern brewpubs. The house where Wagner first brewed the legendary lager is long gone, but a state historical marker at the site details the history.

Little League

1939
Little League Field (now Carl E. Stotz Field)
W. 4th Street
Williamsport

Peter J. McGovern Little League Museum
525 Route 15
South Williamsport

Carl E. Stotz founded Little League baseball at this field in 1939. At the time, three teams sponsored by local businesses comprised the organization; today, Little League baseball is played by nearly 3 million children in 103 countries, and it's estimated that in the past six decades more than 30 million children have participated.

Stotz served as Little League commissioner until 1955, establishing many of the rules in place today. The first twelve Little League World Series (1947–58) were held on the field which now bears his name. A state historical marker has been placed at the site. You can also visit the Peter J. McGovern Little League Museum on U.S. 15 in South Williamsport. The annual Little League World Series, televised by ABC and ESPN, is now played at Howard J. Lamade Stadium, located behind the museum.

Marine Corps

1775
Tun Tavern
Penn's Landing (Front Street between
    Chestnut and Walnut Streets)
Philadelphia

The U.S. Marine Corps was born on November 10, 1775, in the legendary brewhouse named Tun Tavern that stood near here. Built by Samuel Carpenter in 1685 to boost development of the Philadelphia waterfront, the Tun was famous as the first brewhouse in the city, and it became a familiar Philadelphia gathering place. Benjamin Franklin utilized the tavern to organize the Pennsylvania Militia and to recruit soldiers needed to suppress Indian uprisings, and the tavern later hosted George Washington, Thomas Jefferson, and occasionally the Continental Congress. In 1775, the congress commissioned Robert Mullan to raise the first two battalions of marines to serve under the leadership of Samuel Nicholas, the man considered the first commandant of the Continental Marines.

Today, almost every U.S. Marine knows of the historical significance of Tun Tavern. Every November 10, they are said to toast the Corps' birthplace. A state historical marker is located near the site.

Christy Mathewson

1880–1925
Intersection of Routes 6 & 11
Factoryville

Baseball legend Christopher "Christy" Mathewson was born in Factoryville on August 12, 1880. He rose to fame on the diamond as a star at Bucknell University in central Pennsylvania. Mathewson then joined the New York Giants, and the elegant, handsome pitcher was arguably as popular as any baseball player in the early 1900s. Mathewson won 373 games over seventeen seasons, primarily for the Giants. With his famous fadeaway pitch, "Matty" won at least twenty-two games for twelve straight years beginning in 1903, winning thirty games or more four times. He played in four World Series, winning his only championship in 1905 when he hurled three shutouts in six days against the Athletics.

In 1936, Mathewson joined Babe Ruth, Honus Wagner, Ty Cobb and Walter Johnson in the first class of baseball Hall of Famers; unfortunately, he had died in 1925 at the age of forty-five, succumbing to tuberculosis contracted during his service in World War I. Reminders of Mathewson exist throughout Factoryville: In addition to the historic marker at this site, there is a sign upon entering the small town; a park named in his honor featuring a statue of the hurler; and a Little League field named for him.

Tom Mix

1880–1940
Mix Run Road (off Route 555)
Driftwood

Thomas Edwin "Tom" Mix, the famous cowboy star of cinema and circus, was born here on January 6, 1880. Mix served as a soldier during the Spanish-American War, though he never went overseas. In 1910 he acted in his first Western and quickly won renown for his roles in hundreds of motion pictures—both silent and sound—until 1935. Mix died in an auto accident in Arizona on October 12, 1940. A state historical marker is located at the famous cowboy's birthplace, and Mix's home is still standing.

Monopoly

1934
Germantown

In 1934, at the height of the Great Depression, an unemployed salesman named Charles B. Darrow invented the board game Monopoly. He drew on childhood memories of Atlantic City to lay out the streets on his kitchen tablecloth, creating a makeshift prototype and modeling the playing pieces on items from around his house. Soon, Darrow's friends took to the game of buying, renting and selling real estate—a popular diversion for the many victims of the Depression. Darrow sold copies of his game to department stores for $4, and eventually signed a deal with Parker Brothers in 1934. In 1970, a few years after Darrow's death, Atlantic City erected a commemorative plaque in his honor on the Boardwalk near the corner of Park Place (where else?).

Petroleum Industry

1859
Drake Well Museum
205 Museum Lane
Titusville
(814) 827-2797
www.drakewell.org

On August 27, 1859, Edwin L. Drake drilled an oil well that launched the modern petroleum industry. Today at the Drake Well Museum and Park in Titusville, a boulder sits at the spot where Drake had the foresight and persistence to drill to a depth of sixty-nine feet. The museum tells the history with orientation videos, exhibits, operating oil field machinery, and historic buildings in a park setting. Nearby Oil Creek State Park offers recreational opportunities and bike and hiking trails, which begin at the museum. Visitors can also enjoy picnic pavilions, fishing, and canoeing on Oil Creek, and a ride on the Oil Creek & Titusville Railroad.

Philly Cheesesteak

1933
Pat's King of Steaks
1237 E. Passyunk Avenue
Philadelphia
(215) 468-1546
www.patskingofsteaks.com

Pat and Harry Olivieri, founders of Pat's King of Steaks, created the Philly Cheesesteak sandwich here at Wharton and Passyunk Avenues in 1933. As the family story goes, they originally ran a hot dog stand. One day the brothers decided to try something new. Harry bought some inexpensive steak at the market, and he and Pat sliced it thin and grilled it with chopped onions. The aroma caught the nose of a cabdriver, who bought the sandwich for 10 cents. Pat and Harry switched from hot dogs to their new creation. In 1940, they earned enough to open a restaurant at the same spot as their stand. By the 1950s, competitors sold similar steak sandwiches. Longtime rival Geno's Steaks claims to be the first to add cheese, though Harry's son, Frank, claims he first added Cheese Whiz in the 1960s. The two restaurants became cultural and culinary landmarks. In the 1980s, the Olivieri business was divided up; Harry and his son kept the original location, today run by Harry's grandson, while Pat's son, Herbert, opened Olivieri's Prince of Steaks.

Eddie Plank

1875–1926
Carlisle Street and West Lincoln Avenue
Gettysburg

Southpaw Eddie Plank posted more shutouts and completed more games than any other left-hander in baseball history. Astonishingly, Plank never played baseball before prep school. He joined the Philadelphia Athletics after leaving Gettysburg College in 1901. In seventeen seasons, he helped pitch the A's to six pennants and three World Series titles while compiling a 326-194 record. He was elected to the Hall of Fame in 1946.

Plank was born on August 31, 1875, in a home (no longer standing) located near modern Business Route 15 a few miles north of town. This address is the location of the state historical marker commemorating his life and achievements; it is adjacent to Gettysburg College, where he first excelled on the baseball diamond. Plank is buried at the Evergreen Cemetery south of town.

Pro Football

1892
Recreation Park
Intersection of Grant and
**   Pennsylvania Avenues**
Pittsburgh

Pro football began on November 12, 1892, in Pittsburgh when former Yale star William "Pudge" Heffelfinger was paid $500 to play in a single game for the Allegheny Athletic Association. The field was located near the former site of Three Rivers Stadium, and today a plaque commemorates the historic event. Heffelfinger led Allegheny to victory in the contest, scoring the winning touchdown.

Slinky

1943
800 Beaver Street
Hollidaysburg

You may have heard that Slinky is "the favorite of girls and boys," but do you know how the legendary toy came to be? It was invented in 1943 by Richard James, a naval engineer who was conducting an experiment with tension springs. When one of the springs fell to the floor and began to "walk," James got an idea. His wife Betty thought that it would make a great toy. She found the name "slinky" after scouring a dictionary (it's a Swedish word meaning stealthy, sleek, and sinuous), and toy history was made. In 1945, the Slinky debuted at Gimbels Department Store in Philadelphia, where they sold all four hundred of the first shipment in ninety minutes. Since then, more than 300 million Slinky toys have been sold worldwide. Slinky is still manufactured today in Hollidaysburg using the original equipment created by James. It remains largely unchanged, and plastic versions have been added. But the Slinky can do more than walk down your stairs; it has been used as an antenna by soldiers in Vietnam, and as a therapy tool and for coordination development. In 2001, Slinky was named the official state toy of Pennsylvania.

Jimmy Stewart

1908–97
845 Philadelphia Street
Indiana

James Maitland Stewart was born in Indiana, Pennsylvania, on May 20, 1908. The front steps to the Stewart home, which no longer stands, remain along Philadelphia Street and are topped by a plaque that commemorates his birthplace. Near the site, at 845 Philadelphia Street, is the James Stewart Museum, (800) 83-JIMMY. The museum highlights Stewart's accomplishments in film, radio and television. Stewart's versatile career included classics such as *Mr. Smith Goes to Washington* (1939), *It's a Wonderful Life* (1946), *Harvey* (1950), *Rear Window* (1954), *Vertigo* (1958), and *The Man Who Shot Liberty Valance* (1962). He won an Oscar for his performance in *The Philadelphia Story* (1940). His roles as military hero, civic leader, family man, and world citizen are also woven into displays, film presentations and gallery talks. There's also a special room dedicated to his family's long and colorful history in western Pennsylvania. From the museum's windows, visitors can glimpse the family hardware store site and the bronze statue dedicated to Jimmy on his 75th birthday.

Jennie Wade

1843–63
242–246 Baltimore St
Gettysburg

Mary Virginia "Ginnie" Wade—known as "Jennie" Wade, the only civilian killed during the Battle of Gettysburg—was born here on May 21, 1843. Her birthplace was built around 1820. The Wade family rented the northern half from a tailor named John Pfoutz, who used the southern side for his shop. Today, the house is open for tours. The house Wade was killed in was her sister Georgia McClellan's home at 528 Baltimore Street. Now known as the Jennie Wade House, it is a popular tourist attraction and museum.

The Civil War came to Gettysburg in July 1863. On July 3, while Jennie was baking bread for Union soldiers, a bullet that traveled through two wooden doors killed her instantly. The brick house was located between both armies in an area known as "No Man's Land." As the armies fired on each other, the home was riddled with bullets. The north side received most of the damage as it faced the Confederate position, and today is marked with more than 150 bullet holes.

Honus Wagner

1874–1955
Mansfield Boulevard and Chartiers Street
Carnegie

Honus Wagner, nicknamed "The Flying Dutchman," was one of the Baseball Hall of Fame's five original inductees in 1936. Over a twenty-one-year career, the gritty, barrel-shaped Pittsburgh Pirates shortstop put together a lifetime batting average of .329, stole 722 bases, and amassed eight National League batting championships (to name but a few achievements). In 1905, Honus Wagner also became the first baseball player to have his personal signature burned into a Louisville Slugger baseball bat.

Wagner's modern-day fame is due much to the fact that his 1909 tobacco card (T206) is the world's most valuable baseball card. One of the cards sold for $2.8 million at auction in 2007. Wagner is also memorialized with a statue at the Pirates' modern home, PNC Park. The state historical marker here is located near his birthplace at 605 Beechwood Avenue. Honus Wagner was laid to rest at Jefferson Memorial Cemetery in Pittsburgh.

West Virginia

Pearl S. Buck

1892–1973
Rural Route 219
Hillsboro
(304) 653-4430
www.pearlsbuckbirthplace.com

Pearl Sydenstricker Buck, who wrote the Pulitzer Prize-winning book *The Good Earth*, was born here at the Stulting Place on June 26, 1892. The birthplace house was built on a 16-acre farm by the Stulting family, who emigrated from Holland to America in 1847. Buck's parents were Caroline Stulting and Absalom Sydenstricker. Buck was the first American woman to receive the Nobel Prize for Literature, based on her six books on China. While in China, she married missionary John Lossing Buck.

Today, Buck's Birthplace is an historic house museum featuring period rooms with some of the original furniture and Buck memorabilia, as well as West Virginia crafts, first-day covers of Pearl Buck stamps, and other souvenirs. The Stulting Barn, restored in 1977, features 1890s farm implements. The Sydenstricker House, birthplace of Pearl Buck's father, was transported to this location from Greenbrier County for use as a cultural center.

Father's Day

1908
301 Fairmont Avenue
Fairmont

On December 6, 1907, a West Virginia mine explosion killed more than 360 men, 210 of whom were fathers. A local woman named Grace Golden Clayton approached her pastor at the Memorial Methodist Episcopal Church South, Dr. Robert Thomas Webb, about a special day to honor fathers. Reverend Webb agreed it would be a good idea. To that end, he held a special service to honor all fathers here on July 5, 1908, and it is generally considered to be the first formal celebration of Father's Day. Over the years, the holiday continued to gain popularity and was finally officially established by President Richard Nixon in 1972. Today, Central United Methodist Church, constructed in 1922, occupies the location. A state historical marker is located in front of the church.

Nancy Hanks

1784–1818
Mike's Run
Antioch

Nancy Hanks, mother of Abraham Lincoln, was born on February 5, 1784, in a log cabin in Hampshire County, Virginia (now Mineral County, West Virginia). The cabin was located on Joseph and Lucy Hanks's 100-acre farm on Mike's Run east of Saddle Mountain. Her family later moved to Kentucky where she married Thomas Lincoln in 1806. Abraham was born in 1809. In 1816, the Lincoln family migrated to Indiana. Two years later, on October 5, 1818, Nancy died of "milk sickness," contracted by drinking tainted milk from a cow that had fed on a poisonous root. She was buried in a pioneer cemetery on a hilltop near the Lincoln farm. Abraham Lincoln knew little of her background, since she died when he was nine, and in later years he referred to her as his "Angel Mother." A memorial marker was erected to commemorate her birthplace site.

Stonewall Jackson

1824–63
Harrison County Courthouse
Clarksburg

General Thomas J. "Stonewall" Jackson, American war hero and legendary Confederate general, was born on January 21, 1824, in Clarksburg. Jackson went from being an orphan to a military hero and one of the most valued generals in the Confederate Army. After serving bravely in the Mexican War, he joined the Confederacy in 1861. During the First Battle of Bull Run in Virginia, he received his nickname. Amidst the gunfire and confusion of the battle, Brigadier General Barnard E. Bee said, "There is Jackson, standing like a stone wall." Jackson was mortally wounded at Chancellorsville, Virginia, in 1863. Today, a state historical marker and a mounted statue sits at his birthplace site on West Main Street at the junction of South Third Street in the courthouse square in Clarksburg.

Anna Jarvis

1864–1948
U.S. Routes 119 and 250
Grafton
(304) 265-5549
www.annajarvishouse.com

Anna Jarvis, the founder of Mother's Day, was born here on May 1, 1864, in a two-story wooden house built by her father, Granville E. Jarvis, in 1854. Jarvis's lifelong quest was sparked at an early age. During a class prayer given by Ann Maria Reeves Jarvis in the presence of her daughter, she closed with the prayer "I hope that someone, sometime will found a memorial mothers day commemorating her for the matchless service she renders to humanity in every field of life. She is entitled to it." Anna never forgot that prayer, and at her mother's graveside service, she vowed to fulfill her mother's wish. After years of working with local churches and government, Jarvis succeeded in organizing the first Mother's Day program at the Andrews Methodist Episcopal Church in Grafton on May 10, 1908. Ironically, Anna Jarvis never became a mother herself. Today, the Anna Jarvis Birthplace Museum has been restored by a non-profit organization.

Mother's Day

1908
**The International Mother's Day Shrine
and Museum**
Andrews Methodist Episcopal Church
11 E. Main Street
Grafton
(304) 265-1589
www.mothersdayshrine.com

The International Mother's Day Shrine and
Museum incorporates a monument and the
church building where the first Mother's Day program was held. Originally known as the Andrews
Methodist Episcopal Church, the museum commemorates the first celebration of Mother's Day,
which took place here back on May 10, 1908.
President Woodrow Wilson made it a national
holiday in 1914.

SOUTHEAST

Virginia

North
Carolina

South
Carolina

Alabama

Georgia

Florida

Alabama

W. C. Handy

1873–1958
Handy Home, Museum, and Library
620 West College Street
Florence
(256) 760-6434
www.florenceal.org/community_arts/art_
    galleries_museums/WC_Handy/index.html

William Christopher Handy was born in a small log cabin in Florence on November 16, 1873. Handy, the child of former slaves, left home as a teenager to perform in traveling minstrel shows, teaching school and leading a variety of bands, until settling in Memphis, Tennessee. While in Memphis, Handy founded a music publishing company with Harry Pace (they later moved to New York City). Although he lost his eyesight when he was thirty, Handy continued to lead bands and write music. His music combined elements of folk ballads and spirituals with ragtime, and Handy is credited with adding flatted thirds and sevenths, creating what has since been known as the blues. His pioneering role in this distinctively modern American music earned him the nickname of "The Father of the Blues." Handy composed "Memphis Blues," "Hesitating Blues," "St. Louis Blues," and other hits of the early twentieth century. The museum at his birthplace houses the world's most complete collection of Handy's personal papers and artifacts.

Helen Keller

1880–1968
Ivy Green
300 West North Commons
Tuscumbia
(256) 383-4066
www.helenkellerbirthplace.com

This is the home made famous by the inspirational Helen Keller, who became blind and deaf after falling ill around the age of two. She was born here on June 27, 1880, in the house built by her grandparents, and today it is kept much the way it was when Helen grew up here. The small cottage eventually became the living quarters for Helen and her teacher, Anne Sullivan, whose huge strides with Helen began by simply spelling out the word "water" in Helen's hand as she pumped water on it. The famous water pump, made legendary in the 1962 film *The Miracle Worker,* is also here on the grounds. The main house, the cottage, and the grounds are open to the public, and an annual Helen Keller Festival is held in June.

Jesse Owens

1913–80
Jesse Owens Memorial Park
7019 County Road 203
Danville
(256) 974-3636
www.jesseowensmuseum.org

James "Jesse" Owens, a civil rights pioneer and legendary Olympic athlete, was born on September 12, 1913, in Oakville—just minutes from Danville, site of the Jesse Owens Memorial Park and museum. One of ten children born to Henry and Emma Owens, Jesse grew up much like other black kids of his time—his parents were sharecroppers and he was the victim of racial intolerance. In 1922, his family moved to Cleveland, where Owens started his track career in junior high school. After breaking records in the 100-yard and 200-yard dash, he attended Ohio State University. But Owens is best known for his performance at the 1936 Olympic games in Berlin, with Adolf Hitler in attendance, where he captured the attention of the world by winning four gold medals—an Olympic first. His triumph not only paved the way for American black athletes, but also gave hope to oppressed minorities around the world by contradicting the fundamental beliefs of racism.

On June 29, 1996, thousands gathered to honor Jesse Owens at the dedication of the park, marked by the arrival of the Olympic torch on its journey to the Atlanta games. The park honors Owens with a museum, statue, and a 1936 torch replica. The park also mirrors Owens' dedication to the community with athletic facilities, a playground, and soon, an Olympic track.

Hank Williams

1923–53
Hank Williams Boyhood Home and Museum
127 Rose Street
Georgiana
(334) 376-2396
www.hankmuseum.com

Hiram "Hank" Williams was born in a double-pen log house on a hill southwest of Georgiana, on September 17, 1923. The house burned down, and today a red barn occupies the location. Nearby, Williams is remembered at the Hank Williams Boyhood Home and Museum. Hank's mom, Lillie Williams, moved her family to this home in Georgiana in 1930. It was here that young Hank got his first guitar, and black street musician Rufus "Tee Tot" Payne taught him his first chords. In his short career, Williams went on to record hits such as "Your Cheatin' Heart," "Long Gone Lonesome Blues," "Hey Good Looking," and "Jambalaya (On the Bayou)." He died on January 1, 1953, at the age of twenty-nine after long bouts with alcoholism and prescription drug addiction.

The city of Georgiana purchased the family home and opened the Hank Williams Boyhood Home and Museum in 1993. On display in the museum are Hank's clothes, documents, photos, recordings, and memorabilia from his life.

Florida

Burger King

1954
3090 N.W. 36th Street
Miami

Inspired by McDonald's, James McLamore and David Edgerton opened the first Burger King hamburger stand here on December 4, 1954. Originally called Insta Burger King, the hamburger stand couldn't really compete with McDonald's on price (they sold burgers for 18 cents, while their rival's burgers were only 15 cents) so they looked elsewhere for an edge. Burger King became the first chain to offer a dining room. In 1957, they introduced the Whopper aimed at bigger appetites (at a whopping 37 cents) and a year later, they began their storied journey of innovative advertising.

Department of Defense

1948
Truman Little White House
111 Front Street
Key West
(305) 294-9911
www.trumanlittlewhitehouse.com

Built in 1890 as quarters for Navy officers, this building was used later by American presidents William Howard Taft, Harry S. Truman, Dwight Eisenhower, John F. Kennedy, Jimmy Carter, and Bill Clinton. Truman used the facility as a vacation home and functioning White House between 1946 and 1952. National legislation was drafted and official government business was conducted daily from the site. Perhaps the most important of these actions occurred on December 5, 1951, when Truman enacted a civil rights Executive Order requiring federal contractors to hire minorities. The house is considered the birthplace of the U.S. Department of Defense and the U.S. Air Force as a result of the Key West Accords of 1948. President Eisenhower used the site in 1956 while recuperating from a heart attack. In 1961, the house was the venue for a summit between President Kennedy and British prime minister Harold Macmillan during the Bay of Pigs incident. Kennedy returned in 1962 after the Cuban Missile Crisis. Secretary of State Colin Powell and foreign leaders held an international summit here in 2001. The Little White House was listed on the National Register of Historic Places in 1974. Visitors can tour the house and grounds.

Gatorade

1965
University of Florida
Gainesville

School spirit can really pay off! In 1965, James Robert Cade, a professor of medicine and physiology at the University of Florida, invented Gatorade to help the Florida Gators football team. When players began collapsing after practice in the hot sun, an assistant coach asked for help. Cade's team of scientists had free rein to research and experiment on the Gators' freshmen squad. The "volunteers" were monitored as the hydrating brew was concocted in the subbasement of the university's old pharmacy building. The scientists placed rubber gloves on the players' hands to collect sweat and measure electrolytes, took blood samples, and monitored plasma volumes, determining that dehydration was the problem. They developed a mixture that allowed water and sodium to be better absorbed in the intestines. After the university turned down the rights to the drink, Cade signed a deal with Stokley-Van Camp. Sales took off, and he used profits to set up scholarships and businesses. The university eventually sued to receive royalties from Gatorade, and it now receives millions of dollars annually. Cade appeared in the recent "Legend of Gatorade" television commercials, uttering the phrase, "Naturally, we called our stuff *Gator*ade." Today, Gatorade is owned by PepsiCo, and is sold in some eighty countries. In 2007, the University of Florida dedicated a historical marker near the O'Connell Center to note the birthplace of Gatorade.

IBM PC

1981
Yamato Road and T Rex Avenue
Boca Raton

This 620,000-square-foot facility is the birthplace of the IBM personal computer (IBM 5150), completed in 1981 in a project led by IBM executive Don Estridge. To meet the deadline, his team "broke all the rules" of IBM product development: they used outside vendors for parts and went to outside software developers (including a small company called Microsoft) for the operating system. This enabled them to develop the PC in less than twelve months—faster than any other hardware product in IBM's history. The IBM PC became the industry standard, and was one of the reasons *Time* magazine chose the "personal computer" as its 1982 Man of the Year. The computer's $1,565 price included a system unit, a keyboard and color/graphics capability, an Intel 8088 microprocessor, and 16K of user memory. Two decades earlier, an IBM computer cost about $9 million and required an air-conditioned quarter-acre of space, all maintained by a staff of sixty. In 1987, IBM moved its personal computer operation to North Carolina, but maintained the Boca Raton facility until 1996.

Jim Morrison

1943–71
Old Melbourne Hospital
1250 U.S. Route 1
Melbourne

This nondescript office building was once the only hospital in Melbourne. Singer Jim Morrison was born here on December 8, 1943. Morrison (whose father was a U.S. naval officer who fought in World War II) moved to Los Angeles in the early 1960s, where he enrolled himself in the film program at UCLA. In 1965, after Jim graduated from UCLA, he drifted into the hippie scene at Venice Beach and one day ran into Ray Manzarek, a keyboardist and former classmate from UCLA. Soon, they recruited guitarist Robbie Krieger and drummer John Densmore and began calling themselves the Doors. Through the 1960s, the Doors crafted moody, dark hit records including "The End," "L.A. Woman" and "Riders On the Storm." They also had a smash hit with "Light My Fire."

Onstage, Jim gained a reputation for erratic performances. On December 9, 1967, Jim was arrested onstage during a concert in New Haven, Connecticut, for attempting to incite a riot. On March 1, 1969, during a concert in Miami, Florida, Jim was arrested again, this time for exposing himself to the audience and using profanity. In August 1970, he was brought to trial for the Miami incident where he was acquitted of charges of lewd and lascivious behavior, but found guilty of indecent exposure and profanity, and was sentenced to eight months in prison. He remained free on bail while the verdict was being appealed, but when the last of his appeals was denied and with the possibility of jail hanging over him, Jim moved to Paris, France. On July 3, 1971, Morrison was found dead in his bathtub in his apartment in Paris at the age of twenty-seven. The local police listed the cause of death as a heart attack, likely alcohol or drug related.

Georgia

Erskine Caldwell

1903–87
Erskine Caldwell Birthplace and Museum
Camp Street (town square)
Moreland
(770)254-8657
www.newnan.com/ec

Erskine Caldwell, the author of *Tobacco Road* and *God's Little Acre*, was born in this modest frame house on December 17, 1903. He was one of the most successful and controversial American writers of the twentieth century—in fact, his books have been made into three movies, and the stage adaptation of *Tobacco Road* made American theater history when it ran for more than seven years on Broadway. He was named to the American Academy of Arts and Letters and was honored by the governments of France and Bulgaria for his writing.

Also known as "The Little Manse," the birthplace of Caldwell has been restored to its 1903 appearance and relocated to the town square in Moreland as a museum. Its collections include books by and about Caldwell, photographs from various periods of his life, art from book covers, dramatizations of stories, and personal items.

PRESIDENTIAL BIRTHPLACE
Jimmy Carter

39TH

1924–
Lillian G. Carter Nursing Center
  (formerly Wise Sanitarium)
225 Hospital Street
Plains

Jimmy Carter, the thirty-ninth president of the United States and recipient of the 2002 Nobel Peace Prize, was born October 1, 1924, at the Wise Sanitarium in the small farming town of Plains. He was born to James Earl Carter Sr., a farmer and businessman, and Lillian Gordy, a nurse. Carter was the first president ever born in a hospital. He spent his early years in a home without plumbing or electricity. He rose from the son of a peanut farmer to attend the U.S. Naval Academy. After his naval service he entered Georgia politics, becoming governor of the state in 1970. He was elected president in 1976.

As president, Carter expanded the national park system to include protection of 103 million acres of Alaskan lands, created the Department of Education, and bolstered the Social Security system. He also appointed record numbers of women, blacks, and Hispanics to government jobs. In foreign policy, he was known for the Panama Canal treaties, the Camp David Accords, the Egypt/Israel peace treaty, and the establishment of U.S. diplomatic relations with the People's Republic of China.

The hospital where Carter was born, built only three years before his birth, was converted to a nursing home in 1957 and is now the Lillian G. Carter Nursing Center.

Ty Cobb

1886–1961
1350 Highway 105 (Ty Cobb Parkway)
Narrows

Tyrus Raymond "Ty" Cobb was born at this site on December 18, 1886. Nicknamed "The Georgia Peach," Cobb is regarded by many historians as the best player of baseball's "dead-ball era" and as one of the greatest players of all time. Cobb garnered the most votes of any player on the 1936 inaugural Hall of Fame Ballot, receiving 222 out of a possible 226 votes. Cobb, who played most of his career with the Detroit Tigers, is credited with ninety Major League Baseball records during his career and he still holds several, including the highest career batting average (.367). Cobb's legacy as an athlete has sometimes been overshadowed by a reputation for a nasty temperament and an overly aggressive playing style. A roadside marker at this site describes the original location of the cabin in which the Cobb family lived and where Ty was born. The Ty Cobb Museum is located in nearby Royston; call (706) 245-1825 or visit www.tycobbmuseum.org.

Coca-Cola

1886
107 Marietta Street
Atlanta

Many today feel they "need" their daily dose of Coca-Cola, and the soft drink indeed had its beginnings as a "cure-all" tonic—and it all started here in Atlanta. On May 8, 1886, a former Confederate officer and druggist, Dr. John Stith Pemberton, invented "Coca-Cola" syrup in a thirty-gallon brass kettle hung over a backyard fire. He took one of the first jugs of the concoction to Jacob's Pharmacy and convinced Willis E. Venabele to mix it with water and sell it for five cents a glass. Marketed as a "brain and nerve tonic" in drugstores, sales averaged nine drinks per day. Pemberton's bookkeeper, Frank M. Robinson, suggested the name "Coca-Cola" because the words represented two ingredients of the drink—coca leaves and cola nuts. He also suggested the name be written in Spencerian script, a popular penmanship of the era; it was from his pen that the "Coca-Cola" signature originated. Pemberton liked the memorable name, and history was made. The drink evolved further on November 15, 1886, when an allegedly drunk man named John G. Wilkes stumbled into a drugstore complaining of a headache, and requested a bottle of Coca-Cola syrup. Impatient for relief, he asked the soda jerk to mix up a glass on the spot. Rather than walk to the other end of the counter to mix it with cold tap water, the clerk used soda water. The man marveled at the tasty elixir, and Coca-Cola was first enjoyed in its fizzy, carbonated form. The building at 107 Marietta where the drink was invented is no longer there. Jacob's Pharmacy, where Coca-Cola formula was dispensed for the first time, was located at the southwest corner of Peachtree and Marietta Streets, now the site of the Wachovia tower.

Gone with the Wind

1936
Margaret Mitchell House and Museum
990 Peachtree Street
Atlanta
(404) 249-7015
www.gwtw.org

The birthplace of the classic novel *Gone with the Wind* is a two-block historic site in downtown Atlanta listed on the National Register of Historic Places. Tours here include the furnished apartment where Margaret Mitchell wrote her Pulitzer Prize–winning novel, and the house built in 1899 by the son of an Irish immigrant that—along with Mitchell's Irish ancestors—inspired the characters in the novel. There are also numerous exhibit galleries. On display is original movie set doorway from Tara, Rhett's trousers, the original life-size portrait of Scarlett, movie scripts, collectibles, and posters from around the world. Guided tours, which last 1 to 1½ hours, begin in the visitor center.

Oliver Hardy

1892–1957
Laurel and Hardy Museum
250 North Louisville Street
Harlem
(706) 556-0401
www.laurelandhardymuseum.org

The great comic actor Oliver Hardy of the famed duo Laurel and Hardy was born Norvell Hardy here in Harlem on January 18, 1892, at his mother's parents' home. The youngest of five children, Hardy lost his father to a heart attack in 1892 (Norvell was only ten months old). After his father died, Norvell's mother took the family to Milledgeville where she became the manager of the Baldwin Hotel. Young Oliver was enthralled by the visiting troupes of performers who stayed there. Later, as the manager of the town's first movie theater, Hardy performed regularly. After attending the Georgia Military Academy, the Atlanta Conservatory of Music, and, for a short time, the University of Georgia, Hardy left Georgia in 1913 for the newly established film colony in Jacksonville, Florida. After working at various studios on the east coast, he left for Hollywood in 1918. "Babe," as his friends knew Hardy, worked for several years as a supporting actor until he was accidentally teamed with a young Englishman, Stan

Laurel. Laurel and Hardy remained partners and friends until Hardy's death in Hollywood in 1957. Though the home where Hardy was born no longer stands, a marker at the museum details his history in the town of Harlem.

Charles Holmes Herty

1867–1938
West Hancock Street
Milledgeville

A Georgia state historical marker near the old Baldwin County Courthouse marks the site where Charles Holmes Herty, one of America's outstanding chemists, was born on December 4, 1867. Herty attended the Middle Georgia Agricultural and Military College in Milledgeville and the University of Georgia in Athens. After earning a doctorate from Johns Hopkins University, Herty returned to Georgia to become a chemistry professor at the University of Georgia. In addition to his teaching duties, Herty played a pivotal role in development of UGA's athletic programs: he was the coach of the school's first baseball team, and in 1890 he organized Georgia's first college football team.

As a chemist, Herty helped revive or create several Southern industries. He developed a more efficient and environmentally conscious system of extracting resin from pine trees, buoying both the turpentine and lumber industries. Herty also proved and advocated the effective use of Southern pine trees for making newsprint and white paper, leading to the birth of a new economic engine.

Kazoo

1840s
Macon

The kazoo (or membranophone) is a simple musical instrument that adds a "buzzing" timbral quality to a player's voice when one hums into it. The kazoo is a type of mirliton—a device that modifies the sound of a person's voice by way of a vibrating membrane. The membranophone label is a key element in the kazoo being called a musical instrument. An African American named Alabama Vest invented the version we know today in Macon in the 1840s and had Thaddeus Von Clegg, a German clockmaker in town, manufacture his kazoos. The instrument was introduced to the South at the Georgia State Fair in South Mountain in 1852.

Martin Luther King Jr.

1929–68
Martin Luther King Jr. National Historic Site
501 Auburn Avenue
Atlanta
(404) 331-6922
www.nps.gov/malu

The greatest icon of the American civil rights movement, Dr. Martin Luther King Jr., was born on January 15, 1929, in an upstairs bedroom of this Queen Anne-style house owned by his grandfather, A. D. Williams. Today, King's birth home, the nearby Ebenezer Baptist Church (where he, his father, and grandfather all officiated), and his gravesite comprise the Martin Luther King Jr. National Historic Site and Preservation District.

The son of Reverend and Mrs. Martin Luther King Sr., Dr. King (born Michael Luther King Jr.) grew up in the Sweet Auburn community, the African-American hub of Atlanta. His Christian upbringing and theological education greatly influenced his speeches and his work in the civil rights movement, and the teachings of Gandhi were instrumental in King adopting his nonviolent methods of protest.

King rose to a position of leadership and high visibility in the civil rights movement by spearheading the 1955–56 Montgomery, Alabama, bus boycott. He is

today best remembered for his "I have a dream" speech, delivered on the steps of the Lincoln Memorial during the 1963 March on Washington. He was also awarded the Nobel Peace Prize in 1964. King's work and life were tragically cut short on April 4, 1968, when he was assassinated in Memphis, Tennessee.

Today, visitors to the national historic site can peruse exhibits about King and the civil rights movement. Park rangers lead tours of the home on the trail of the Freedom Walk, an interpretive route through Sweet Auburn toward downtown Atlanta.

Sidney Lanier

1842–81
Sidney Lanier Cottage
935 High Street
Macon
(478) 743-3851
www.historicmacon.org/slc.html

This modest home is the birthplace of the great southern poet Sidney Lanier. The cottage where Lanier was born has been converted to a museum, which is owned and operated by the Historic Macon Foundation. Lanier was a poet, musician, and scholar who was nationally known and particularly beloved in the South. He served in the Confederate Army until he was captured aboard a blockade runner and confined at Fort Lookout, Maryland. Lanier was best known for his regional poems, including "The Marshes of Glynn," "The Song of the Chattahoochee," and "Sunrise." The cottage features an interesting array of Lanier memorabilia.

Juliette Gordon Low

1860–1927
10 East Oglethorpe Avenue
Savannah
(912) 233-4501
www.juliettegordonlowbirthplace.org

This historic home is the birthplace of Juliette Gordon Low, founder of Girl Scouts of the USA. It was also the first National Historic Landmark in Savannah. Built in 1821, the house blends Regency architecture and Victorian-style additions. Not coincidentally, the Girl Scouts organization was born a few blocks away at the Andrew Low House. The Girl Scouts of the USA purchased this historic site in 1953, restored it to its late 1880s decor, and opened it to the public in 1956.

Juliette Low was laid to rest in the family plot at Laurel Grove Cemetery in Savannah. She was buried in her full Girl Scout uniform. A telegram in her pocket from Sir Robert Baden-Powell (founder of the scout movement) states: "You are not only the first Girl Scout, you are the best Girl Scout of them all."

Jackie Robinson

1919–72
Hadley Perry Road
Cairo

Born on January 31, 1919, to sharecroppers and slave grandparents on what was once a plantation, Jack Roosevelt "Jackie" Robinson was just two years old when his mother packed up he and his four siblings, hopped on a train, and headed to California.

Robinson went on to become a collegiate sports star at UCLA, and he served a two-year stint in the Army before joining the Kansas City Monarchs of the Negro League in 1945. Jackie achieved everlasting fame in 1947, when he broke Major League Baseball's color barrier as a member of the Brooklyn Dodgers.

The second baseman was National League Rookie of the Year in 1947 and NL MVP in 1954, and he helped Brooklyn win its only World Series title in 1955. Robinson was elected to the Hall of Fame in 1962; in 1997, the fiftieth anniversary of Robinson breaking the color barrier, Major League Baseball retired his number 42.

The tin-roofed wooden house where he was born in this small southwest Georgia town burned down in 1996, leaving only the brick chimney and double fireplace as a physical reminder of Jackie Robinson's birthplace. A recently unveiled marker, placed by the Georgia Historical Society, identifies the exact spot of the house.

Robert Winship Woodruff

1889–1985
1414 Second Avenue
Columbus

Coca-Cola became the "real thing" around the world in large part because of Robert Winship Woodruff, born here on December 6, 1889. When he was only thirty-three, the former truck salesman took command of The Coca-Cola Company in 1923 and shaped the young soft drink enterprise and its bottler franchise system into a corporate giant with the world's most widely known trademark. He pioneered such revolutionary concepts as the six-bottle carton, the open-top cooler (the precursor to the vending machine), the signature fountain glass, and the automatic fountain dispenser. By establishing a "foreign department," his vision shepherded Coca-Cola into the huge international brand that it is today. A man of enormous stature and personal magnetism, Woodruff's influence over the affairs of The Coca-Cola Company was absolute until his death in 1985. His birthplace is honored with a historical marker.

North Carolina

Civil Rights Movement

1960
F. W. Woolworth Store
132 S. Elm Street
Greensboro

International Civil Rights Center & Museum
301 N. Elm Street, Suite 303
Greensboro
(800) 748-7116
www.sitinmovement.org

Although the Civil Rights Movement has had many heroes and historic moments, its inception can be traced to four brave college students who defied a national injustice here on February 1, 1960. That afternoon, four freshmen from North Carolina Agricultural and Technical College—Ezell Blair Jr., David Richmond, Joseph McNeil, and Franklin McCain—entered the F. W. Woolworth store on South Elm Street. They seated themselves at the "whites only" Woolworth lunch counter, igniting a movement to protest segregated public eating facilities and unequal access for African Americans across the country. The next day, they returned with nineteen supporters, and by the third day, about eighty-five white and black students from neighboring colleges turned out to support them. Before the week was out, there were more than four hundred supporters. Meanwhile, students staged smaller sit-ins in seven other North Carolina cities as well as in Hampton, Virginia, and Nashville, Tennessee. By summer, thirty-three southern cities had integrated their restaurants and lunch counters. One year later, 126 cities had taken the same step. To commemorate the students' actions, the International Civil Rights Center & Museum was established near the site of that original sit-in.

John Coltrane

1926–67
Hamlet Avenue at Bridges Street
Hamlet

A plaque here marks the birthplace of jazz saxophonist and composer John Coltrane on September 23, 1926. Coltrane began playing tenor saxophone as a teen and worked with numerous big bands, including Dizzy Gillespie's band, before coming into his own in the mid-1950s. He became as a major stylist while playing as a sideman with Miles Davis. Coltrane made a number of influential recordings, among them the modal-jazz classics *My Favorite Things* (1961) and *A Love Supreme* (1964). In 2007, Coltrane received a posthumus citation from the Pulitzer Board for his "masterful improvisation, supreme musicianship, and iconic centrality to the history of jazz."

Flight

1903
Wright Brothers National Memorial
1401 National Park Drive
Manteo
(252) 441-7430
www.nps.gov/wrbr

Flying was born here. Wilbur and Orville Wright made the first successful sustained powered flights in a heavier-than-air machine here on December 17, 1903. The world-changing achievement of these two visionaries from Dayton, Ohio, is commemorated by a sixty-foot granite monument, dedicated in 1932 and perched atop the ninety-foot Kill Devil Hill. Also in the park is a commemorative boulder, placed at the approximate site of the revolutionary 1903 liftoff. The Wright Brothers Visitor Center tells the story through a series of exhibits, which include replicas of the brothers' 1902 glider and 1903 flying machine.

PRESIDENTIAL BIRTHPLACE
Andrew Johnson

17TH

1808–75
Fayetteville Street
Raleigh
(919) 857-4364

Andrew Johnson, the seventeenth president of the United States and the man who succeeded Abraham Lincoln, was born in the kitchen of a small wooden house in Raleigh on December 29, 1808. At the time of his birth, the building was a kitchen and residence behind Casso's Inn in downtown Raleigh. Johnson's mother worked as a weaver and his father was the inn hostler, caring for the horses, as well as a janitor at the state capitol. The original birthplace has been relocated to Mordecai Historic Park, about a mile away, but a state historical marker is located near the site of his original birthplace.

Andrew Johnson ran a tailor shop in Greeneville, Tennessee, before entering politics. He served in the House of Representatives and Senate before becoming vice president under Abraham Lincoln. Following President Lincoln's assassination, President Johnson led attempts to reunify the nation torn by civil war. In 1868, he was impeached and removed from office, charged by some Radical Republican members in the House of Representatives with violating the Tenure of Office Act.

Pepsi-Cola

1898
256 Middle Street
New Bern
(252) 636-5898

Pepsi-Cola was invented at a pharmacy on this site in 1898 by Caleb Bradham, a pharmacist who originally called his new concoction "Brad's Drink." In 1903, he would patent the drink as "Pepsi-Cola." Typical of pharmacists of the era, Bradham operated a soda fountain in his drugstore where he served homemade beverages, and the customers' favorite was Brad's Drink. His recipe included carbonated water, sugar, vanilla, rare oils, pepsin, and cola nuts. (The pepsin and cola nuts inspired the name "Pepsi-Cola.") Unfortunately, Bradham lost everything in the stock market in 1923, and in 1929 Pepsi-Cola went bankrupt; it was bought in 1931 by the Loft Candy Company. Today, at the actual birthplace of Pepsi, visitors can enjoy a re-created soda fountain and purchase a wide variety of Pepsi memorabilia inside the store, which opened its doors on the one hundredth anniversary of Pepsi-Cola.

PRESIDENTIAL BIRTHPLACE
James K. Polk

11TH

1795–1849
President James K. Polk
  State Historic Site
12031 Lancaster Highway
Pineville
(704) 889-7145
www.nchistoricsites.org/polk

James K. Polk, eleventh president of the United States, was born here on November 2, 1795, on a 150-acre farm worked by his parents, Jane and Samuel. Polk became known as the first "dark horse" in American politics when he defeated Martin Van Buren for the 1844 Democratic nomination to run against Henry Clay, the Whig nominee. With the re-annexation of Texas and the re-occupation of Oregon as hot issues in the 1844 election, Polk took a strong stand in favor of both, and he rode into the White House.

At the President James K. Polk State Historic Site, a reconstructed log cabin, period log buildings, and furnishings similar to what the Polks might have had illustrate the early life of the future president.

J. E. B. Stuart

1833–64
Laurel Hill
1091 Ararat Highway
Ararat
(276) 251-1833
www.jebstuart.org

Confederate Major General James Ewell Brown "Jeb" Stuart, the most famous cavalry commander of the Civil War, was born on February 6, 1833, at this site. The house, built around 1830, was destroyed by fire in the winter of 1847–48.

Stuart graduated from the U.S. Military Academy at West Point in 1854, and then served as a U.S. Army officer until 1861, when he joined the Confederate Army. In 1862, he became cavalry commander of the Army of Northern Virginia, where he made his mark on history.

Stuart once commented to his brother about his birthplace, "I would give anything to make a pilgrimage to the old place, and when the war is over quietly spend the rest of my days there." Sadly, he never made it, as he was mortally wounded at the Battle of Yellow Tavern, Virginia, in 1864. In 1992, the J. E. B. Stuart Birthplace Preservation Trust purchased the seventy-acre property to preserve and interpret the birthplace of General Stuart.

South Carolina

Dizzy Gillespie

1917–93
337 Huger Street
Cheraw

This park marks the site of jazz great Dizzy Gillespie's birthplace in Cheraw. The park includes a historical marker and features sculpture and park benches that symbolize his life. There is also a statue of Gillespie on the Cheraw Town Green on Market Street. Born here in 1917 as John Birks Gillespie, "Dizzy" attended public schools, graduating from Robert Smalls in 1933. His family attended the Wesley United Methodist Church on Green Street, and as a child, he was employed to keep kids from sneaking into the Lyric Theater. Now the Theater on the Green, the restored circa 1920 facility is used for performances. Gillespie's musical talents earned him a scholarship to the Laurinberg Institute in North Carolina. In 1990, Gillespie received the National Medal of the Arts (the highest award bestowed upon an American artist) and was honored by the Kennedy Center for his contributions to the performing arts. A guide to the sites connected to his life is available at the Cheraw Chamber of Commerce.

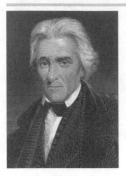

PRESIDENTIAL BIRTHPLACE
Andrew Jackson

1767–1845
Andrew Jackson State Park
196 Andrew Jackson Park Road
Lancaster
(803) 285-3344
www.southcarolina_parks.com/park-finder/
    state-park/1797.aspx

7TH

Andrew Jackson Memorial
8215 Waxhaw Highway (Route 75 East)
Waxhaws, North Carolina
(704) 843-1832
www.museumofthewaxhaws.com

"Old Hickory," Andrew Jackson, the seventh president of the United States, was born in the Waxhaws area near the border of North and South Carolina on March 15, 1767. Historians still debate on which side of the state line the birth took place. The two most likely locations are Craw-

ford Plantation in Lancaster County, South Carolina, and the George McCamie cabin, located in what is now Union County, North Carolina. The sites are just a few miles from each other, and the state line had yet to be drawn at the time of Jackson's birth.

As a soldier, Jackson is known for leading American troops to a resounding victory over the British at the Battle of New Orleans in 1814—a battle that took place, unbeknownst to the combatants, after a peace treaty had been signed. Jackson's presidency saw many firsts. He was the first populist president; his rise from humble upbringings and his inclusive style of governing lent his name to "Jacksonian Democracy." He was also the first to have his vice-president resign (John C. Calhoun), he was the first to have married a divorcée, he was the first to be nominated at a national convention (his second term), and the first to use the pocket veto to kill a congressional bill.

Today, visitors can decide Jackson's true birthplace location themselves by visiting the Andrew Jackson Memorial at the Museum of the Waxhaws and the historical marker placed by the Daughters of the American Revolution and a bold equestrian statue of the president at Andrew Jackson State Park.

Virginia

William Randolph Barbee

1818–68
Lee Highway (U.S. Route 211)
   and Skyline Drive
Luray

Sculptor William Randolph Barbee was born near here at his home, Hawburg, on January 17, 1818. The house was built by his father and often served as a stopping point for those preparing to cross the Blue Ridge Mountains.

Barbee is known for his works portraying classical figures, and he is best remembered for the pieces *Coquette* and *Fisher Girl*. Barbee was a lawyer by trade. He became a sculptor after a wealthy Lynchburg art patron, impressed with Barbee's carving skills, sent him to Italy to study sculpture. Barbee quickly became a noted artisan, and he maintained a studio in the United States Capitol in the 1850s. He was at work on a frieze for the pediment of the House of Representatives when the Civil War broke out in 1861. The Virginian left Washington at the onset of the war, and his piece was never finished. William's son, Herbert, also became a sculptor and completed two of his father's unfinished works—*The Star of the West* and *The Lost Pleiad*.

In 1972, the Virginia Historical Landmarks Commission erected a marker near William's birthplace site.

William Clark

1770–1838
Ladysmith Road
Chilesburg

William Clark, one half of the famed duo that led the Corps of Discovery on its exploration of the American West, was born on August 1, 1770, at a family plantation about one mile north of the Virginia state historical marker at this location. After his family moved to Kentucky in 1784, Clark began his career as a military man, serving in several Indian campaigns as a member of the Kentucky militia.

In 1803, Clark's friend Meriwether Lewis (see page 118) asked him to help lead the overland expedition to the Pacific Ocean. The three-year journey—and the discoveries made during its time—won Clark widespread fame and respect. He later served as Indian agent for the Louisiana Territory, governor of the Missouri Territory, and superintendent of Indian Affairs. He died in St. Louis on September 1, 1838, and is buried there in Bellefontaine Cemetery.

William Clark was the younger brother of famed frontier soldier George Rogers Clark (1752–1818). George was not born at this site; his birthplace was in central Virginia near Charlottesville.

PRESIDENTIAL BIRTHPLACE
William Henry Harrison

9TH

1773–1841
Berkeley Plantation
12602 Harrison Landing Road
Charles City
(804) 829-6018
www.berkeleyplantation.com

William Henry Harrison, the ninth president of the United States, was born on February 9, 1773, at this plantation to a distinguished family. His father, Benjamin Harrison, was a signer of the Declaration of Independence, and his grandson, also named Benjamin Harrison, became the twenty-third president. William Henry Harrison was the oldest man to take office, at age sixty-eight—a record that stood for 140 years until Ronald Reagan took office at age sixty-nine. He also served the shortest presidential term in history, dying only thirty-one days into his term. However, before becoming president, Harrison had a distinguished career.

He served as secretary of the Northwest Territory, and from 1801–12 served as governor of the Indiana Territory. Harrison also won fame for his military success at the Battle of Tippecanoe (1811) and as a general in the War of 1812. Harrison is credited with opening up the Indian territories to settlement.

Harrison's birthplace mansion was built in 1726 on a hilltop overlooking the James River. The date of the building and the initials of the owners, Benjamin Harrison IV and his wife, Anne, appear in a datestone over a side door. It is believed to be the oldest three-story brick house in Virginia that can prove its date, as well as the first with a pediment roof. Today, visitors can tour Berkeley Plantation and see an incredible array of eighteenth-century antiques as well as an exhibit of Civil War artifacts.

Sam Houston

1793–1863
U.S. Route 11
Lexington (Timber Ridge)

Sam Houston, the commander-in-chief of the Texas Army who secured Texas independence at the Battle of San Jacinto, was born here on March 2, 1793, in a cabin. Houston served as president of Texas from 1836–38 and from 1841–44. He was also a U.S. Senator and governor of Texas. Today, a 38,000-pound piece of Texas pink granite commemorates the birthplace of the Texas hero at the Sam Houston Wayside.

PRESIDENTIAL BIRTHPLACE
Thomas Jefferson

3RD

1743–1826
U.S. Route 250
Charlottesville

Thomas Jefferson, author of the Declaration of Independence and third president of the United States, was born at Shadwell Plantation near Charlottesville on April 13, 1743. His father, Peter Jefferson, a surveyor, planter, and officeholder, purchased the Shadwell tract where Jefferson was born by 1741. He built a house soon after and developed the plantation into a successful agricultural operation.

As a Founding Father and the author of the Declaration of Independence, Jefferson helped shape the government and philosophies of the United States. His presidency saw many defining moments in the formative years of the country, including the Louisiana Purchase and the Lewis and Clark Expedition. Jefferson was also wartime governor of Virginia, the first secretary of state, the second vice president, and the founder of the University of Virginia. However, Jefferson was more than a politician, also establishing himself as an architect, scientist, and inventor of the swivel chair, pedometer, dumbwaiter, and hideaway bed. He could read more than five languages and was the U.S. minister to France for several years.

Thomas Jefferson spent his early years at Shadwell, but when the house burned to the ground in 1770, he moved to Monticello, the house he designed and at which he is buried. Today, a marker sits at the former site of Shadwell on U.S. Route 250 (sign on eastbound side) just west of Charlottesville.

Simon Kenton

1755–1836
U.S. 15 (northbound)
   at the junction with Route 234
Hopewell Gap

Simon Kenton, legendary frontiersman and friend of Daniel Boone, was born April 3, 1755, in Fauquier County, Virginia. He grew up without any formal schooling, instead working with his father on their family farm. Kenton left home in 1771 and befriended Daniel Boone, George Rogers Clark, Simon Girty, and Spencer Records. He established his legacy through his service as a scout and as one of the founders of Kentucky. Today, a historical marker sits at the birthplace site of Kenton near Hopewell Gap at U.S. Route 15 and Route 234.

Fitzhugh Lee

1835–1905
4700 Franconia Road
Alexandria

Fitzhugh "Fitz" Lee, nephew of Confederate Civil War general Robert E. Lee, was born at Clermont near Alexandria on November 19, 1835. He graduated from the U.S. Military Academy in 1856. During the Civil War, Fitzhugh Lee was commissioned as a lieutenant in the Confederate army and rose to the rank of major general by 1863. He served with Maj. Gen. J. E. B. Stuart and commanded cavalry at Antietam, Chancellorsville, and Gettysburg. Lee is known to have led the last charge of the Confederates at Farmville, Virginia, shortly before the surrender at Appomattox.

Lee was the governor of Virginia from 1886 to 1890. He later served as Consul General in Havana (1896–1898) and commanded the U.S. Army VII Corps in Cuba during the Spanish-American War. Today, a historical marker is located at his birthplace site, now the entrance to Mark Twain Middle School on Franconia Road.

Robert E. Lee

1807–70
Stratford Hall Plantation
483 Great House Road
Stratford
(804) 493-8038
www.stratfordhall.org

Robert E. Lee, legendary commander of the Confederate Army of Northern Virginia during the Civil War, was born on January 19, 1807, at Stratford Hall Plantation. He was the fourth child of Revolutionary War hero Henry "Light Horse Harry" Lee and Ann Hill Carter Lee.

Lee, a West Point graduate and veteran of the Mexican War, famously declined President Abraham Lincoln's offer of command of the Union Army and remained loyal to his home state of Virginia when it seceded from the Union (a move which Lee actually opposed). He first served as military advisor to Confederate President Jefferson Davis, and then went on to achieve military victories in the Second Battle of Bull Run, the Battle of Fredericksburg, and the Battle of Chancellorsville. His forces were defeated at the Battle of Gettysburg, but made an escape to Virginia. Lee eventually surrendered to General Ulysses S. Grant on April 12, 1865, at Appomattox Court House, thus ending the Civil War. Lee's birthplace, today known as Stratford Hall, is a majestic house on a bluff above the Potomac River. Its unique architecture and style distinguish it from typical colonial houses. It is still managed as a farm today, and visitors can relish more than 1,600 acres of original farmland.

Meriwether Lewis

1774–1809
Locust Hill Farm
U.S. Route 250
Charlottesville

Meriwether Lewis, leader of the Lewis and Clark Expedition, was born in Virginia on August 18, 1774. Called "the greatest pathfinder this country has ever known," Lewis, along with William Clark (see page 114), was chosen by President Thomas Jefferson to lead an expedition to the Pacific Ocean in 1804. The duo led a party of thirty-one men west, reached the coast on November 15, 1805, and returned safely in a rigorous trip in 1806. After a hero's welcome, Lewis was named governor of Louisiana. In 1809, Lewis traveled to Washington, D.C. to answer complaints about his actions as governor. He died a mysterious death when he was shot in his room at a tavern near Nashville. While Jefferson (and many scholars today) believed he committed suicide, his family maintained that he was murdered, and the facts remain uncertain. In 1942, the Virginia Conservation Commission placed a historical marker to honor the birthplace of Lewis. It is located on U.S. 250 near Ivy, west of Charlottesville. Locust Hill Farm is a private residence.

PRESIDENTIAL BIRTHPLACE
4TH
James Madison

1751–1836
U.S. Route 301
Port Conway

James Madison, Father of the Constitution and fourth president of the United States, was born here in Port Conway on March 16, 1751. Madison is best known for his leadership in shaping the new republic following the American Revolution. Along with Alexander Hamilton and John Jay, Madison wrote *The Federalist Papers*, a series of eighty-five essays that encouraged the adoption of the U.S. Constitution. In Congress, James Madison helped secure passage for the Bill of Rights. As president, Madison asked Congress for the declaration that entered the

United States into the War of 1812; he and his family were later forced to flee the White House when the British burned it during the invasion of Washington in 1814. A historical marker at the intersection of U.S. Route 301, James Madison Parkway, and Walsingham Road commemorates the site of his birthplace.

John Marshall

1755–1835
John Marshall Birthplace Park
Germantown Road (County Route 649)
Midland

John Marshall, the longest serving Chief Justice in Supreme Court history (1801–35), was born in a log cabin near here on September 24, 1755, at Licking Run, near Germantown (now Midland) in what became Fauquier County. Marshall was instrumental in shaping constitutional law and defining the American legal system, as well as helping establish the Supreme Court's power. He is noted for advocating for the court's right to judicial review. Marshall's military background included serving as captain in the Continental Army during the Revolutionary War and spending the winter of 1777–78 with the troops in Valley Forge. Marshall also served as secretary of state. In 1950, the Virginia Conservation Commission erected a historical marker nearby at John Marshall Birthplace Park.

Matthew Fontaine Maury

1806–73
Furnace Road
Spotsylvania

Matthew Fontaine Maury, the "Pathfinder of the Seas," who helped found the U.S. Weather Bureau, was born in this area on January 14, 1806. The pioneering scientist won his fair share of nicknames for his many contributions to charting winds and ocean currents. He is known as the "Father of the Naval Observatory," "Father of Modern Oceanography and Naval Meteorology," and "Scientist of the Seas," especially due to his groundbreaking study of oceanography titled *Physical Geography of the Sea* (1855). He plotted the present North Atlantic ocean lanes, conceived the idea of an Atlantic cable, and lent his expertise to laying the first cable, which made overseas communication possible. During the Civil War, Maury accepted the position of commander in the Confederate States Navy, and was sent to England as a Confederate spokesperson. Today, his birthplace site is designated by several historical markers in Spotsylvania and is a stop on the Fredericksburg and Spotsylvania County Battlefields Memorial Tour.

PRESIDENTIAL BIRTHPLACE

5TH

James Monroe

1758–1831
Route 205
Near Colonial Beach,
   Westmoreland County

James Monroe, the fifth president of the United States, was born here on April 28, 1758. In 1811, President James Madison appointed Monroe as secretary of state, and in 1816 he became the president. He was easily re-elected in 1820, winning 231 of 232 electoral votes, and his administration was termed "The Era of Good Feelings." He is known for the Monroe Doctrine (1823), which proclaimed U.S. hostility toward any European intervention in the Americas.

In 1976, The College of William & Mary began an archaeological survey of the James Monroe Birthplace and uncovered the ruins of the Monroe family home. The twenty by fifty-eight-foot house foundation coincided with the known 1845 etchings of the home. The study indicated that Monroe's beginnings were humble. The family resided in a small four-room, rough-cut wooden farmhouse with a few outbuildings on a 500-acre farm filled with wetlands. Today, Monroe's birthplace, already recognized as a state and national archaeological site, is in the process of being restored and is planned for designation as a national landmark. A state historical marker is located about one mile from Monroe Hall.

Naval Aviation

1910
Ocean View Boulevard
Norfolk

On November 14, 1910, a Curtiss biplane piloted by E. B. Ely took off from the deck of the cruiser U.S.S. *Birmingham* at anchor off Old Point Comfort. The plane flew two miles to Willoughby Spit before landing on the beach near this location, now part of Naval Air Station Norfolk.

World War II brought a renewed interest in shipboard operations, and Naval Air Station Norfolk began developing and testing catapult and arresting-gear systems for the Navy. Additionally, NAS Norfolk began to provide anti-submarine patrols to clear the vital seaways off the Mid-Atlantic coast. Although Naval Air Station Norfolk was dis-established on February 5, 1999, Chambers Field continues to operate as a detachment of Naval Air Station Oceana.

Walter Reed

1851–1902
Intersection of Routes 616 and 614
Belroi
(804) 693-3992
www.apva.org/walterreed

Dr. Walter Reed, the esteemed U.S. Army physician who helped eradicate yellow fever, was born on September 13, 1851. He earned fame as the bacteriologist who headed the 1900 Yellow Fever Commission; he proved the disease was transmitted by mosquitoes, thus enabling completion of the Panama Canal. He was also a medical hero of the Spanish-American War for his study of typhoid. His discoveries saved millions of lives and dramatically advanced the fields of epidemiology and biomedicine. APVA Preservation Virginia maintains the pre-1850 historic two-room cottage and loft building where Reed was born. It is open by appointment.

Secretariat

1970–89
Meadow Farm
Route 30
Doswell

Secretariat, considered by many to be the most inspiring and beloved racehorse of all time, was born here on March 3, 1970. Secretariat finished first in sixteen out of twenty-one starts, earned a total of $1,316,808, and captured the Triple Crown in 1973. Secretariat's times in the Kentucky Derby and Belmont Stakes are still the fastest in history. "Big Red's" thirty-one-length victory in the Belmont is regarded as one of the greatest sporting performances of all time. A state historical marker was erected near his birthplace, located on Route 30 east of the King William/Caroline County line.

"Taps"

1862
Berkeley Plantation
12602 Harrison Landing Road
Charles City
(888) 466-6018
www.berkeleyplantation.com

The haunting military bugle piece called "Taps" was composed by Brigadier General Daniel A. Butterfield at Berkeley in 1862, while General George B. McClellan and 140,000 Union troops were quartered there during the Peninsula Campaign. It was played for the first time here in July 1862 by bugler Oliver W. Norton. Berkeley is Virginia's most significant historic plantation for other reasons, as well. On December 4, 1619, early settlers from England came ashore at Berkeley Plantation and observed the first official Thanksgiving in America. It is also the birthplace of Benjamin Harrison, signer of the Declaration of Independence, and President William Henry Harrison (see page 114).

PRESIDENTIAL BIRTHPLACE
Zachary Taylor

1784–1850
Montebello Plantation
Gordonsville

12TH

Zachary Taylor, twelfth president of the United States and a decorated war hero, was born on November 24, 1784, in a log cabin. Taylor was known as "Old Rough and Ready" for his homespun dress and readiness for a fight, as demonstrated by his forty-year military career during which he fought or led troops to victory in the War of 1812, the Second Seminole War, and the Mexican War. He was the first president who had not been previously elected to any other public office, the second president to die from illness while in office, and the second president to actually die in the White House. Although Taylor's actual birthplace is often disputed, the state of Virginia has concluded that the Montebello Plantation was the probable site and that the birth may have taken place in a secondary house while the family was quarantined because of a measles scare. The site is closed to the public, but a state historical marker sits near it on U.S. Route 33, a few miles west of Gordonsville.

PRESIDENTIAL BIRTHPLACE
John Tyler

10TH

1790–1862
John Tyler Memorial Highway
Charles City

John Tyler, the tenth president of the United States, was born on March 29, 1790, on a plantation on the James River. He was the second son of Mary Armistead Tyler and Judge John Tyler, a personal friend of Thomas Jefferson. Tyler served as a state legislator, governor of Virginia, U.S. Senator, and vice president under William Henry Harrison. Tyler was the first vice president to take office as president upon the death of the chief executive. Up to that point, the interpretation of the Constitution on that subject was largely unclear, so Tyler decided to have himself sworn in as president instead of merely serving as an "acting president" and holding new elections. Although his decision was bitterly denounced by some, it set a precedent that has been followed ever since. As president, Tyler would go on to oversee the annexation of Texas. At the time of his death he was serving as a Confederate congressman. The home where John Tyler was born is still standing but is privately owned and is closed to the public. There is a marker on Route 5 near the house.

Booker T. Washington

1856–1915
Booker T. Washington National Monument
12130 Booker T. Washington Highway
Hardy
(540) 721-2094
www.nps.gov/bowa

Booker Taliaferro Washington, the country's most prominent African American educator and orator of the late nineteenth and early twentieth centuries, was born a slave on the Burroughs Plantation on April 5, 1856. He grew up there during the Civil War in the farm's one-room cabin with his mother and two half siblings. He graduated from Hampton Institute in 1875 and later established a school for blacks in Alabama, which became the Tuskegee Institute. He spent his lifetime urging blacks to help themselves through educational attainments and economic advancement. Washington was also an advisor on race relations to Presidents Theodore Roosevelt and William Howard Taft. In his 1901 biography, *Up from Slavery*, Washington recalls, "I was born a slave on a plantation in Franklin County, Virginia. I am not quite sure of the exact place or exact date of my birth, but at any rate I suspect I must have been born somewhere and at some time." Today, the Booker T. Washington National Monument at the former Burroughs Plantation features reconstructions of the nineteenth-century farm buildings similar to those from Washington's childhood.

PRESIDENTIAL BIRTHPLACE
George Washington

1ST

1732–99
**George Washington Birthplace
National Monument
1732 Popes Creek Road
Washington's Birthplace
(804) 224-1732
www.nps.gov/gewa**

George Washington, the father of our country and the first president of the United States, was born on February 22, 1732, to Augustine and Mary Washington. He served as the commander-in-chief of the Continental Army during the Revolutionary War, presided over America's Constitutional Convention, and oversaw a long series of "firsts" that set historical precedents. Washington only lived three years at his original birthplace, located on Popes Creek just off the Potomac River. Washington's father, Augustine, purchased the land in 1718 and built the house in 1726. Washington's half brother, Augustine Jr., inherited the property after his father's death. The original dwelling was a U-shaped timber-frame house, which burned in 1779. On May 14, 1932, build-

ings and the 367 acres once owned by the Washington family were presented to the secretary of the interior, and George Washington Birthplace National Monument officially became a national park. The birthplace site was excavated in 1936 and in 1974, but the foundation was covered over to preserve it. The location of the home and the size and shape of the foundation are marked by crushed oyster shells. The foundation over which a memorial house (right) was constructed has since been determined to be that of an outbuilding.

PRESIDENTIAL BIRTHPLACE
Woodrow Wilson

28TH

The Woodrow Wilson Presidential Library
18–24 North Coalter Street
Staunton
(540) 885-0897
www.woodrowwilson.org

Woodrow Wilson, the twenty-eighth president of the United States who oversaw America's entry into World War I, was born in this Greek Revival manse on December 28, 1856. The home was built in 1846 to house the pastors of Staunton's First Presbyterian Church. In 1855, Wilson's parents, Rev. Dr. Joseph Ruggles Wilson and Janet Woodrow Wilson, moved in.

Wilson's presidency saw the passing of major legislation establishing the Federal Reserve System and the Federal Trade Commission, as well as laws including the Clayton Antitrust Act and the Underwood Tariff. Although he believed in neutrality, in 1917 he asked Congress to formally declare war on Germany and the Central Powers, and the U.S. officially entered World War I. On a lighter note, Wilson was the first president to throw out a first ball at a World Series. He was also the first to watch a movie in the White House, D. W. Griffith's controversial

The Birth of a Nation (1915). Wilson won the Nobel Peace Prize in 1919 for conceiving of the League of Nations. Today, the Woodrow Wilson Birthplace is a National Historic Landmark. The manse was acquired by the Woodrow Wilson Birthplace Foundation in 1938 and was dedicated as a museum by President Franklin D. Roosevelt in 1941.

MID-SOUTH

Missouri

Kentucky

Tennessee

Arkansas

Mississippi

Louisiana

Arkansas

PRESIDENTIAL BIRTHPLACE
Bill Clinton

42ND

1946–
1001 South Main Street
Hope

William Jefferson Clinton, the forty-second president of the United States, was born at the Julia Chester Hospital in the small town of Hope, Arkansas, on August 19, 1946. His birthname was William Jefferson Blythe III, named after the father who died in an auto accident three months before Bill was born. The future president changed his surname to Clinton when he was a teenager, after his stepfather, Roger Clinton.

Clinton served as Arkansas attorney general and governor before his election as president in 1992. Clinton easily won reelection in 1996, but was impeached by the House of Representatives in 1998 after lying under oath about an affair with a White House intern; he was then acquitted by a Senate trial. Clinton would leave office with high approval ratings, thanks to a domestic economic boom, budget surplus, and relative peace abroad.

The hospital where Clinton was born has since been demolished; there is a state historical marker noting the site today. Nearby at 117 S. Hervey Street is Clinton's First Home Museum (right), a two-and-a-half-story home built in 1917 by Clinton's biological grandparents. Clinton lived at the home until 1950. The site, now open to the public, is sometimes erroneously referred to as the "Clinton Birthplace."

Douglas MacArthur

1880–1964
MacArthur Museum of Arkansas Military History
503 E. Ninth Street
Little Rock
(501) 376-4602
www.arkmilitaryheritage.com

Douglas MacArthur was born January 26, 1880, in the Little Rock Barracks—originally a Civil War arsenal, today the MacArthur Museum of Arkansas Military History. The first room on the right upon entering the museum is known as the birthplace of MacArthur, although some say his parents were assigned an upstairs room. MacArthur started his life the same way he lived it—surrounded by the U.S. Army (his earliest memory was the sound of military bugles).

MacArthur was one of the greatest American war heroes of the twentieth century, and he played crucial and sometimes controversial roles in World War I, World War II, and Korea. His father, General Arthur MacArthur, earned the Congressional Medal of Honor as a teenager fighting in the Civil War, and would eventually become military governor of the Philippines. MacArthur's father spent eighteen months at the Little Rock Barracks before transferring.

After 1892, the birthplace structure remained vacant for fifty years until it opened in 1942 as the Museum of Natural History and Antiquities. The historic structure reopened in 2001 as the MacArthur Museum of Arkansas Military History, preserving the birthplace of a military hero and honoring Arkansas' military heritage.

Wal-Mart

1951
105 N. Main Street
Bentonville
(501) 273-1329

This museum is on the site of Sam Walton's original 5&10 store in Bentonville, the town now home to Wal-Mart world headquarters. Walton opened this store (as part of the Ben Franklin franchise) in 1951 and went on to form his own company, opening his first Wal-Mart Discount City Store in Rogers, Arkansas, in 1962. The Wal-Mart Visitors Center at this site traces the origin and growth of Wal-Mart, telling the story behind the company that is now the world's largest private employer.

Kentucky

Cheeseburger

1934
Kaelin's Restaurant
1801 Newburg Road
Louisville
www.kaelins.com

When it comes to the invention of the cheeseburger, who was really the Big Cheese? Carl and Margaret Kaelin *may* have beaten Louis Ballast of Denver (see page 202) by one year. According to the story, in 1934, Carl Kaelin was cooking a hamburger in his new restaurant when he decided to throw on a slice of American cheese—he apparently liked the extra "tang" from the cheese. He christened his new creation the "cheeseburger." A proclamation from the mayor of Louisville designated every October 12, the date of Carl Kaelin's invention, as Kaelin's "Cheeseburger Day" in Louisville.

Jefferson Davis

1808–89
Jefferson Davis State Historic Site
Highway 68 E
Fairview
(270) 889-6100
http://parks.ky.gov/findparks/historicparks/jd

Jefferson Davis, the first and only president of the Confederate States of America, was born at this site on June 3, 1808.

Davis's family moved to Mississippi when he was young, and Jefferson attended schools in Mississippi and Kentucky before enrolling at West Point. Following graduation from the academy he served in the Mexican War, and he later held offices as a Mississippi congressman, senator, and secretary of war during the Franklin Pierce administration. Davis was selected president of the Confederacy in 1861, and he held that post until he was arrested and detained by Federal forces in 1865.

While the house where Davis was born no longer stands, the site is now a Kentucky state park and is marked by an impressive 351-foot-high concrete obelisk. Visitors may climb to the top of the monument. A visitors center details Davis's life and career.

Johnny Depp

1963–
Owensboro Mercy Hospital (formerly
  Our Lady of Mercy Hospital)
811 E. Parrish Avenue
Owensboro

Johnny Depp was born June 9, 1963, at Our Lady of Mercy Hospital in Owensboro (today Owensboro Mercy Hospital). His mother was a waitress named Betty Sue Palmer and his father was a civil engineer named John Christopher Depp Sr. To this day, Depp claims that he doesn't know the origin of his surname, but jokes that it translates to "idiot" in German (it actually translates to a lighthearted insult similar to "fool"). Depp, a three-time Academy Award-nominated actor, is best known for his portrayals of eccentric and offbeat characters in the *Pirates of the Caribbean* films, as well as numerous Tim Burton-directed films like *Edward Scissorhands, Ed Wood,* and *Charlie and the Chocolate Factory*.

"Happy Birthday to You"

1893
The Little Loomhouse
328 Kenwood Hill Road
Louisville

The melody of "Happy Birthday to You"—the most popular song in the English language, according to the *Guinness Book of World Records*—was written in 1893 by sisters and schoolteachers Patty and Mildred J. Hill at Esta Cabin, now part of the Little Loomhouse complex. Their original verse, "Good Morning to All," was a classroom greeting, first published in their songbook, *Song Stories for the*

Kindergarten. Nobody knows who wrote the modern lyrics of "Happy Birthday to You," but that version first appeared in a songbook edited by Robert H. Coleman in 1924. By the mid 1930s, the new song had appeared in a Broadway musical and had been used for Western Union's first singing telegram. In 1934, Jessica Hill, a third Hill sister, secured the copyright of "Happy Birthday to You." Chicago-based music publisher Clayton F. Summy Company published and copyrighted the song in 1935 as an arrangement by Preston Ware Orem.

Kentucky Fried Chicken

1930
688 U.S. 25 W
Corbin

Corbin is the birthplace of Kentucky Fried Chicken. Colonel Harlan Sanders was born on September 9, 1890, in Henryville, Indiana (see page 165). It wasn't until 1930, however, that Sanders moved to Corbin, where he would one day forge the culinary empire for which he became famous. Once in Corbin, Sanders opened a service station, which was located on a spot near where the current Kentucky Fried Chicken is located. In the back of that service station, he operated a lunchroom, which consisted of one table surrounded by six chairs. It wasn't long, however, before word spread and Sanders found it necessary to expand his capacity. By 1937, he had built Sanders' Cafe, which seated 142 customers. At this restaurant, it was soon discovered that Sanders's fried chicken was the most popular selection on the menu.

Each year, thousands of customers make a stop at the Harland Sanders Café and Museum, where they can view a variety of items from the early days of Sanders' restaurant business, including a barrel of his famous recipe, a life-size statue of the Colonel, and a replica of his original kitchen. You can view Harland Sanders exhibits, take advantage of the convenient drive-thru service, or even enjoy a meal in the Colonel's original dining room.

133

PRESIDENTIAL BIRTHPLACE
Abraham Lincoln

1809–65
Abraham Lincoln Birthplace
  National Historic Site
2995 Lincoln Farm Road
Hodgenville
(270) 358-3137
www.nps.gov/abli

16TH

In the fall of 1808, Thomas and Nancy Lincoln settled on the 348-acre Sinking Spring Farm. On February 12, 1809, Abraham Lincoln was born in a one-room log cabin near the spring. The Lincolns lived here and farmed before moving to land a few miles away at Knob Creek. An early nineteenth-century Kentucky cabin, symbolic of the one in which Lincoln was born, is today enshrined inside the Memorial Building at the site of his birth. The National Park Service's Lincoln Birthplace Unit features 116 acres of Sinking Spring Farm. It also includes a visitor center, the Sinking Spring itself, site of the Boundary Oak tree, and other reminders of the sixteenth president's beginnings. A nearby unit preserves the site of the Knob Creek Farm as Abraham Lincoln's Boyhood Home.

Lincoln rose from his frontier beginnings to become one of the best-known men in American history. His political career began in the Illinois legislature, but he rose to prominence after an unsuccessful run for the U.S. Senate in 1858. That campaign was notable for Lincoln's debates against Stephen Douglas, which focused on the increasingly divisive issues surrounding slavery.

Though Lincoln lost the election to Douglas, the debates launched him onto the national stage. The fledgling Republican Party made him its presidential nominee in 1860, and he became the president after winning a plurality of the national vote. Thus began his extraordinary presidential term, during which the nation became embroiled in civil war. Lincoln held firm to his belief in the preservation of the Union, guiding the nation through the terrible four-year conflict. Lincoln also issued the Emancipation Proclamation, which began the process of freedom for America's slaves (and also allowed black soldiers to fight for the Union). Many of Lincoln's speeches are considered landmarks, among them the House Divided Speech, the Cooper Union Address, the First Inaugural Address, the Gettysburg Address, and the Second Inaugural Address. Lincoln was elected to a second term in 1864, but never got a chance to finish out that term. He was assassinated in Washington, D.C.'s Ford's Theatre by John Wilkes Booth on April 14, 1865—just five days after the Confederate surrender at Appomattox.

Loretta Lynn

1935–
Millers Creek Road
Butcher Hollow
Van Lear
(606) 789-3397

Loretta Lynn, the "First Lady of Country Music" and a Country Music Hall of Fame inductee, was born April 14, 1935, in Butcher Hollow (known as "Butcher Holler" by the locals), a small mining community in Johnson County, Kentucky. She and her siblings, including sister Crystal Gale, were born to Ted and Clara Webb, who named Loretta after movie actress Loretta Young. Many of the songs she has written were inspired by her stormy relationship with her husband Doolitle, such as the 1966 hits "You Ain't Woman Enough (To Take My Man)" and "Don't Come Home a-Drinkin' (With Lovin' on Your Mind)." Lynn's popularity soared with her 1976 autobiography *Coal Miner's Daughter* and the related film. She was also the first country star to appear on the cover of *Newsweek* magazine, as well as the first woman to win the Country Music Association's "Entertainer of the Year" award. Today, her brother Herman Webb conducts tours of the home, which has been preserved with most of its original furnishings to show what life was like during Lynn's childhood.

Louisiana

Jazz

Before 1800
Congo Square
New Orleans

Congo Square is an open space within Louis Armstrong Park, which is located in the Treme neighborhood of New Orleans, just across Rampart Street from the French Quarter. Why is the area known as Congo Square thought to be the birthplace of jazz? During slavery days, multi-racial crowds gathered here to make music, dance, and kindle the tribal rhythms that were the lifeblood of African culture. The musical seeds planted in this park are what grew into what we know as jazz, and Congo Square is listed on the National Register of Historic Places for its musical and cultural significance.

Sazerac Cocktail

1800s
Fairmont Hotel
123 Baronne Street
New Orleans
(504) 529-4764

One of America's first cocktails, the Sazerac, was created here in the Big Easy. It happened in the early 1800s thanks to a man named Antoine Peychaud.

The Sazerac was named for his favorite French brandy, Sazerac-du-Forge et fils. In 1870, the drink was changed when American rye whiskey was substituted for cognac, and a dash of absinthe was added by local bartender Leon Lamothe, who today is regarded as the Father of the Sazerac. Absinthe was banned in 1912, so Peychaud substituted his special bitters in its place. In 1893, the Grunewald Hotel was built in the New Orleans, and the hotel earned the exclusive rights to serve the Sazerac (in 1965 the hotel was renamed the Fairmont Hotel). Today, the Sazerac is enjoyed in many of New Orleans'

finest restaurants and bars, most notably the Sazerac Bar in the Fairmont Hotel, where celebrities, locals, and tourists enjoy the drink.

Tabasco

1860s
McIlhenny Company
Avery Island
(337) 365-8173
www.tabasco.com

Tabasco, the world's most popular hot sauce, has deep roots in Louisiana. It is still made at its birthplace on Avery Island, a small community about 140 miles west of New Orleans. The Tabasco story begins in the mid-to-late 1860s, when local banker and amateur gardener Edmund McIlhenny was given *Capsicum frutescens* pepper seeds from Latin America. He cultivated the plants and loved the peppers they produced. McIhenny created a hot sauce from the peppers, and it proved so popular that he quit his day job to make the sauce full time. The name of the sauce is alleged to come from a Mexican Indian word meaning either "place where the soil is humid" or "place of the coral or oyster shell."

Today the sauce is still made with the original ingredients in the same factory where it was born. Tabasco's worldwide popularity—the sauce is sold in 160 countries—has even caused a bit of a land crunch on the island: all seeds are cultivated on Avery Island, but because of lack of space, many are then shipped to Latin America to be grown into peppers.

The McIlhenny family still owns and operates the company, and they also own a large swath of Avery Island. Visitors to the island can tour the pepper sauce factory and visit Jungle Gardens and Bird City, a 250-acre nature preserve begun by I. A. McIhenny (Edmund's son) in 1895.

Mississippi

William Faulkner

1897–1962
Cleveland Street
New Albany

William Faulkner, the Nobel Prize winner whom many consider the greatest writer of the twentieth century, was born in a clapboard house in New Albany on September 25, 1897. He is revered for such works as the novels *The Sound and the Fury* (1929) and *As I Lay Dying* (1930), and the short stories "A Rose for Emily" and "Red Leaves." When he was born, Faulkner's parents lived in a simple frame house on the corner of Jefferson and Cleveland Streets, a few blocks from the railroad. Historians believe the house was one of the first built on the north side of town. The house was demolished in the 1950s and a state historical marker commemorates the site. Visitors can learn more about Faulkner at the Union County Heritage Museum, located just a block away from the site of his birthplace, at 114 Cleveland Street in New Albany. Call (662) 538-0014 or visit www.ucheritagemuseum.com.

Robert Johnson

1911–38
The Robert Johnson Center
138 North Ragsdale Road
Hazlehurst

The "King of the Delta Blues Singers," Robert Johnson, was born in Hazlehurst on May 8, 1911. The influential musician is known for a handful of songs recorded between November 1936 and June 1937, such as "Kind Hearted Woman Blues," "Cross Road Blues" and "Love in Vain." One legend says that he sold his soul to the Devil "at the crossroads" in exchange for his remarkable talent on the guitar. Many rock legends, including Eric Clapton and the Rolling Stones, have covered his songs, and in 1986, he was inducted into the Rock and Roll Hall of Fame. Today, the Robert Johnson Foundation maintains the Robert Johnson Center in the historic Hazlehurst Depot. It contains memorabilia related to Johnson and is the starting point of the Robert Johnson Walking Tour.

Kermit the Frog

1955
Jim Henson Delta Boyhood Exhibit
415 SE Deer Creek Drive
Leland
(662) 686-7383
www.lelandms.org/kermit.html

Kermit the Frog, the original Muppet, was "born" on the banks of Deer Creek in the small town of Leland, where Muppet creator Jim Henson spent much of his childhood. In this charming town twelve miles east of Greenville, Henson met his boyhood friend Kermit Scott, who is believed to have lent his name to Kermit the Frog. Today, Leland pays tribute to Henson (and Kermit) with an exhibit located at the Washington County Tourist Center/Chamber of Commerce, which was donated by The Jim Henson Company as "a gift to the people of Leland." It features a tableau honoring Kermit the Frog's birth on Deer Creek, photographs from the Henson family album, a video center with many of Jim Henson's early works, and a gift shop. A separate room is filled with Muppet memorabilia.

Elvis Presley

1935–77
306 Elvis Presley Drive
Tupelo
(662) 841-1245
www.elvispresleybirthplace.com

Before the days of Graceland, Elvis Presley was born in Tupelo, Mississippi, on January 8, 1935 in this modest two-story house. Presley rocketed to fame from his humble upbringing, first hitting the charts as a hip-swiveling, pompadoured, rock and roll rebel in the mid-1950s. His September 1956 appearance on the *Ed Sullivan Show* (with Presley shot by camera from the waist up to hide his scandalously gyrating hips) instantly made him a household name. His many hit records included "Jailhouse Rock," "Hound Dog," and "Blue Suede Shoes." Presley also appeared

in dozens of movies, including *King Creole* and *Blue Hawaii*. During the late 1960s, with his career on the downturn, Presley reinvented himself as "The King," a melodramatic icon known for his sequined, karate-style jumpsuits, lavish lifestyle, and over-the-top concerts. Elvis Presley died in 1977, and his Memphis home, Graceland, has become a permanent shrine to the singer. The more subdued birthplace has been faithfully restored to the period before the singer's family moved to Memphis. The Elvis Presley Birthplace, part of the Elvis Presley Park, has been designated a Mississippi landmark and includes the Elvis Presley Museum, Memorial Chapel, gift shop, and a life-size statue titled *Elvis at Age 13*.

Teddy Bear

1902
Onward Store
Intersection of U.S. Route 61 and Route 1
Onward

Where, oh where, was the teddy bear born? Down south in a place called Onward, Mississippi. In 1902, President Theodore Roosevelt visited the state to go hunting for wild game. While in the woods, a bear was located by a member of the hunting party for the president to shoot. The bear was exhausted and possibly lame, and some claim it was a mere cub. In any case, Roosevelt refused to shoot the helpless animal because he thought it unfair. News of the president's refusal to shoot the bear spread far and wide. Soon after, Morris Michtom, a New York merchant, made toy history when he created a stuffed toy bear and labeled it "Teddy's Bear" in honor of Roosevelt. Today, a state historical marker next to the general store in Onward (near where Roosevelt met the bear) tells the story of the bear hunt and the birth of the teddy bear.

The picturesque town of Glenwood Springs, Colorado, also claims to be the birthplace of the teddy bear. When Roosevelt stayed at the Colorado Hotel there in 1905, he went hunting bear in the local mountains. Legend says that hotel maids at the Colorado created a bear doll from fabric after one of Roosevelt's unsuccessful hunts, hence the origination of the teddy bear.

Eudora Welty

1909–2001
741 N. Congress Street
Jackson

Pulitzer Prize-winning writer Eudora Welty was born April 13, 1909, in this house near the state capitol. The house was built by her parents Christian and Chestina Welty in 1908. Many of the events memorialized in Welty's 1984 book, *One Writer's Beginnings*, occurred here. She gained fame for her photography and literary works such as *Curtain of Green* (1941), *The Robber Bridegroom* (1942), and *The Optimist's Daughter* (1972). Today, her childhood home is known as the Eudora Welty Writers Center, a working retreat for writers from around the world. The Eudora Welty Foundation operates the house at 1119 Pinehurst Street where Welty lived from 1925 to 2001. For more information, visit www.eudorawelty.org or call (601) 353-7762.

Tennessee Williams

1911–83
Tennessee Williams Home and Welcome Center
300 Main Street
Columbus
(662) 329-1191
www.columbusms.org

Built in 1875, this two-story Victorian house is the birthplace of the great southern playwright, Thomas Lanier "Tennessee" Williams. Moved to its present location in 1995, the home now serves as a state welcome center. Williams lived in this home, then the rectory for St. Paul's Episcopal Church, for three years. Walter Dankin, Williams's grandfather, served as the church's rector. The home, built of wood native to Mississippi, has been restored to its 1911 condition. The first floor is open to visitors. Newspaper and magazine articles about Williams are prominently displayed. The home also maintains a bound collection of works by Williams. Many tourists enjoy walking one block north to see the stately St. Paul's Episcopal Church where young Williams was baptized. Considered one of the most important southern playwrights, Tennessee Williams spent much of his youth outside the South. Williams built a career as a playwright, novelist, poet, and a screenwriter for MGM. He is best known for the plays *The Glass Menagerie* (1945), *A Streetcar Named Desire* (1947), and *Cat on a Hot Tin Roof* (1955).

Oprah Winfrey

1954–
Oprah Winfrey Road
Kosciusko

Oprah Winfrey, beloved talk show host, was born here on January 29, 1954. The pioneering multimedia icon, Emmy Award winner and Oscar nominee was the first black woman to appear on the *Forbes* magazine billionaire list. She founded Harpo Productions, the magazine *O*, and a book club that wields unprecedented power in the publishing industry. On Route 12E just east of town, a sign by a dirt road points visitors to "Oprah Winfrey Road." She lived here until age six. The Kosciusko Chamber of Commerce operates a tourist information center on the Natchez Trace at mile marker 160. The city has gained worldwide fame as the birthplace of Winfrey, and visitors can also see the Buffalo United Methodist Church—which she attended as a young girl—and her family cemetery.

Missouri

Molly Brown

1867–1932
The Molly Brown Birthplace & Museum
505 North 3rd Street
Hannibal
(573) 221-2477
www.visitmollybrown.com

Margaret Brown, better known as "The Unsinkable Molly Brown" who survived the sinking of the *Titanic*, was born Margaret Tobin on July 18, 1867. When she turned eighteen, she moved to Leadville, Colorado. There she met and married mining engineer James J. Brown. The couple became wealthy when gold was found at a mine partially owned by James. Brown (who was never actually called Molly during her life) used her fame to fight for the rights of workers, women, and children, as well as historic preservation. During World War I in France, she worked to rebuild areas behind the front lines, helped wounded soldiers, and was eventually awarded the French Legion of Honour.

Her birthplace was built in the early 1860s by a Hannibal lumberman. The Marion County Historical Society renovated the house in 1964, and opened it to the public for about ten years. Between 1978 and 1998 the house slid into disrepair. Soon after, hundreds of volunteers worked to restore the house as accurately as possible for the period of 1867 to 1885. Today at the Molly Brown Museum, visitors can learn about Molly's rags-to-riches story and tour the cottage furnished with period antiques, including a room dedicated to the voyage and sinking of the *Titanic*. Photographs, newspaper accounts, and displays tell the story of Molly's trip to Europe and the role she played in the efforts to help the widows and orphans from the *Titanic* tragedy.

George Washington Carver

1864–1943
George Washington Carver
  National Monument
5646 Carver Road
Diamond
(417) 325-4157
www.nps.gov/gwca

George Washington Carver became a famous American agricultural chemist. However, he was born a slave in 1864 on this farm in Missouri. In 1896 he joined the staff of Tuskegee Institute as director of the department of agricultural research, retaining that post the rest of his life. His efforts to improve the economy of the South (particularly African Americans) included teaching soil improvement and crop diversification. He discovered hundreds of uses for the peanut, the sweet potato, and the soybean and stimulated the cultivation of these crops. He devised many products from cotton waste and extracted blue, purple, and red pigments from local clay. In 1953 his birthplace was made a national monument. The park consists of 210 acres of the original 240-acre Moses Carver homestead. The visitor center includes a museum with exhibits that trace George W. Carver's life from his birth through his youth at the Carver farm, to his role as an artist, educator, and humanitarian, as well as his world-renowned work as a scientist. Highlights of the monument include the Carver bust, birthplace site, boyhood statue, William's Pond, 1881 Moses Carver dwelling, and Carver family cemetery.

Walter Cronkite

1916–
St. Luke's Hospital (former location)
2400 Frederick Avenue
St. Joseph

Newsman Walter Cronkite was called "the most trusted man in America" during his two decades as anchor of *The CBS Evening News*. A correspondent for United Press International during World War II, he joined CBS television in 1950 as a reporter and was appointed the evening news anchor in 1962. He remained in that role until his retirement in 1981, ending each broadcast with the now-famous catchphrase, ". . . and that's the way it is." Cronkite is vividly remembered by many Americans as breaking the news of the death of President John F. Kennedy on November 22, 1963.

Cronkite was born in St. Joseph on November 4, 1916. He lived in Kansas City until he was ten, when his family moved to Houston, Texas. The hospital where Cronkite was born, St. Luke's, is today an apartment complex called the Frederick Towers. It is the original building that once housed the hospital.

Ice Cream Cone

1904
Forest Park
St. Louis

Who would've thought an unlikely collaboration would help bring about the ice cream cone? It happened at the 1904 St. Louis World's Fair, which is now Forest Park (at 1,370 acres, one of the largest urban parks in the United States). The fair drew more than 20 million visitors from around the world, and many of them must have enjoyed the goods of Charles Menches, an ice cream vendor who ran out of dishes in which to serve his product. In the stall next to Menches was Ernest Hamwi, who was selling waffles. Hamwi offered to help and cleverly rolled up some of his waffles to be used to serve Menches' ice cream, and the ice cream cone was born. In 1920, Hamwi received a patent for the ice cream cone.

Jesse James

1847–82
James Farm and Museum
21216 James Farm Road
Kearney
(816) 628-6065
www.jessejames.org

Notorious outlaw Jesse James was born on this farm on September 5, 1847. One of the most storied and romanticized criminals in American history, James's legendary bank and train robberies won him worldwide fame, and his legend continued to grow after his early demise. His birthplace, today known as the Jesse James Farm and Museum, is a Clay County Historic Site, and features the largest collection of James family memorabilia in the world. Visitors can see three of Jesse's guns, the boots he was wearing when he was killed, a pair of his spurs, the family Bible, and what's left of Jesse's original tombstone. The cabin where James was probably born was built in 1822, and is believed to be the oldest standing structure in Clay County. The James farm was owned by the descendents of Frank and Jesse James until 1978. Clay County purchased the farm, which was nearly in ruins, from Jesse's grandchildren and restored it.

Negro League

1920
Paseo YMCA
1800 Paseo Boulevard
Kansas City

In 1920, team owner (and former Negro League pitcher) Andrew "Rube" Foster met here with other independent team owners to brainstorm a plan to create a stable league of teams to help establish black baseball. This summit resulted in the formation of the Negro National League (NNL). Besides Foster's American Giants, charter members included the Chicago Giants, the Dayton Marcos, the Detroit Stars, the Indianapolis ABCs, the St. Louis Giants, and the Kansas City Monarchs. Prior to this historic session, Negro League teams were mainly a group of rudderless barnstormers. After the organization was formed, they grew into a popular, nationally recognized association. Over the next forty years, the Negro Leagues expanded to include more than 2,600 athletes and dozens of teams. Visit the nearby Negro Leagues Baseball Museum at 1616 E. 18th Street. For more information, call (816) 221-1920 or visit www.nlbm.com.

J. C. Penney

1875–1971
J. C. Penney Museum
312 N. Davis Street
Hamilton
(816) 583-2168

A pioneer of American retail, James Cash "J. C." Penney was born here on September 16, 1875. He was the seventh of twelve children born to James and Mary Frances Paxton Penney. He went into retailing when he was twenty, and is responsible for advancing customer service as a business priority. His first enterprises were called the Golden Rule stores. From his first store in Kemmerer, Wyoming, (see page 236) his business grew into a chain of more than 1,700 J. C. Penney locations. Today at the J. C. Penney Museum in Hamilton, visitors can see Penney's first and last desks, and even sit in his last office chair. The museum has displays featuring Penney's Masonic sword, cases filled with historic J. C. Penney sales literature, and photos of his pedigreed livestock. The museum also houses a public library and community room.

Pony Express

1860
Pony Express Museum
914 Penn Street
St. Joseph
(816) 279-5059
www.ponyexpress.org/history.htm

The purpose of the Pony Express was simple: provide the fastest mail delivery between St. Joseph, Missouri, and Sacramento, California. The service was active from April 3, 1860, to late October 1861. The Pony Express ran day and night, and 183 men are known to have ridden for the organization during its 18-month existence. As far as what it took to be a rider, one recruitment ad read: "Wanted. Young, skinny, wiry fellows. Not over 18. Must be expert riders. Willing to risk death daily. Orphans preferred." While most riders were around twenty years old, the youngest was eleven, and the oldest was in his mid-forties. Riders were paid $100 per month, and a relay system ensured that each rider got a fresh horse every ten to fifteen miles. Four hundred horses were purchased to stock the Pony Express route—thoroughbreds, mustangs, pintos, and morgans were often used across about 165 stations. The total trail length was almost two thousand miles and ran through the present-day states of Missouri, Kansas, Nebraska, Colorado, Wyoming, Utah, Nevada, and California.

The original building in St. Joseph, known as the Pike's Peak Stable, was built in 1858. In 1860, the Central Overland California and Pike's Peak Express Company purchased the building for the Pony Express. On April 3, 1860, William (Billie) Richardson left this stable, rode the short distance to the nearby Patee House, picked up the waiting mochila (knapsack full of mail), and headed west on the first Pony Express run to Sacramento. The original wooden structure was replaced by a brick building in 1888, but some of the original posts and beams were reused and can be seen today at the Pony Express Museum, which faithfully preserves the history of the Pony Express on the very site where it all began.

Route 66

1926
Park Cental Square
Springfield

It is difficult to pinpoint the birthplace of a historic road that passes through eight states and runs more than 2,400 miles—but Route 66 definitely has its roots in this small Missouri town. On April 30, 1926, highway officials from Missouri and Oklahoma held a historic meeting in Springfield to decide on a number for this new road. They sent a telegram to Washington, D.C. requesting the numerical designation of "66"—and thus, the first recorded reference to Route 66 took place here, making Springfield the official "birthplace" of America's most famous highway. Route 66 was officially commissioned U.S. Highway 66 on November 11, 1926, stretching from Chicago to Santa Monica, California. A placard in Park Central Square in Springfield was dedicated to the city by the Route 66 Association of Missouri for its prominent role in the birth of this storied highway.

PRESIDENTIAL BIRTHPLACE
Harry S. Truman

 33RD

1884–1972
Harry S. Truman Birthplace
   State Historic Site
1009 Truman Street
Lamar
(417) 682-2279
www.mostateparks.com/trumansite.htm

President Harry S. Truman, who made some of the most momentous decisions in American history, was born here on May 8, 1884, in a downstairs bedroom in this small house. Truman will be remembered as the president who gave the order

to drop atomic bombs on Japan in 1945 after the Japanese refused an urgent plea to surrender, thus bringing a swift end to the increasingly brutal World War II.

Truman was born the son of John Anderson and Martha Ellen (Young) Truman. His birthplace was built between 1880 and 1882. His parents purchased the modest house in 1882 for $685. His father bought and sold livestock, primarily horses and mules, in a lot located diagonally across the street. Visitors can tour the house, which has been restored and redecorated to the period of its ownership and occupancy by the Truman family. During that period, the house did not have electricity or indoor plumbing. In 1959, the United Auto Workers donated the home to the state for preservation as a state historic site. President Truman himself attended the dedication on April 19, 1959. Today, the house is listed on the National Register of Historic Places.

Mark Twain

1835–1910
Mark Twain Birthplace State Historic Site
37352 Shrine Road
Florida
(573) 565-3449
www.mostateparks.com/twainsite.htm

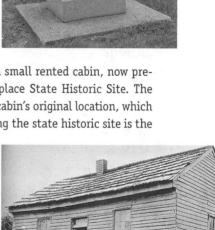

Mark Twain, in response to speculation that his birthplace was a particular ramshackle cabin in the town of Florida, remarked: "No, it is too stylish, it is not my birthplace." Twain was born in a small rented cabin, now preserved in the museum at the Mark Twain Birthplace State Historic Site. The museum is located about a quarter-mile from the cabin's original location, which is marked by a red granite monument. Surrounding the state historic site is the 2,775-acre Mark Twain State Park, which offers camping, hiking, swimming, fishing and access to Mark Twain Lake—a beautiful tribute to America's most beloved author-humorist.

Born Samuel Langhorne Clemens, Twain wrote some of the greatest novels in American history, as well as some of the most scathing quips. Among his most celebrated works are *The Adventures of Huckleberry Finn* (1884), *A Connecticut Yankee in King Arthur's Court* (1889), and *Puddn'head Wilson* (1894). The museum features first editions of his works, including a handwritten manuscript of *The Adventures of Tom Sawyer*, as well as furnishings from his Hartford, Connecticut, home. A public reading room is available for personal study and research.

Tennessee

Bluegrass Music

1945
The Ryman Auditorium
116 Fifth Avenue N.
Nashville
(615) 889-3060
www.ryman.com

Bluegrass music was officially "born" in December 1945, when Bill Monroe (the Father of Bluegrass) and his new lineup of "Bluegrass Boys" played the Grand Ole Opry at the Ryman. Although Monroe and his band had played the Grand Ole Opry several years earlier, it was his new lineup with the addition of banjo player Earl Scruggs that is considered the true originators of the classic bluegrass sound. Scruggs innovated the three-finger picking style on the banjo—a dazzling sound that energized audiences. Also in the band were Lester Flatt on guitar and lead vocals, Chubby Wise on fiddle, and Howard Watts (also known as Cedric Rainwater) on acoustic bass. Monroe's unique sound utilized traditional acoustic instruments, distinctive harmonies, rhythms from string bands, gospel, work songs and "shouts" of black laborers, and country and blues music repertoires. In 2006, the Tennessee Historical Commission dedicated a historical marker in front of the Ryman Auditorium, officially naming the venue the "Birthplace of Bluegrass."

Charlie Bowman

1889–1962
Fitz Road and Route 75
Gray

Charlie Bowman, the legendary fiddler who helped pioneer the sound of country music in the 1920s and 1930s, was born on July 30, 1889, on a small farm here in Gray. This farmer-turned-musician was also known as "the champion fiddler of East Tennessee" and "Fiddlin' Charlie Bowman." Able to coax unnatural sounds from a fiddle, like hound dogs, turkey cacklings, and a bantam hen, Bowman could also play fifteen other not-so-conventional instruments, including saws, washtubs, brooms, a one-string bass, and even an underfeed furnace. In 1925, he joined the Hillbillies (also known as the Bucklebusters), who became the first professional country string band to achieve popularity on both records and radio. Bowman's version of "Nine Pound Hammer" became a standard (he apparently learned the tune from a black railroad construction crew in Tennessee). Bowman, along his brothers and daughters, were part of the famous Columbia Records "Johnson City Sessions" of 1928 and 1929. A state historical marker honoring Charlie Bowman was unveiled near his birthplace in 2004. The event, attended by many dignitaries, featured the Bowman Brothers (James, Ray, Tony, Robert, sons of Elbert and Gladys Bowman) and fiddling by Jim Bowman, who performed some of Charlie's most famous songs.

Country Music

1927
W. State Street
Bristol

Country music was born here in 1927 with the discovery of Jimmie Rodgers and the Carter Family, the first two bona fide stars of the genre. This "big bang" of country music took place when Ralph Peer, a scout with Victor Records, traveled to Bristol to check out the new talent. The Bristol Recording Sessions, by virtue of Rodgers's and the Carters' impact, laid the groundwork for what became the country music industry. The building in which those sessions occurred is no longer standing, but a monument marks the spot on State Street. In 1998, the United States Congress passed a resolution officially recognizing Bristol, Tennessee, as the "Birthplace of Country Music." In downtown Bristol, the city has put up a mural and monument to commemorate this historic claim to fame.

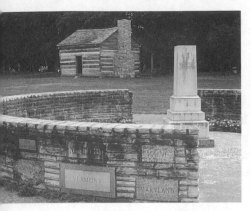

Davy Crockett

1786–1836
1245 Davy Crockett Park Road
Limestone
(423) 257-2167
www.tennessee.gov/environment/parks/
DavyCrockettSHP

The "King of the Wild Frontier," Davy Crockett, was born here in a log cabin on August 17, 1786. One of the most storied folk heroes in American history, Crockett was a legendary hunter, successful businessman, and U. S. congressman. He fought in the Texas Revolution, dying at the Battle of the Alamo in 1836. His birthplace has been preserved by the Tennessee Department of Environment and Conservation as a historic site. The park consists of 105 partially wooded acres along the Nolichucky River in Greene County. Visitors to the park can tour a museum with exhibits chronicling different aspects of Crockett's life. There's also a replica of the birthplace cabin, restored and furnished in a period style that depicts the typical 1786 home in which Crockett was born. The engraved footstone to the original cabin is located in front of the replica. There are also picnic and camping areas, as well as swimming, hiking, and fishing.

Holiday Inn

1952
4941 Summer Avenue
Memphis

In August of 1952, the world's first Holiday Inn opened in Memphis, offering exciting innovations like bathrooms, telephones, and air conditioning in each of its 120 rooms. Memphis entrepreneur Kemmons Wilson had implemented an ambitious vision, simply because he thought the world needed a better place to stay. Today there are more than 1,300 Holiday Inns located around the world. This original location would later become a Royal Oaks Motel, and then in 1995 the building was torn down to make way for the funeral home that currently occupies the site.

Cordell Hull

1871–1955
Cordell Hull Birthplace and Museum
  State Park
1300 Cordell Hull Memorial Drive
Byrdstown
(931) 864-3247
www.cordellhullmuseum.com

Cordell Hull, the "Father of the United Nations,"
was born October 2, 1871, in a log cabin in present-day Pickett County (formerly
Overton County). Hull served longer than any other U. S. secretary of state, having been appointed by President Franklin D. Roosevelt in 1933 and serving until
1944. In 1945 he was awarded the Nobel Prize for Peace for his role in establishing the United Nations.

The Cordell Hull Birthplace and Museum State Park is now a historic site
owned by the state of Tennessee. It features a representation of Hull's log cabin
birthplace, an activities center, and a museum that includes his Nobel Peace
Prize. Also in the park is Bunkum Cave Trail, which leads to an overlook and
the entrance of historic Bunkum Cave, where Hull's father made moonshine
years ago.

Rock and Roll

1954
Sun Studio
706 Union Avenue
Memphis
(901) 521-0664
www.sunstudio.com

Although disc jockey Alan Freed is credited with
coining the phrase in 1951 to describe music
that originated as early as the 1940s (see page 188), the most pivotal, seminal
recordings of the genre came from Sun Studios, including those of Jerry Lee
Lewis, Johnny Cash, Roy Orbison, and Carl Perkins. On July 5, 1954, a nervous
teenager named Elvis Presley came into Sun Records to lay down a few vocal
tracks. Needless to say, it went well. This tiny Memphis studio had other glory
days as well. Opened in 1950 by a local radio station engineer named Sam
Phillips, some of the most legendary moments in rock and roll history were captured here. Today, the studio has been restored as a museum, where you can
even touch the microphone that Elvis used to make his first record.

Self-Serve Grocery Stores

1916
Piggly Wiggly
79 Jefferson Street
Memphis

"Help yourself" is a concept we take for granted, but the completely self-service market was a revolutionary idea when it was born here in Memphis on September 6, 1916. Clarence Saunders, founder of Piggly Wiggly, pioneered the unusual and instantly popular concept: shopping baskets and open shelves. No more clerks who had to get everything for the customers. It was so successful that Saunders patented the concept in 1917. The Piggly Wiggly self-service markets paved the way for the first supermarkets. A state historical marker is located nearby, and a replica of the store can be found at the Pink Palace Museum, 3050 Central Avenue. For more information, call (901) 320-6362 or visit www.memphismuseums.org.

Sequoyah

Circa 1776
The Sequoyah Birthplace Museum
576 Route 360
Vonore
(423) 884-6246
www.sequoyamuseum.org

The great Cherokee warrior Sequoyah (also known as George Gist), inventor of the Cherokee writing system, was born here around 1776 at the village of Tuskegee. He was the son of Nathaniel Gist, a Virginia fur trader, and Wut-teh, daughter of a Cherokee chief. Sequoyah married a Cherokee, had a family, and became a silversmith. Sequoyah and other Cherokees heroically fought for the United States under General Andrew Jackson against the British troops and the Creek Indians in the War of 1812. Sequoyah had the idea to invent a Cherokee written language when he realized that Cherokee soldiers, unlike white soldiers, were not able to write letters home, read military orders, or record events. After the war, he set out in earnest on his quest, developing symbols that could form words and reducing thousands of Cherokee concepts to eighty-five symbols representing sounds. He taught his daughter Ayoka the new alphabet by making a game of this new writing system. The Sequoyah Birthplace Museum is owned and operated by the Eastern Band of the Cherokee Indians. It is Tennessee's only tribally owned historic attraction featuring Cherokee history and culture.

MIDWEST

Minnesota

Wisconsin

Michigan

Iowa

Illinois

Indiana

Ohio

Illinois

Corn Dog on a Stick

1946
Cozy Dog Drive In
2935 S. Sixth Street
Springfield
(217) 525-1992
www.cozydogdrivein.com

The corn dog, originally named the "crusty cur" and then the "cozy dog," first leapt into American culture at this restaurant after being invented by Ed Waldmire Jr. Waldmire first came across the corn dog—a hot dog baked in cornbread—in Muskogee, Oklahoma. Waldmire was a fan of the concoction, but believed it took too long to prepare, so he began searching for a way to cover a hotdog with batter and cook it in a short time. Waldmire and college friend Don Strand developed a mix that would stick to a hot dog while it was being fried. They made their new creation on a stick, and called it a "crusty cur." The treat quickly gained in popularity, although its name was changed to "Cozy Dog" after Waldmire's wife objected to the original moniker. Cozy Dogs were officially launched on June 16, 1946, at the Lake Springfield Beach House. Today at the Cozy Dog Drive In, a classic American restaurant operated by the Waldmire family, you'll still find the delicious, innovative hot dog on a stick. The original location opened in 1949; the current drive-in was built in 1996.

Walt Disney

1901–66
2156 N. Tripp Avenue
Chicago

Walt Disney, who introduced the animated character Mickey Mouse and a host of others to the world, was born in this modest, two-story home in 1901. The house was built by his father, Elias, in 1892. The family moved to Missouri in 1906. The home's history was mostly forgotten until 1991, when a city official recommended landmark status for the home. (The owner declined the designation because of the legal restrictions it brings, and Disney company officials expressed little interest in the home.) Still, many people from around the world make the pilgrimage here. What they can see of the private home from the residential street is a simple structure covered with white aluminum siding and fronted by large bushes for privacy.

Wyatt Earp

1848–1929
406 S. 3rd Street
Monmouth

Deputy U.S. Marshal Wyatt Earp, the internationally famous lawman, was born at the Pike-Sheldon House in Monmouth on March 19, 1848. Earp is probably best known for his participation in the controversial "Gunfight at the O.K. Corral," which took place at Tombstone, Arizona, on October 26, 1881. In this legendary Old West encounter, Wyatt Earp, his brothers Virgil and Morgan, and Doc Holliday faced off against Ike and Billy Clanton and Tom and Frank McLaury. The shootout and the bloody events that followed, combined with Wyatt Earp's penchant for storytelling, resulted in his reputation for being one of the Old West's toughest and deadliest gunmen. Earp would go on to become the archetypal Western hero in countless novels and films. His birthplace and boyhood home was listed on National Register of Historic Places in 1999.

Ernest Hemingway

1899–1961
Ernest Hemingway Birthplace Home
339 N. Oak Park Avenue
Oak Park
(708) 848-2222
www.ehfop.org

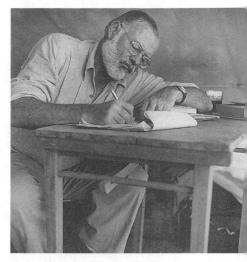

Oak Park is home to the world's largest collection of Frank Lloyd Wright-designed buildings and houses, with twenty-five structures built between 1889 and 1913. But it's also the birthplace of legendary writer Ernest Hemingway. The Queen Anne-style Ernest Hemingway house was the home of Hemingway's maternal grandparents and where the writer was born on July 21, 1899. Though Hemingway spent most of his boyhood and high school years a few blocks away at 600 N. Kenilworth Avenue, his birthplace has been carefully restored to replicate its appearance at the end of the nineteenth century. A tour of the house features the room in which the famed author of *The Sun Also Rises* (1926) and *For Whom the*

Bell Tolls (1940) was born. Just a short walk from the birthplace at 200 N. Oak Park Avenue, the Ernest Hemingway Museum is host to permanent and temporary exhibits that explore the author's life. Kiosks fashioned from historic doors hold exhibits of rare photos and artifacts, including Hemingway's childhood diary and the famous letter from nurse Agnes von Kurowsky—later portrayed in *A Farewell to Arms*—terminating their engagement. Special exhibits highlight Hemingway's love of nature and the arts, along with his involvement in both World Wars and the movies.

Nuclear Reaction

1942
Joseph Regenstein Library
University of Chicago
1100 East 57th Street
Chicago

Enrico Fermi and a team of scientists achieved mankind's first controlled, self-sustaining nuclear chain reaction here on December 2, 1942. The historic moment occurred on what used to be Stagg Field (the university's athletic field from 1892 to 1967), a site now occupied by the Joseph Regenstein Library. It was here that Fermi supervised the design and assembly of an "atomic pile," a code word for a device that, in peacetime, would be known as a nuclear reactor. The bronze memorial *Nuclear Energy*, by famed sculptor Henry Moore, marks the exact spot on the west edge of the 12-acre site of the library.

PRESIDENTIAL BIRTHPLACE
Ronald Reagan

40TH

1911–2004
Ronald Reagan Birthplace
111 S. Main Street
Tampico
(815) 438-2130

Ronald Wilson Reagan was born in a second-floor apartment in the Graham Building, a late nineteenth-century commercial building in Tampico. The building was constructed in 1896, and it housed a tavern from that time until 1915. On February 6, 1911, the fortieth president of the United States was born in the apartment above the tavern to John E. and Nelle Wilson Reagan. The Reagans moved out of the apartment and into a house in Tampico a few months after Ronald was born.

Reagan enjoyed a successful acting career and was elected president of the Screen Actors Guild. In 1966 he became governor of California, and he was elected president in 1980. Reagan's small-government, lower-tax policies and commitment to national defense made him an icon among political conservatives. Reagan's presidency also marked the last days of the Cold War.

Today, Reagan's two-story birthplace building is part of a historic district in Tampico. The building's first-floor interior has been restored as the First National Bank, which occupied the property from 1919–31. On the second floor the Reagan apartment has been restored to the period when the president was born. The site offers tours to the public.

Carl Sandburg

1878–1967
Carl Sandburg Historic Site
331 E. Third Street
Galesburg
www.sandburg.org

This modest home is the birthplace of Carl Sandburg, the Pulitzer Prize-winning poet and Lincoln biographer, children's author, and folk song
collector. His parents were Swedish immigrants
and his father worked as a blacksmith's assis-
tant at the nearby Chicago, Burlington, & Quincy Railroad shops. Sandburg
attended local primary schools and Lombard College in Galesburg. His first books
of poetry were published in Galesburg. He later became a journalist and prolific
author. His *Complete Poems* (1950) and his biography *Abraham Lincoln: The War
Years* (1939) won Pulitzer prizes. He also wrote a novel (*Remembrance Rock*), an
autobiography, children's stories, and folk songs.

The small frame home contains three rooms—parlor, bedroom, and kitchen.
Several original family items are on display, along with other simple, utilitarian
furnishings typical of the era. Behind the cottage is a tranquil garden where the
ashes of Sandburg and his wife lie beneath a red granite boulder, dubbed Remembrance Rock, after the title of his only novel. A series of flagstones inscribed with
quotations from Sandburg's writings is known as "Quotation Walk."

Albert Spalding

1850–1915
133 E. 2nd Street
Byron

One of the premier pitchers of the 1870s and an "organizational genius of baseball's pioneer days," as his Hall of Fame plaque states, Spalding's amazing forty-
seven victories led the 1876 Chicago White Stockings to the first-ever National
League championship. Spalding left the game to join the White Stockings front
office in 1882, as well as to tend to the thriving sporting goods business he
had founded in 1876—today, that company is the official basketball supplier for
the NBA. A plaque marks this private home, about eighty miles west of Chicago,
where Spalding was born on September 2, 1850.

Indiana

Coca-Cola Bottle

1915
Root Glass Company
Corner of Third and Voorhees Streets
Terre Haute

The "hobbleskirt," or contour, bottle—the signature bottle of Coca-Cola—was born here in Terre Haute. Modeled after the shape of a coca bean, the bottle was invented specifically for Coca-Cola by Chapman J. Root, T. Clyde Edwards, Earl R. Dean, and Alexander Samuelson of the Chapman Root Glass Company. They first patented the bottle on November 16, 1915, and renewed the patent on December 25, 1923. The actual shape of the bottle was patented in 1960. Today, a state historical marker notes the former location of the bottling company, long-since replaced by a gas station and restaurant. At the Vigo County Historical Society Museum, located at 1411 South 6th Street, visitors can see a huge collection of original Coca-Cola artifacts, including a rare mold of the original bottle.

James Dean

1931–55
Corner of Fourth and McClure Streets
Marion

The house where film star James Byron Dean was born on February 8, 1931 stood at this corner. A stone with a plaque and a star in the sidewalk now commemorate the spot where the apartments, known as "The Seven Gables," once stood. Dean lived there until he was six, when the family moved to California. He had a brief but iconic career before his untimely death in a car crash on September 30, 1955.

Each September 30, to commemorate the day Dean was killed in Cholame, California, the town honors its favorite son with a festival. The nearby Fairmount Historical Museum at 203 E. Washington Street in Fairmount features the James Dean Memorial Gallery, where you can see the actual speeding ticket issued to Dean just before his fatal crash and the Lee Rider jeans he wore in *Giant*.

Democratic Party Rooster

1840
Riley Memorial Park
Greenfield

A marker here notes the first use of the rooster as a Democratic party symbol. The bird was introduced in Greenfield for the 1840 campaign. The rooster was later adopted by the state and national Democratic parties. However, the rooster was used only sporadically and by 1880 the donkey was well-established as the mascot of the party.

Paul Dresser

1857–1906
Dresser Birthplace
First Street and Dresser Drive
Terre Haute
www.indstate.edu/community/vchs/ dresser.htm

Paul Dresser is best known for composing what would become the state song of Indiana, "On the Banks of the Wabash, Far Away." His younger brother was novelist Theodore Dreiser, also born at this site. Dresser worked as an actor, playwright, songwriter, producer, and music publisher. He composed more than one

hundred songs on Tin Pan Alley in New York City. At the peak of his fame, in the 1890s, he was the most popular songwriter in America. He created his own publishing house in 1901 to produce his works. Despite his fame, he was financially unwise. He gave much of his money away to friends and family, and when his publishing house failed, he was left destitute. He died in New York City at age forty-nine. The home where he was born, which the Vigo County Historical Society now owns and maintains in his honor, is listed on the National Register of Historic Places.

Gasoline Automobile

1893–94
Elwood Haynes Museum
1915 S. Webster Street
Kokomo
(765) 456-7500

Elwood Haynes built the world's first gasoline automobile here in his garage on Main Street in 1893–94. In addition to creating the first horseless carriage, Haynes is also known for inventing stainless steel and an alloy called stellite that is today used in the space program. The museum looks at his life and contributions to science and industry, including exhibits on the auto industry.

James Whitcomb Riley

1849–1916
Riley Birthplace and Museum
250 W. Main Street
Greenfield
(317) 462-8539
www.greenfieldin.org

Greenfield is the birthplace and boyhood home of the famed "Hoosier Poet," James Whitcomb Riley. He was born here on October 7, 1849 and he started his career in 1875 writing newspaper verse in Indiana dialect for the *Indianapolis Journal*. His verse tended to be humorous or sentimental, and of the approximately one thousand poems that Riley published, more than half are in dialect.

Claiming that "simple sentiments that come from the heart" were the secret of his success, Riley satisfied the public with down-to-earth verse that was "heart high." Although Riley was a bestselling author in the early 1900s and earned a steady income from royalties, he also traveled and gave public readings of his poetry. Riley befriended bestselling Indiana authors such as Booth Tarkington, George Ade, and Meredith Nicholson. Many of his works were illustrated by Howard Chandler Christy. Riley died in 1916, and the home where he was born was purchased by the city of Greenfield in 1936. The Riley home is listed on the National Register of Historic Places and is open to visitors.

Harland Sanders

1890–1980
South side of Route 160 just east of I-65
Henryville

Harland Sanders, who was known to the world as "Colonel Sanders," and who created the Kentucky Fried Chicken fast-food chain, was born on a farm in Henryville, Indiana, on September 9, 1890. His father died when he was six years old, and because his mother worked, he was required to cook for his family. He dropped out of school in seventh grade. During his teen years, Sanders worked many jobs, including steamboat driver, insurance salesman, railroad firefighter, and farmer, and he enlisted in the Army as a private in 1907 in Cuba. Later, at the age of forty, Sanders cooked chicken dishes and others for people who stopped at his service station in Corbin, Kentucky (see page 133). Since he did not have a restaurant, he served customers in his living quarters in the service station. Eventually, his local popularity grew, and Sanders moved his operation to a restaurant that seated 142 people and where he served as the chef. Over the next nine years, he perfected his method of cooking chicken. He also made use of a pressure fryer that allowed the chicken to be cooked much faster than by pan frying.

Kentucky governor Ruby Laffoon gave him the honorary title "Kentucky Colonel" in 1935. Sanders chose to call himself "Colonel" and to dress in a stereotypical Southern gentleman costume as a way of self-promotion. After the original restaurant was bypassed, Sanders began franchising Kentucky Fried Chicken restaurants (see page 235). Sanders sold the Kentucky Fried Chicken Corporation in 1964, although he remained its corporate spokesman until his death. Today, a plaque marks his birthplace.

Tomato Juice

1917
French Lick Springs Hotel
8670 West State Road 56
French Lick
(800) 457-4000
www.frenchlick.com

In 1917, world-famous chef Louis Perrin of the French Lick Resort ran out of oranges to serve for breakfast—so he prepared tomato juice. The renowned hotel established in 1845 has hosted dignitaries like Franklin D. Roosevelt, Lana Turner, Bing Crosby, and Bob Hope. The hotel still welcomes guests to its elegant facilities.

Wilbur Wright

1867–1912
Wilbur Wright Birthplace and Museum
1525 N. 750 E
Hagerstown
(765) 332-2495
www.wwbirthplace.com

Wilbur Wright was born at this site on April 16, 1867, in a small farmhouse near Millville. He was the third of seven children born to Milton Wright and Susan Catherine Koerner Wright. Visitors to the site today can tour the reconstructed home of Wilbur Wright, view a replica of 1903 Kitty Hawk Flyer, and enjoy plenty of Wright memorabilia. Wright, along with his brother Orville (see page 191), is credited with inventing and building the world's first successful airplane and making the first controlled, powered, and sustained heavier-than-air human flight on December 17, 1903. In the ensuing two years, the brothers developed their flying machine into the first practical fixed-wing aircraft. Although not the first to build and fly experimental aircraft, the Wright brothers were the first to invent aircraft controls that made mechanical fixed-wing flight possible.

Iowa

Buffalo Bill

1846–1917
North Cody Road
Le Claire

Buffalo Bill was born William Frederick Cody on February 26, 1846, in a log cabin on a farm in Napsinekee Hollow outside of Le Claire. Buffalo Bill is best known for his Buffalo Bill's Wild West Show, an international sensation that coined the term "Wild West" and helped forge the mythical stature of the American West. However, Buffalo Bill was more than a showman; he served in the Civil War and received the Medal of Honor in 1872 for his service as a scout in the Indian Wars. He was also a noted buffalo hunter and Indian fighter.

The original Cody farm and site of his log cabin birthplace was sold in 1852 and incorporated into a larger farm. Today, a historical marker can be found near the site in the 100 block of North Cody Road. The actual site of the log cabin is about a quarter-mile north of the marker. The Buffalo Bill Museum at 199 N. Front Street features Buffalo Bill and local history exhibits. Call (563) 289-5580 or visit www.buffalobillmuseumleclaire.com. Visitors can also tour the Cody Homestead, Buffalo Bill's boyhood home, which is on the National Registry of Historic Places. It is located at 28050 230th Avenue at Bluff Road near Princeton, Iowa; call (563) 225-2981.

4H Emblem

1907
Gazebo Park at the intersection of Routes 3 and 38
Clarion

4-H in the United States is a youth organization administered by the Cooperative Extension System of the United States Department of Agriculture (USDA). Its mission is "engaging youth to reach their fullest potential while advancing the field of youth development." Today, the organization serves more than 6.5 million members in the United States from ages five to nineteen in approximately 90,000 clubs. The official 4-H emblem is a green four-leaf clover with a white H on each leaf representing head, heart, hands, and health. White and green are the 4-H colors: the white symbolizes purity, and the green represents nature's most common color and is emblematic of youth, life, and growth. Wright County superintendent of schools O. H. Benson created the logo in 1907, and today in Clarion you'll find a plaque engraved on a boulder, and the old schoolhouse where the logo was born.

PRESIDENTIAL BIRTHPLACE
Herbert Hoover

31ST

1874–1964
Herbert Hoover National Historic Site
210 Parkside Drive
West Branch
(319) 643-2541
www.nps.gov/heho

Herbert Hoover, who served during the Great Depression and was the first president born west of the Mississippi River, was born in a small two-room cottage on August 10, 1874. Hoover was a mining engineer, humanitarian, statesman, and our thirty-first president. Herbert's father Jesse and grandfather Eli Hoover built the birthplace cottage in 1871. The Hoover family lived in it until 1879. Today, the Herbert Hoover National Historic Site buildings and grounds in West Branch are preserved by the National Park Service to commemorate the life of Herbert Hoover. The site includes the small cottage where Hoover was born in 1874, a blacksmith shop similar to the one owned by his

father, the first West Branch schoolhouse, and the Quaker meetinghouse where the Hoover family worshipped. Also located on the grounds are the Herbert Hoover Presidential Library and Museum, the gravesites of Hoover and his wife, Lou Henry Hoover, and an 81-acre tallgrass prairie. As Herbert Hoover Birthplace, the site was declared a National Historic Landmark on June 23, 1965.

Captain James T. Kirk (future birthplace)

2228–
Riverside

Riverside, Iowa, has officially proclaimed itself the future birthplace of Captain James T. Kirk, a character from the television show *Star Trek* played by William Shatner. Gene Roddenberry, the creator of *Star Trek*, asserted in his book *The Making of Star Trek* that the character of Kirk had been born in the state of Iowa. In March 1985, when the town was looking for a theme for its annual town festival, Steve Miller, a member of the Riverside City Council who had read Roddenberry's book, suggested to the council that Riverside should proclaim itself the future birthplace of Kirk. Miller's motion passed unanimously. The council later wrote to Roddenberry for his permission to be designated as the official birthplace of Kirk, and Roddenberry agreed.

The proclamation declaring the town the "Official Future Birthplace of Captain James T. Kirk," signed by Gene Roddenberry, is housed, along with a carved wooden statue of James T. Kirk, at the Riverside Area Community Club on Route 22 in downtown Riverside. A large stone and plaque in the rear of the building purports to be the site of the future farmstead and birthplace of James Kirk, March 22, 2228.

Glenn Miller

1904–44
122 West Garfield Street
Clarinda
(712) 542-2461
www.glennmiller.org/birthome.htm

Alton Glenn Miller, revered Big Band leader from the swing era, was born on March 1, 1904, in Clarinda. One of the best-selling artists of the early 1940s, he is remembered for such Big Band hits as "In the Mood," "Tuxedo Junction," "Chattanooga Choo-Choo," and "Moonlight Serenade." Miller, however, will also

be remembered as a war hero. In October 1942, he disbanded his group and joined the Air Force to serve by entertaining the troops during World War II. On December 15, 1944, while flying to France, Miller's plane disappeared in bad weather and no trace was ever found. In 1989, his daughter, Jonnie Dee Miller, purchased her father's birthplace. Soon after, in 1991, the Glenn Miller Foundation was formed to oversee restoration. They carefully returned the house to its original condition and style of 1904, restoring the original roofline and adding period furnishings. Visitors are asked to call in advance for tours.

Billy Sunday

1862–1935
**South Duff Avenue (south of the
   entrance to Interstate 30)
Ames**

William Ashley "Billy" Sunday, the most influential American evangelist in the early twentieth century—and a professional baseball player—was born here in a log home on his grandparents' farm just south of Ames on November 19, 1862.

Sunday is estimated to have reached millions of people through his sermons, all without the aid of television, radio, or even loudspeakers. Historians regard his frenetic revivals as important landmarks of the emotional era during the country's transition from rural communities to an industrialized society. Sunday was a strong supporter of Prohibition, almost certainly playing a significant role in the adoption of the Eighteenth Amendment in 1919. Sunday's birthplace is no longer in existence, and at one time the Ames Municipal Airport stood near the site. In 1992, the Ames Heritage Association dedicated a plaque honoring his birthplace.

John Wayne

1907–79
216 S. Second Street
Winterset
(515) 462-1044
www.johnwaynebirthplace.org

Marion Robert Morrison, later known as John Wayne, was born here on May 26, 1907. The son of a pharmacist, he grew up to become one of Hollywood's greatest movie stars, an Oscar winner who starred in more than two hundred films over fifty years. At his restored birthplace, you can see an impressive collection of John Wayne memorabilia, such as a prop suitcase used in *Stagecoach* (1939), the eye patch he wore in *True Grit* (1967), and his hat from *Rio Lobo* (1970). You can also browse hundreds of rare photographs of the Duke, as well as letters from Lucille Ball, Gene Autry, Maureen O'Hara, Jimmy Stewart, Kirk Douglas, Bob Hope, Ronald Reagan, and George Burns. Since its opening, this historic site has been visited by countless celebrities and dignitaries. In 1984, President Ronald Reagan commented that the birthplace of John Wayne "is an inspiring tribute to a good friend and a great American."

Michigan

Paul Bunyan

1906
Paul Bunyan Birthplace & Festival
Paul Bunyan Park (Furtaw Field)
4440 North U.S. 23
Oscoda
(989) 739-7322

Oscoda, Michigan, is known as the birthplace of the Paul Bunyan legend, first written by *Oscoda Press* reporter James MacGillivray in 1906, and appearing again in 1910 in the *Detroit News*. Historians believe the legend is based on the exploits of Fabian "Joe" Fournier, a French-Canadian logger born in Quebec around 1845. In 1914, W. B. Laughead, a former lumberjack who worked in advertising for a lumber company, used stories and cartoons about Bunyan for a booklet advertising his company's products. By 1922, the company was publishing handsome illustrated booklets about Bunyan that circulated to libraries and readers outside the timber industry. Today, Oscoda hosts an annual Paul Bunyan Festival, featuring numerous lumberjack competitions. Several other towns also claim to be the birthplace of the mythical lumberjack (see page 7).

Thomas Dewey

1902–71
313 West Main
Owosso

Thomas Emund Dewey, the subject of the famously inaccurate 1948 newspaper headline, "DEWEY DEFEATS TRUMAN," was born here in a room above his grandfather's general store on March 24, 1902. Although he is remembered as the subject of the *Chicago Daily Tribune*'s legendary blunder, Dewey was actually a respected prosecutor and politician. During the 1930s he achieved national prominence for his prosecution of organized crime in New York. Dewey was elected governor of New York three times, serving from 1942 through 1954; twice, in 1944 and 1948, he received the Republican nomination for the presidency but was defeated in both elections. He played a major role in nominating Dwight D. Eisenhower for the presidency in 1952. A state historical marker is located at the site of his birthplace in Owosso.

Henry Ford

1863–1947
Greenfield Village
20900 Oakwood Boulevard
Dearborn
(313) 982-6001
www.hfmgv.org

A state historical marker at Ford and Greenfield Roads in Dearborn marks the original location of the farmhouse where Henry Ford was born on July 30, 1863, to William and Mary Ford. In 1944, the house was moved to nearby Greenfield Village where it can be toured today. In a space of less than ten years at the beginning of this century, the founder of Ford Motor Company developed three separate and distinct concepts, any of which would have assured him an honored niche in history. He designed and built the Model T Ford, "the car that put the world on wheels." He inaugurated the moving automotive assembly line and developed the process of mass production on which modern industry is based; and by instituting the five-dollar wage for an eight-hour day, he pioneered a new economic concept that opened the door to mass distribution.

Ford Automobile

1892
220 Bagley Avenue
Detroit

In 1892, Henry Ford began building his first gas-propelled automobile here, the site of his small, one-story brick workshop. After experimenting with the motorized vehicle, he came up with an invention that was rather simple compared to the modern automobile: a two-cylinder machine mounted in a light frame geared to bicycle wheels. That unpretentious yet promising invention signaled the start of the Ford Motor Company, a great American industrial force that propelled the automobile industry to its world-changing destiny. A state historical marker marks the spot of Ford's momentous innovation. A replica of the shop can be toured at Greenfield Village.

Kellogg Company

1906
235 Porter Street
Battle Creek

A state historical marker at this site notes the beginnings of the world's largest cereal maker. In 1906, Will Keith Kellogg launched the Battle Creek Toasted Corn Flakes Company in a building on Bartlett Street in Battle Creek, producing his signature brand—Kellogg's Corn Flakes. Will manufactured the first boxes of the cereal at the rate of thirty-three cases per day. After part of that original factory building was destroyed by fire in 1907, Kellogg built a plant at this site. Rapid expansion followed, and by 1917 Kellogg's was an international company manufacturing nine million boxes of cereal per day. Today, the Kellogg Company manufactures a host of well-known brands, including Frosted Flakes, Rice Krispies, Froot Loops, and the original Kellogg's Corn Flakes.

Madonna

1958–
Bradley House (formerly Mercy Hospital)
100 15th Street
Bay City

This building, formerly Mercy Hospital, is where Madonna Louise Ciccone, the singer and actress today known as Madonna, was born on August 16, 1958. The red brick structure is now senior apartments called the Bradley House, located just off Water Street in Bay City.

In 1977, Madonna dropped out of college at the University of Michigan to move to New York to study dance. She was a member of several bands before signing a solo contract with Sire Records in 1982. Her musical breakout came with the release of 1984's *Like a Virgin*, which reached number one on the record charts and eventually sold 12 million copies. Madonna went on to become one of the most successful female artists in history, selling more than 250 million albums worldwide. She has also appeared in a number of feature films including *A League of Their Own* (1992) and *Evita* (1996). Madonna was inducted into the Rock and Roll Hall of Fame on March 10, 2008.

"The Old Rugged Cross"

1912
1101 East Michigan Avenue
Albion

One of the greatest hymns of the Christian church, "The Old Rugged Cross," was composed at this location in Albion in 1912 by George Bennard (1873–1958), a traveling Methodist evangelist. Reverend Bennard, who lived in an apartment at the home of Professor Delos Fall (formerly the Andrew Mason Fitch house), wrote the first verse and the chorus while sitting in the kitchen. The structure later became a fraternity house and was eventually demolished in 1960.

Minnesota

Bob Dylan

1941–
St. Mary's Hospital
407 E. 3rd Street
Duluth

The great singer/songwriter Bob Dylan was born Robert Zimmerman on May 24, 1941, in Duluth, and spent his first six years in this port city at the end of Lake Superior. When Dylan was in kindergarten, his family moved to his mother's hometown of Hibbing, a mining town about seventy-five miles north of Duluth. After living briefly with relatives, they settled into a home on the corner of Seventh Avenue and 25th Street, where Dylan spent the remainder of his youth and high school years. Bob Dylan became one of the giants of late twentieth-century popular music, writing such classics as "Blowin in the Wind," "The Times They Are A-Changin'," "Like a Rolling Stone," "All Along The Watchtower," "Lay Lady Lay," and "Tangled Up in Blue." Dylan has been recording and performing since 1962, combining folk, country, blues, and rock. His albums *Highway 61 Revisited* (1965), *Blonde on Blonde* (1975), and *Blood on the Tracks* (1975) have been continuously ranked by critics among the all-time greatest rock recordings. In 1988, he was inducted into the Rock and Roll Hall of Fame; in 1991, he was given a Lifetime Achievement Grammy; in 1997, his album *Time Out of Mind* won three Grammys; and in 2001, he won an Oscar for "Things Have Changed" from the movie *Wonder Boys*. In 2006, he released his first album in five years, *Modern Times*, which became yet another critical and commercial smash.

F. Scott Fitzgerald

1896–1940
481 Laurel Avenue
St. Paul

F. Scott Fitzgerald, author of *This Side of Paradise* (1920), *The Great Gatsby* (1925), and *Tender Is the Night* (1934), was born here on September 24, 1896. Fitzgerald drew his material from his imagination and from his life in St. Paul's Ramsey Hill neighborhood. He was born in a second-floor apartment in this building, which was originally known as the San Mateo Flats. Fitzgerald was named for his famous distant cousin, Francis Scott Key, who wrote *The Star Spangled Banner*. The Fitzgeralds lived here for about two years until F. Scott's father lost his job as a wicker furniture salesman and he moved the family to New York.

Fitzgerald would go on to become one of the greatest American novelists of the twentieth century, known for his depiction of the Jazz Age of the 1920s and 30s. His stories often featured people like himself: middle-American types obsessed with the wealth and status of upper-crust society. Fitzgerald was a major celebrity in his day; in fact, he and his wife, Zelda, gained notoriety for their extravagant lifestyle, bouts of drinking, and erratic behavior. Today, his birthplace is a private residence, devoutly restored and maintained by Richard McDermott. In 2004, the site was dedicated as a National Literary Landmark by the Friends of Libraries U.S.A.

Judy Garland

1922–69
Judy Garland Museum
2727 U.S. Route 169
Grand Rapids
(800) 664-5839
www.judygarlandmuseum.com

This cozy house was the birthplace of Frances Ethel "Baby" Gumm—better known to the world as Judy Garland. Born on June 10, 1922, she spent her first four and a half years living in the two-story white frame house that had been built thirty years earlier. "Baby Gumm" gave her first public stage performance at age two and a half in her father's New Grand Theater when she sang "Jingle Bells", wearing a little white dress created by her mother. She went on to become a world-famous singer and star of *The Wizard of Oz* (1939), *Meet Me in St. Louis* (1944), and *A Star is Born* (1954).

Today you can visit the house and a one-acre memorial garden that includes a field of poppies and the famous Judy Garland roses. Oral histories and photographs allow visitors to experience the house as it once was, right down to precise details like the ukulele perched on top of the small grand piano. The nearby Judy Garland Museum houses classic *Wizard of Oz* memorabilia and artifacts, including the original carriage used in the 1939 movie classic and a complete *Wizard of Oz* memorabilia exhibit.

General Mills

1866
Washburn "A" Mill
Mill City Museum
704 South 2nd St.
Minneapolis
(612) 341-7555
www.millcitymuseum.org

General Mills, parent company of more than one hundred of the world's best-loved brands—such as Betty Crocker, Häagen-Dazs, Pillsbury, Green Giant and Cheerios—was born with a bang here in Minneapolis. In 1866, Cadwallader Washburn and his brother harnessed the power of St. Anthony Falls on the Mississippi River to build the Washburn "B" Mill. After the surprising success of the massive mill, they built the even bigger Washburn "A" Mill in 1874. A year later, the "A" Mill exploded, killing seventeen workers and also leveling several nearby buildings. In 1879, Washburn joined with John Crosby to build a new Washburn "A" Mill, which would produce Gold Medal Flour and become the home of Betty Crocker's kitchen. In 1928, General Mills was created when Washburn-Crosby president James Ford Bell directed his company to merge with twenty-six other mills. The original Washburn "A" Mill burned in 1991 and the Mill City Museum was built within its walls.

Greyhound

1914
Greyhound Bus Museum
1201 Greyhound Boulevard
Hibbing
(218) 263-5814
www.greyhoundbusmuseum.org

The Greyhound Bus System first began operation in 1914. It all began in Hibbing with one "Hupmobile" and two enterprising men who began transporting miners from one town to another. Eventually, Carl Eric Wickman and Ralph Bogan's small local business evolved into the country's widely recognized Greyhound Bus Company. The Greyhound Bus Museum traces the history of the bus industry from its humble beginnings using pictorial displays and hundreds of artifacts and memorabilia. The museum also features vintage Greyhound buses.

Target

1962
1515 West County Road B
Roseville

The first Target store opened at this location on May 1, 1962, in Roseville, a suburb of St. Paul. The company has its origins in 1902, when George Dayton opened his first store in downtown Minneapolis, called "Goodfellows." He soon formed The Dayton Company, which would go on to start the Target franchise. Today, more than 1,107 Target stores operate in forty-seven states, including Target Greatland stores and SuperTarget stores. A SuperTarget operates at this location.

Ohio

Alcoholics Anonymous

1935
Mayflower Hotel
263 South Main Street
Akron

Alcoholics Anonymous originated here on May 11, 1935; not by vote, committee, or proclamation, but by the private gut-wrenching decision of one man. That night, Bill W. found himself at a crossroads. An alcoholic who had nearly drunk himself to death, he had finally begun a sober life after four detox hospital stays. But, alone on a business trip here in Ohio, his newfound sobriety was being threatened. He found himself standing in the lobby of the Mayflower Hotel, desperately wanting a drink. With burning anxiety, he weighed all of his options and decided he had a choice: order a cocktail in the hotel bar, or call someone and ask for help in his battle to stay sober. Sensing that this was his last chance, he gathered his strength and passed by the hotel bar. Minutes later he was on the phone with Henrietta Seiberling, an Oxford Group adherent. (The Oxford Group was an early self-help group.) She arranged a meeting with a Dr. Bob Smith to take place the next day at the Gate Lodge, a three-bedroom house located at the Stan Hywet Hall where she lived. (The doctor was also an alcoholic and she felt the meeting might benefit both men.) Alcoholics Anonymous grew out of that meeting. Today, the Mayflower Hotel has become the Mayflower Manor apartments.

The Gate Lodge
Stan Hywet Hall and Gardens
714 North Portage Path
Akron
(330) 836-5533

The heart and soul of Alcoholics Anonymous originated with Bill W.'s personal triumph at the Mayflower Hotel. However, the "birth" of the organization occurred when Henrietta Seiberling brought Bill W. and Dr. Bob Smith together for the first time. The historic collaboration took place on Mother's Day of 1935 in the Stan Hywet Hall Gate Lodge, a small home originally intended to accommodate the estate's caretaker at the entrance to the property. Here, the two men began their journey to develop the founding principles of AA—the twelve-step program. Their common goal was to provide support for recovering alcoholics, as well as their family and friends—and as we all know, they have had a huge impact on the world. The house is open for tours. The Stan Hywet Hall and Gardens estate is considered one of the finest examples of Tudor Revival architecture in America. The sixty-five-room mansion, adorned with treasures from around the world, is located on 70 artfully landscaped acres that include a fully-restored English garden, a Japanese garden, a lagoon, vistas, and scenic alleys.

Ambrose Bierce

1842–circa 1914
Horse Cave Creek
Meigs County

Ambrose Gwinnett Bierce, a writer, editorialist, journalist, and satirist, was probably born in Horse Cave Creek on June 24, 1842. However, controversy has long clouded the facts of his birth, as well as his death. Bierce is best known for his works "An Occurrence at Owl Creek Bridge," "The Devil's Dictionary," and "Tales of Soldiers and Civilians." After some debate about whether he was really born in Meigs County, the Ohio Bicentennial Commission finally dedicated a historical marker to him in 2003 at Eastern District High School on Route 7 in Reedsville, approximately ten miles from his assumed birthplace (his actual birth site is unknown, but believed to be on private property). Bierce's death has also been the subject of debate, as he disappeared in 1913–14 after joining Pancho Villa's army in revolutionary Mexico. A photo of Bierce and a memorial marker also reside in the Chester County Courthouse, Ohio's oldest standing courthouse building.

George Custer

1839–76
Custer Birthplace Monument
Route 646
New Rumley
(740) 945-6415

You have heard of "Custer's Last Stand," but George Armstrong Custer's first stand was on December 5, 1839, when he was born in New Rumley in northern Harrison County. Custer graduated from West Point and served in the Union Army in the Civil War, gaining fame as a daring cavalryman. His famed and sometimes controversial military career ended in 1876 at the Battle of Little Bighorn, where he died facing forces led by Sitting Bull. At the site of his birthplace, visitors are greeted by a majestic bronze statue. Unfortunately, only the foundation of his house remains at this roadside park and picnic area. A memorial pavilion also features exhibits outlining the colorful, storied life of the young soldier whose final, fatal battle ironically won him eternal fame and made his name a household word. The Custer Memorial Association holds annual events, including Custer Days in June and a celebration of General Custer's birthday. The Custer Birthplace Monument is located on the north side of Route 646 at the western edge of New Rumley, eleven miles north of Cadiz.

Thomas Edison

1847–1931
Edison Birthplace Museum
9 Edison Drive
Milan
(419) 499-2135
http://tomedison.org

Thomas Alva Edison, perhaps the greatest inventor in history, was born here in Milan in 1847. After a tumultuous and precocious childhood, Edison would go on to invent the phonograph, the first practical incandescent lightbulb (see page 47), the motion picture camera, and many other devices. After Edison's death in 1931, his wife, Mina Miller Edison, and their daughter, Mrs. John Eyre Sloane, made it their personal project to ensure the opening of his birthplace to the public as a memorial and museum. It opened on the centennial of the inventor's birth in 1947. Today, visitors to the Edison Birthplace Museum can experience a collection of rare treasures, including examples of many of Edison's early inventions, documents, and family mementos. This historic site is operated by the Edison Birthplace Association, Inc.

PRESIDENTIAL BIRTHPLACE
James A. Garfield

20TH

1831–81
James A. Garfield Memorial Cabin
**   and Birth Site**
4350 S.O.M Center Road
Moreland Hills
(440) 248-1188

James Abram Garfield, the youngest of five children and the last of the "log cabin" presidents, was born on November 19, 1831, on a frontier farm in Cuya-hoga County, Ohio (now called Moreland Hills). The home no longer stands, but a historical marker sits at the original site, and the Moreland Hills Village Hall features a replica of the cabin.

Garfield was the twentieth president of the United States and the second to be assassinated. He was shot on July 2, 1881, by a disgruntled attorney in a Washington railroad station. Garfield lay in the White House for weeks, as doctors probed the wound with their fingers to find the bullet, introducing the bacteria that probably killed him. Alexander Graham Bell, inventor of the telephone, tried in vain to find the bullet with an induction-balance electrical device which he had designed. In September, Garfield was moved to the New Jersey shore, near Long Branch, as it was believed the sea air would help him recover, but he finally succumbed to infection and died there.

PRESIDENTIAL BIRTHPLACE
Ulysses S. Grant

18TH

1822–85
Grant Birthplace
1551 Route 232
Point Pleasant
(513) 553-4911
http://ohsweb.ohiohistory.org/places/sw08

Ulysses S. Grant, legendary Civil War general and eighteenth president of the United States, was born April 27, 1822, as Hiram Ulysses Grant in Point Pleasant, near the mouth of Big Indian Creek at the Ohio River. The tenacious Union general will always be remembered for his magnanimous handling of General Lee's surrender at the Appomattox Court House in 1865. Although his tenure as president was initially marred by a tolerance for corruption, he is regarded as having eventually served the office with integrity. Today, visitors can tour his birthplace and see the restored one-story, three-room cottage, which was built in 1817 and is now furnished with period items. At the time of Grant's birth, the cottage was located next to the tannery where Grant's father worked. At one time, the house made an extensive tour of the country on a railroad flatcar, even being temporarily displayed on the Ohio state fairgrounds. The house is now owned by the state of Ohio and maintained by the Ohio Historical Society.

PRESIDENTIAL BIRTHPLACE
Warren G. Harding

29TH

1865–1923
Route 97 S
Blooming Grove

Warren G. Harding, twenty-ninth president of the United States, was born in a small saltbox clapboard cottage on November 2, 1865, in Corsica, Ohio (now called Blooming Grove). Harding pursued a career in publishing before turning to politics. During his presidential campaign, he famously promised a "Return to Normalcy" in the aftermath of World War I, and launched himself into the White House with his famous "front porch" campaign conducted from his Victorian home in Marion, Ohio. Historians regard him as an ineffective president who became embroiled in scandal after he discovered corruption among the friends he had appointed to government positions. Harding was the only president to have appointed a previous president to the Supreme Court (William Howard Taft, 1921), and is rumored to have once gambled away the White House china in a card game. His birthplace was demolished in 1896, and today there is a state historical marker and a small stone marker resting on the southwest corner of the actual location of the cottage. It can be found on Route 97, just south of Blooming Grove and just north of Route 288.

William Rainey Harper

1856–1906
Main Street and College Drive
New Concord
(740) 872-3117

William Rainey Harper, an icon of American higher education and founder of the University of Chicago, was born in a five-room log cabin on July 26, 1856. A child prodigy, he graduated from Muskingum College at the age of fourteen. In 1876, Harper got his postgraduate degree from Yale University, then began his innovative teaching career at Morgan Park Academy in Chicago. Harper initiated summer school classes and created correspondence courses. He would later serve as the first president of the University of Chicago in 1891. One of Harper's ideas was that students should be able to attend the first two years of college in their own communities to be better prepared for the rigors of college. This approach led to the creation of the community college system in the United States—a system which included Harper College, a two-year college in Palatine, Illinois, named after him. In 1919, Muskingum College acquired Harper's birthplace cabin and turned it into a museum to honor their illustrious alumnus. It remains intact in its original location, across the street from the college, and is furnished with Civil War-era pieces. A historic marker is located at the intersection of Main Street (U.S. 40) and College Drive. Harper's Cabin is open to the public for scheduled tours.

PRESIDENTIAL BIRTHPLACE
Benjamin Harrison

1833–1901
Symmes and Washington Avenues
North Bend

23RD

Benjamin Harrison, the twenty-third president of the United States, was born here on August 20, 1833, at the home of his grandfather and ninth president of the United States, William Henry Harrison. Benjamin Harrison's father, John Scott Harrison (an Ohio congressman) is the only man in American history to be both son and father of a president. If that weren't enough of a dynasty, Benjamin was named after his great-grandfather, Benjamin Harrison V, a signer of the Declaration of Independence. Harrison's presidency saw many innovations: He was the first president to sign his papers under an electric light, and he saw the construction of the first four American battleships, the first Pan-American Conference, the addition of six states to the Union (Washington, North Dakota, South Dakota, Montana, Idaho, and Wyoming), the International Copyright Act, and the settlement of Oklahoma. The "Big House," as the birthplace home was called, had sixteen rooms and wainscoting on the interior walls. Sadly, it was destroyed by fire in 1858 while President William Henry Harrison's wife, Anna, was still living there. Today, there is a historical marker at the site of President Harrison's birthplace near Symmes and Washington Avenues.

PRESIDENTIAL BIRTHPLACE
Rutherford B. Hayes

1822–93
East William Street
Delaware

19TH

Rutherford B. Hayes, nineteenth president of the United States and a veteran of the Civil War, was born on October 4, 1822, the fifth child of Rutherford and Sophia Birchard Hayes (he was born two months after the death of his father). A historical marker can be found at the site where his birthplace brick house once stood, now occupied by a gas station. He triumphed in one of the most fiercely disputed presidential elections in American history (a title perhaps challenged in recent years), and brought dignity, honesty, and moderate reform to the office. To the delight of the Woman's Christian Temperance Union, First Lady Lucy

Webb Hayes carried out her husband's orders to banish wines and liquors from the White House. As president, Hayes dealt with weighty issues, such as the aftermath of Reconstruction in the South, the oppression and rights of black citizens, and the plight of the American Indian. Hayes tried to curb inflation, vetoed the Chinese Immigration Exclusion Act, and promoted Civil Service reform. Before his election, Hayes espoused a single six-year term for presidents—and, true to his word, he retired after one term.

PRESIDENTIAL BIRTHPLACE
William McKinley

25TH

1843–1901
McKinley Birthplace Home and Research Center
40 S. Main Street
Niles
(330) 652-1704
www.mckinley.lib.oh.us

William McKinley, the twenty-fifth president of the United States and the last Civil War veteran to hold the office, was born on January 28, 1843, in a two-story frame house. McKinley's presidency is remembered for the highest tariff in history, as well as the one hundred-day war with Spain in which the U.S. destroyed the Spanish fleet outside of Cuba, seized Manila in the Philippines, and occupied Puerto Rico. His life came to a tragic end in September 1901 when he was assassinated by a deranged anarchist in Buffalo. McKinley's birthplace house was moved twice before it burned down in 1937. For years, the McKinley Bank Building and National City Bank occupied the space until they donated the land to the city of Niles in 1994. In 2001, the city donated the land to the McKinley Memorial Library, which constructed a replica of his birthplace in 2003. A historical marker sits at the original site of the house. The McKinley Birthplace Home and Research Center is open to the public.

Annie Oakley

1860–1926
Spencer Road off Route 205
Darke County

Annie Oakley, the legendary female sharpshooter, was born Phoebe Ann Mosey (or Mozee) on August 13, 1860. After her father's death when she was six years old, her impoverished mother turned her over to the county orphanage. There, Annie gained an education, but eventually ran away to reunite with her mother. Annie helped support her family by shooting game in the nearby woods and selling it to a local shopkeeper. Her marksmanship paid off the mortgage on her mother's house, and soon led to fame and fortune as the world's first female superstar in Buffalo Bill Cody's Wild West Show. She performed for seventeen years, dazzling audiences by shooting the corks off bottles, snuffing candles, and splitting the edges of playing cards—and even theatrically pouting when she deliberately missed a shot. Today, the house where Oakley was born is long gone, but a plaque is located about one thousand feet away from the original site. Annie Oakley Memorial Park, at 520 S. Broadway in Greenville, features a marker and a statue of Oakley. She is buried in Brock Cemetery on Greenville–St. Mary's Road in Versailles.

"Rock and Roll"

1951
300 Prospect Avenue
Cleveland

Was this the real birthplace of the term "rock and roll"? At one time an influential record store owned by a man named Leo Mintz stood here. Many claim that it was Mintz, not disc jockey Alan Freed, who first coined the term "rock and roll." Mintz also revolutionized how records were marketed. It was here that he saw an increasing number of white teenagers buying rhythm and blues records. Based on this, Mintz convinced Freed to start playing these records on his radio show on WJW in Cleveland. On July 11, 1951, calling himself "Moondog," Freed went on the air and became among the first to play rhythm and blues for a white teenage audience and call it rock and roll. Other small stations followed, eventually forcing the larger stations to join in. To learn more, visit the nearby Rock and Roll Hall of Fame at 751 Erieside Avenue, or visit their website at www.rockhall.com.

William Tecumseh Sherman

1820–91
Sherman House Museum
137 E. Main Street
Lancaster
(740) 654-9923
www.fairfieldheritage.org

William Tecumseh Sherman, the Union general of the Civil War who uttered the famous aphorism, "War is hell," was born on February 8, 1820. Although undistinguished in his service in the Mexican War, Sherman gained a reputation as a ferocious Civil War battlefield commander who implemented a "scorched earth" policy and brought the Confederacy to its knees. His refusal to engage in politics and run for president after his military service was considered quite unusual. Today, his birthplace is on the National Register of Historic Places, and is preserved as the Sherman House Museum. Built in 1811, the Sherman House features two bedrooms, a kitchen, and a Victorian parlor, all restored to their period appearance and furnished with items owned by Sherman and his wife. There's also a parlor set originally owned by General Ulysses S. Grant. Visitors can see an extensive display of family memorabilia, a re-creation of Sherman's Civil War field tent containing several items that he used during the war, and a stunning exhibit of Civil War artifacts, guns, and GAR memorabilia.

Superman

1934
10622 Kimberly Avenue
Cleveland

Although Superman was officially born on the planet Krypton, the Superman character was actually born here in Cleveland in 1934. High-school students Jerry Siegel and Joe Shuster teamed up to create the iconic character in Siegel's house, which is now listed on the National Register of Historic Places. The pair came up with the concept of Superman and even had it developed before they graduated from high school. During four years of trying to sell their idea to the newspaper syndicates, they were repeatedly rejected. In the meantime, they were producing work for the fledgling Detective Comics, Inc. (predecessor to today's DC Comics), with their most notable creation being "Slam Bradley." Finally, in early 1938, Siegel and Shuster sold the rights to Superman to DC for a reported $130, as well as a contract to supply the publisher with material. The first story, cobbled together by re-pasting the newspaper strip samples, appeared in Action Comics No. 1.

PRESIDENTIAL BIRTHPLACE
William Howard Taft

35TH

1857–1930
William Howard Taft National Historic Site
2038 Auburn Avenue
Cincinnati
(513) 684-3262
www.nps.gov/wiho

William Howard Taft, the only man to serve as both president and chief justice of the United States, was born here on September 15, 1857. Taft is known as a somewhat reluctant president, who had always dreamed of serving on the Supreme Court. He found himself in the position of president after a series of successes in appointed positions, including civil governor of the Philippines under President McKinley and secretary of war

under President Theodore Roosevelt. Today, visitors can tour the two-story brick house where Taft was born, which has been restored to its nineteenth-century appearance. It features a museum honoring his life and career, as well as the Taft Education Center, which features exhibits on later generations of the Taft family.

Traffic Light

1914
105th Street and Euclid Avenue
Cleveland

Did you know that Cleveland was the location of America's first traffic light? It was installed on August 5, 1914, when the American Traffic Signal Company installed red and green traffic lights at each corner of the intersection of 105th

Street and Euclid Avenue in Cleveland. The lights were very primitive—in fact, they were "railroad switch stand" types of signals that had to be rotated manually by a policeman 90 degrees to show the indication "STOP" or "GO." The first "actuated" signals to be used (not requiring manpower) were installed on February 22, 1928, at the corner of Falls Road and Belvedere Avenue in Baltimore, Maryland.

Wendy's

1969
257 East Broad Street
Columbus

What other fast-food restaurant can say that it was inspired by a father's love for his daughter? Wendy's was born here on November 15, 1969, when the late, great Dave Thomas decided to open a restaurant named for his daughter. The building, once a car dealership, housed the first Wendy's from 1969 to 2007, when it closed. Wendy's signature menu includes made-to-order square burgers, chicken sandwiches, thick fries, meaty chili, stuffed baked potatoes, and their ultra-thick chocolate Frosty. Memorabilia from the first restaurant was moved to the company's headquarters in Dublin, Ohio.

Orville Wright

1871–1948
7 Hawthorn Street
Dayton

Orville Wright, one of history's most famous pioneering aviators, was born here on August 19, 1871, in the upstairs front bedroom of the family home of Milton Wright and Susan Catharine Koerner Wright. He and his brother Wilbur (see page 166) are credited with making the first verified, powered, sustained, and controlled flight of an airplane on December 17, 1903, at Kitty Hawk, North Carolina. Orville was at the controls for the first flight at 10:35 A.M. that morning. In the years afterward, they developed their flying machine into the world's first practical fixed-wing aircraft, and participated in many other aviation milestones.

Orville, who grew up in a nurturing atmosphere with two libraries in his house, once commented: "We were lucky enough to grow up in an environment where there was always much encouragement to children to pursue intellectual interests; to investigate whatever aroused curiosity." The Wrights stayed in Dayton until 1878, when Milton was elected bishop in the United Brethren in Christ Church and moved the family to Iowa. However, the Wrights soon moved back to their former home in Dayton in 1884, and lived in the house until 1914. The original home was moved to Greenfield Village in Dearborn, Michigan, in 1937. For more information, call (313) 982-6001, or visit their Web site at www.hfmgv.org.

Wisconsin

Flag Day

1885
Route 1, half-mile east of Waubeka
Fredonia

The great patriot who championed the celebration of the American flag was neither a brave soldier nor a crusading politician. Rather, he was a nineteen-year-old, $40-a-month schoolteacher. Bernard J. Cigrand (1866–1932) held the first Flag Day exercises at Stony Hill Schoolhouse near Fredonia in 1885. He chose June 14—the day the Continental Congress adopted the Stars and Stripes in 1777—as the day to honor the American flag.

Cigrand eventually left his teaching job to attend dentistry school, but he continued his quest to have the flag honored every June 14. Cigrand became a prolific author and editor, often using his platforms to advocate the observance of Flag Day. In 1916, President Woodrow Wilson proclaimed June 14 as Flag Day. The observance was turned into an annual national holiday in 1949, when Congress and President Truman proclaimed the flag would be displayed on all government buildings every June 14, and the day to be known as National Flag Day.

Stony Hill School has been restored to its 1885 appearance and is now a historic site. A state historical marker was erected there in 1962.

Gideon Bible

1898
Boscobel Hotel
1005 Wisconsin Avenue
Boscobel

No, the Gideon Bible in your hotel room did not just miraculously appear—it was actually placed there by a real organization, the Gideons International, whose earliest roots can be traced to an informal encounter in 1898 here at the Boscobel Hotel. In September of that year, a traveling salesman named John H. Nicholson found that no single rooms were available at the Central House, and so he shared a room with Samuel E. Hill, also a salesman. Discovering their shared Christian faith, the two men struck up a friendship and discussed the need for an organization that would provide support for Christian travelers. In 1899, the two men met again and, along with W. J. Knights, formed the Christian Commercial Travelers' Association of America. Although the first organizational meeting took place in Janesville, Wisconsin, the Gideons have always identified the Boscobel Hotel as the location of their founding. From their modest beginnings in Boscobel and Janesville, the Gideons have grown into an internationally-recognized organization. The Gideon Bible, distributed by the organization, is now familiar to every American traveler. A plaque in Room 19 commemorates where the historic meeting took place.

GTE

1918
Krouskop Park
U.S. Route 14
Richland Center

GTE, a world leader in telecommunications, was born here in 1918 when John F. O'Connell and Sigurd L. Odegard pooled $33,500 to purchase the Richland Center Telephone Company. At that time, the company served 1,466 telephones in the dairy belt of southern Wisconsin. The trio envisioned better telephone service for small communities by operating a number of exchanges under one managing body. By 1935, the company had changed its name to General Telephone Corporation, with twelve consolidated companies operating under its control. Today, a historical marker at the site reads in part: "General Telephone & Electronics Corporation, among the world's largest businesses and a leader in telecommunications, is headquartered in Stamford, Connecticut, but was born in Richland Center."

Ice Cream Sundae

1881
1404 15th Street
Two Rivers

Many believe the first ice cream sundae was served here at this address in Two Rivers on July 8, 1881. George Hallauer asked Edward C. Berner, the owner of a soda fountain at 1404 15th Street, to top a dish of ice cream with chocolate sauce, hitherto used only for ice cream sodas. The concoction cost a nickel and soon became very popular, but was sold only on Sundays. One day a ten-year-old girl insisted she have a dish of ice cream "with that stuff on top," saying they could "pretend it was Sunday." After that, the confection lost its Sunday-only association and was sold every day in many flavors. It gained its name when a glassware salesman placed an order with his company for the long canoe-shaped dishes in which it was served, as "sundae dishes." At the nearby Washington House Hotel Museum in Two Rivers, you'll find a replica of Ed Berner's ice cream parlor. The Wisconsin State Historical Society erected a historical marker in Two Rivers Central Memorial Park in 1973. Ithaca, New York, also claims to be the birthplace of the sundae (see page 58).

Kindergarten

1856
Watertown Historical Society
919 Charles Street
Watertown

The first kindergarten (children's garden) was started here in 1856 by German-born school-teacher Margarethe Meyer Schurz (1833–76). After teaching with her sister in the United Kingdom, Margarethe and her husband Carl moved to Watertown. Margarethe started to teach her daughter and other children of relatives and neighbors, using arts and crafts, music, and play to motivate the kids. Historically, this was the first time that young children got together and learned rules by having fun, which constituted the first modern kindergarten. This system was adopted quickly throughout the United States and remains a staple of American education today. The original schoolhouse, which was moved to this site in 1956, is open for tours.

Republican Party

1854
The Little White Schoolhouse
303 Blackburn Street
Ripon
(920) 748-6764

The Republican Party, founded by anti-slavery activists and individuals who believed that government should grant western lands to settlers free of charge, was born here on March 20, 1854, in this small town northwest of Milwaukee. Alvan Earle Bovay, a local lawyer, led a majority of the area's one hundred eligible voters in forming this new political organization to "protect the voters against the Nebraska swindle," referring to the Kansas-Nebraska Act which threatened to extend slavery. The first informal meeting of the party took place in this schoolhouse, where the group definitively cut loose from old parties and advocated a new party under the name Republican. The building was designated as a National Historic Landmark in 1974, and is open to the public.

Ringling Brothers Circus

1884
Circus World Museum
550 Water Street (Route 113)
Baraboo
(866) 693-1500
www.circusworld.wisconsinhistory.org

More than one hundred circuses had their start in Wisconsin, with the town of Delavan serving as the winter quarters for twenty-six circuses between 1847 and 1894. One of the first was the United States Olympic Circus, brought here by New York brothers Edmund and Jeremiah Mabie. The concept for P. T. Barnum's Asiatic Caravan was developed in 1871 by William Cameron Coup. One of the most famous circuses, the Ringling Brothers' World Greatest Shows, began in 1884.

Today at the Circus World Museum, visitors can experience a vast complex that houses exhibits such as the world's largest collection of one-of-a-kind antique circus wagons, rare circus posters and graphics, and displays that tell the story of the Ringling Brothers. The museum was opened in 1959 by the Wisconsin Historical Society.

Typewriter

1869
318 State Street
Milwaukee

A state historical marker at N. 4th and State Streets notes that C. Latham Sholes (1819–90) perfected the first practical typewriter at 318 State Street in September 1869. During that summer he was working with Carlos Glidden, Samuel W. Soule, and Matthias Schwalbach in the machine shop of C. F. Kleinsteuber. During the next six years, money for further development of the typewriter was provided by James Densmore, who later gained controlling interest and sold it to E. Remington and Sons of Ilion, New York.

Orson Welles

1915–85
6116 7th Avenue
Kenosha

George Orson Welles, American multimedia pioneer and filmmaker, was born in this duplex on May 6, 1915. Welles was a multi-talented actor, director, writer, producer, and editor. He first made history with his legendary radio broadcast, *War of the Worlds*, a 1938 Mercury Theater production that sent the nation into a panic with its realistic depiction of an alien invasion. In 1941, he wrote, directed, and starred in *Citizen Kane*, generally regarded to be the greatest movie ever made. Several of his other films, including *The Lady from Shanghai* (1948), *Touch of Evil* (1958), and *Chimes at Midnight* (1965), are considered masterpieces. His father Richard was allegedly a free-spirited reveler who retired at age forty-six with a generous settlement from a company buyout. His mother, Beatrice Ives Welles, was an accomplished pianist, suffragette, and community activist who became chairman of the board of education in Kenosha. Today, Welles' birthplace is located within the Library Park Historic District, which is on the National Register of Historic Places. It was originally built in the late nineteenth century, then remodeled several times. Since the early twentieth century, the building has been a duplex.

Laura Ingalls Wilder

1867–1957
The Little House Wayside
County Highway CC
Pepin

"Once upon a time . . . a little girl lived in the Big Woods of Wisconsin in a little gray house made of logs." Writing about herself and her young life here, these are the words Laura Ingalls Wilder wrote at the beginning of *Little House in the Big Woods*, the first of her legendary "Little House" books.

Laura Elizabeth Ingalls was born February 7, 1867 near the village of Pepin, in what people commonly called the "Big Woods" area of Wisconsin. Her actual birth site is commemorated here by a replica log cabin, called the Little House Wayside. Today the area around the site is farmland, not the dense forest that Laura would have grown up with. The site is maintained by the Laura Ingalls Wilder Memorial Society and is closed during winter months. The unfurnished cabin has a fireplace, two bedrooms, a loft, and lots of background information on the history of Wilder and the rest of her family. Interestingly, Wilder was already sixty five years old when her first "Little House" book was published. She would go on to write the following titles in the popular series: *Little House in the Big Woods* (1932); *Little House on the Prairie* (1935); *On the Banks of Plum Creek* (1937); *By the Shores of Silver Lake* (1939); *The Long Winter* (1940); *Little Town on the Prairie* (1941); and *These Happy Golden Years* (1943).

CENTRAL

North Dakota

South Dakota

Nebraska

Colorado

Kansas

Oklahoma

Texas

Colorado

"America the Beautiful"

1893
Pikes Peak
Larkspur
(800) 318-9505
www.pikespeakcolorado.com

Pikes Peak, known as "America's Mountain," is believed to be the inspirational birthplace of "America the Beautiful." Originally a poem, it was written by Katharine Lee Bates (1859–1929), an instructor at Wellesley College in Massachusetts, soon after she visited Pikes Peak in 1893. It was eventually published on July 4, 1895, in a weekly journal called *The Congregationalist*. For several years, Bates would revise the lyrics. It's interesting to note that the poem was not always sung to the now-familiar melody (a tune called *Materna*, composed by Samuel A. Ward in 1882, nearly a decade before the poem was written). In fact, for the first couple of years, the poem was sung to virtually any popular tune that would fit with the lyrics (*Auld Lang Syne* being the most notable). The words of the poem were not formally set to *Materna* until 1910, which is how we know the song today. There is a commemorative plaque on the summit of the mountain.

Cheeseburger

1935
2776 Speer Boulevard
Denver

It seems obvious now, but in 1935, putting cheese on a burger was revolutionary. Some accounts say that Louis Ballast, owner of the Humpty-Dumpty Barrel Drive-In in northwest Denver, was the first person to offer a "cheeseburger." Ballast had previously tried to "spruce up" his hamburgers with toppings like peanut butter and chocolate—but, thankfully, it was cheese that put him on the map. He is said to have trademarked the cheeseburger, though there is an ongoing dispute about its origin (See page 131). Ballast is honored with a small memorial at 2776 Speer Boulevard, where his drive-in once stood. It is now a parking lot.

Root Beer Float

1893
Cripple Creek Brewing Company
Cripple Creek

The root beer float is thought to have been invented by Frank J. Wisner in August of 1893. He was inspired to "float" a scoop of vanilla ice cream on top of his locally-made Myers Avenue Red Soda Company root beer after catching a late-night glimpse of the snow on top of dark Cow Mountain (location of his gold claims) illuminated by the full moon overhead. It was an instant hit with the children of Cripple Creek. Wisner dubbed the treat a "black cow." Today, the black cow is better known as the root beer float. Visit the Cripple Creek District Museum, 5th and Bennett Avenues, (719) 689-2634 or www.cripple-creek.org.

Kansas

Amelia Earhart

1897–circa 1937
223 N. Terrace Street
Atchison
(913) 367-4217
www.ameliaearhartmuseum.org

Famous female aviator Amelia Mary Earhart was born here in her grandparents' home on July 24, 1897. Although she is best known for her mystifying 1937 disappearance, Earhart was in fact the most celebrated female aviator of her time, and she made great strides in opening the new field of aviation to women. In 1932, she became the first woman to fly solo across the Atlantic Ocean. In 1935, she became the first person to fly solo across both the Atlantic *and* Pacific Oceans when she flew from Hawaii to the American mainland. In June 1937, Amelia embarked upon her attempt to make the first around-the-world flight at the equator. After completing nearly two-thirds of her historic circumnavigational flight (more than 22,000 miles), Amelia and her navigator, Frederick Noonan, vanished over the Pacific Ocean near Howland Island.

Her birthplace is a wood-frame, Gothic Revival cottage. It was built in 1861, and the brick Italianate rear addition built in 1873. The Earharts lived in the house until 1912. Visitors can tour the national historic site to learn about the life of Amelia Earhart.

"Home on the Range"

1872
Higley Cabin
Athol

Perhaps the most famous American folk song of all time, "Home on the Range" was written as a poem in 1872 by Brewster M. Higley (1823–1911). Higley, also a surgeon, titled his poem, "My Western Home." It was published a year later in the *Smith County Pioneer* under the title "Oh, Give Me a Home Where the Buffalo Roam." It would be set to music and later known as "Home on the Range." The Kansas legislature voted to adopt the song as the official state song in 1947, since Higley had written the original poem while living in Smith County. You can visit the small log cabin where Higley was inspired to write the poem; it is located on Beaver Creek, just west of Athol. A commemorative plaque interprets this historic cabin.

Walter Johnson

1887–1946
900th and Iowa Streets
Humboldt

Walter Perry Johnson was born November 6, 1887, to Swedish emigrants on a rural farm four miles west of Humboldt. His family left the Humboldt area for the oil fields of California in 1901. In 1907, at the age of nineteen, Johnson began his phenomenal major league baseball career with the Washington Senators. In his twenty-year pitching career, the man nicknamed "The Big Train" posted a dozen twenty-plus win seasons and amassed a total of 417 victories—the most by any pitcher in the twentieth century. Walter Johnson was one of the first five players inducted into the Baseball Hall of Fame in 1936. A commemorative marker is located near his birthplace.

Buster Keaton

1895–1966
U.S. Route 54
Piqua

A plaque marks the birthplace of Joseph F. "Buster" Keaton, who was born in Piqua on October 4, 1895. Buster's parents, Joseph and Myra Keaton, were appearing in a traveling medicine show which included the magician Harry Houdini. According to the story Joseph later told interviewers, a cyclone (tornado) struck Piqua and blew away the performance tent. When he returned to his boarding house after chasing around the countryside looking for the tent, he found his wife had given birth to their first child. Buster Keaton made his first stage the next day in the Catholic Hall, which served as a substitute theater for the evening's performance. When he was five years old, his family began touring vaudeville as "The Three Keatons." He went on to become one of film's greatest comedic talents during the Silent Era, starring in such films as *Our Hospitality* (1923), *Sherlock Jr.* (1924), and *The General* (1927). The Buster Keaton Museum, dedicated to the comic genius's life, is located at 302 Hill Street off U.S. Route 54 in the Water District Building.

Pizza Hut

1958
1845 North Fairmount
Wichita State University
Wichita

The original Pizza Hut, founded at the corner of Kellogg and Bluff Streets in Wichita in 1958, was influenced by the very building that housed it. The franchise started here in Wichita, amidst the late 1950s pizza craze that was sweeping the nation. Two students, brothers Frank and Don Carney, decided to capitalize on the trend. After reading a *Saturday Evening Post* article about the pizza boom, they borrowed $600 from their mother and opened their first Pizza Hut. The structure of the building influenced the name of the future worldwide pizza chain. Since the building's sign would only accommodate nine characters—and the brothers definitely wanted to use the word pizza in the name—that left room for only three more characters. A Carney family member noticed that the building resembled a hut—and so, "Pizza Hut" was born. In the 1980s, this historic building was moved to the Wichita State University campus and is now used as a meeting place. A plaque marks the building.

Nebraska

PRESIDENTIAL BIRTHPLACE
Gerald R. Ford

35TH

1913–2006
Ford Birthsite and Gardens
3202 Woolworth Avenue
Omaha
(402) 444-5955
www.nebraskahistory.org/conserve/birthsite.htm

Gerald Rudolph Ford, born here on July 14, 1913, was far from the clumsy oaf that unjustly became his persona. Ford was actually a levelheaded—and even athletic—man who came into power during one of the most turbulent times in American history. He had been the first vice president selected under the Twenty-fifth Amendment and, in the aftermath of the Watergate scandal, was succeeding the first president ever to resign. He faced the challenges of controlling inflation, reviving a depressed economy, solving energy shortages, and ensuring world peace.

Ford was born Leslie Lynch King Jr. in an ornate three-story, fourteen-room Victorian house—one of the finest homes in Omaha. He eventually took the name Gerald Rudolph Ford after his parents divorced and his stepfather adopted him. In 1971, his birthplace home was razed following a fire. Upon Ford's succession to the presidency in 1974, businessman James M. Paxson purchased the property to build a memorial. In 1977, the birth site was dedicated, and a rose garden was added in honor of former First Lady Betty Ford. The Ford Birthsite and Gardens are open to the public daily from early morning until dusk.

Kool-Aid

1927
508 W. 1st Street
Hastings

Nebraska native Edwin Perkins invented the powdered drink Kool-Aid here in Hastings in 1927. A commemorative sign marks the actual site where Kool-Aid was invented. To honor Kool-Aid on its milestone seventy-fifth birthday, the Hastings Museum, 1330 North Burlington Avenue, permanently dedicated a 3,300 square-foot exhibit to portray the Kool-Aid story. The museum features artifacts such as rare early Kool-Aid packets, a Kool-Aid cartoon suit worn by its jug mascot, and a large interactive exhibit that relates the colorful journey of Perkins. You can reach the museum at (800) 508-4629, or visit their Web site at www.hastingsmuseum.org.

Harold Lloyd

1893–1971
24 Pawnee Street
Burchard

Harold Lloyd, one of the most influential comedy stars of the silent era, was born in this small, three-room house on April 20, 1893. Lloyd is best remembered today as the man desperately dangling from a clock tower in the 1923 comedy *Safety Last*. Known as "The King of Daredevil Comedy," Lloyd was one of the most popular and highest-paid stars of his time. He made more films than Charlie Chaplin and Buster Keaton combined and was a driving force in the advent of the feature-length film. The Harold Lloyd Foundation restored his childhood home, which features memorabilia from Lloyd's life. The home is open to the public.

Reuben Sandwich

1925
Blackstone Hotel
302 S. 36th Street
Omaha

According to one of the competing accounts, the famous Reuben sandwich was born at this historic hotel during a late-night poker game in 1925. To feed the hungry players, a local grocer named Reuben Kulakofsky dreamed up the delicious combination of rye bread, corned beef, Swiss cheese, and sauerkraut. Hotel owner Charles Schimmel loved the sandwich so much that he offered it on the hotel restaurant menu—but the Reuben would finally take its place in American culture with the help of Fern Snider, a one-time waitress at the Blackstone. In 1956, she entered the Reuben in a national sandwich competition, where it took top prize and vaulted into history.

Malcom X

1925–65
3448 Pinkney Street
Omaha

On May 19, 1925, Malcolm X (born Malcolm Little) was born in University Hospital to Earl and Louise Norton Little, who lived at this address. As a civil rights leader, Malcolm X advocated racial separatism over integration and the legitimacy of violence in self-defense. He also championed the beauty and worth of blackness and black Americans' African past. On February 14, 1965, unidentified attackers firebombed Malcolm X's New York house while he and his family were asleep inside. One week later, on February 21, Malcolm X was assassinated by Black Muslim extremists at a rally in New York City's Audubon Ballroom. The childhood home was torn down prior to 1970. A state historical marker at the site commemorates Malcolm X.

North Dakota

Louis L'Amour

1908–88
113 3rd Avenue S.
Jamestown

Famous Western novelist Louis L'Amour was born Louis Dearborn LaMoore in Jamestown on March 22, 1908. He started penning short stories in the late 1930s, but didn't hit the big time as a novelist until the 1960s. He spent decades writing adventure stories before he started mastering the western genre. His first big success came when his story "The Gift of Cochise" was turned into the popular 1953 John Wayne film *Hondo*. When he passed away in 1988, L'Amour's sales totaled more than 200 million books, including *Flint* (1960), *Catlow* (1963), *Down the Long Hills* (1968), and several novels in the Sackett Family series.

Lawrence Welk

1903–92
845 88th Street SE
Strasburg
(701) 336-7470

Lawrence Welk, the bandleader icon of American television, was born here in a sod house on March 11, 1903. Welk is adored by fans as the accordion-playing television host and bandleader whose "champagne music" soothed America for thirty years. His hometown's pride in its favorite son is apparent from the Lawrence Welk Highway and the Lawrence Welk Dam. Welk was raised in a German-speaking household and did not learn English until he was twenty-one, when he left home for good. He went on to play weddings and barn dances until he debuted on national television in 1955. Allegedly, Welk harbored a lifelong resentment toward his birthplace; he never visited and never encouraged the effort his neighbors and friends put into restoring it. He donated money to Strasburg, but requested that none of it go to the farmstead. Today, visitors can tour the main house, barn, windmill, blacksmith shop, and outhouse. A cardboard cutout of Welk in a white suit greets visitors in the dining room, and his accordion rests on a table while champagne music fills the air.

Oklahoma

Brad Pitt

1965–
Unity Health Center (formerly ACH Hospital)
Ninth Street
Shawnee

Dr. R. M. Anderson, Dr. J. E. Hughes, and Dr. F. L. Carson, who had practiced together since 1918, opened the ACH Hospital in 1927 as a clinic. The facility's name came from the first initials of their last names. The two upper floors were added in 1929, and it became a thirty-five-bed hospital with thirteen employees. It served the area until December 4, 1967, when the present-day Unity Health Center, North Campus, opened as Shawnee Medical Center Hospital. The building is on the National Register of Historic Places. But what makes it truly notable? It is where actor Brad Pitt was born on December 18, 1965. Pitt, the star of such films as *Se7en* (1995), *Fight Club* (1999), and *Ocean's Eleven* (2001), grew up in Springfield, Missouri, where the family moved soon after his birth.

Will Rogers

1879–1935
Will Rogers Birthplace Ranch
9501 E. 380 Road
Oologah
(918) 275-4201
www.willrogers.com

He never met a man he didn't like, and there were probably few people who didn't like Will Rogers. He was born here on November 4, 1879, and would fast become one the most popular personalities in American history. He was a movie star, humorist, rodeo rider, vaudeville performer, author, radio personality, pioneer of aviation, and personal friend of three presidents. Rogers was born into a well-to-do ranching family in Indian Territory (now Oklahoma). Today, his birthplace—built in 1875 and known as Dog Iron Ranch—is a living history museum that spans 400 acres on the shores of Lake Oologah. The log-walled, two-story home was moved up the hill when Oologah Lake was filled. Visitors are greeted by longhorn cattle grazing the pastures and other farm animals that help re-create the feel of Rogers' childhood. The birthplace is operated by the Will Rogers Memorial Museums, which also operates the Will Rogers Museum at 1720 W. Will Rogers Boulevard in nearby Claremore. For more information, call (800) 324-9455.

Jim Thorpe

1887–1953
Moccasin Trail, five miles west of Route 995
   (on Jim Thorpe Road)
Prague

Legendary Olympian Jim Thorpe was born near here on May 28, 1887. Thorpe's father, Hiram, was a farmer and his mother, Mary James, was a descendant of the last great Sac and Fox chief, Black Hawk. Thorpe was sent to the Carlisle (Pennsylvania) Indian School in 1904, where he began his illustrious athletic career. He went on to win two gold medals at the 1912 Olympics in Sweden. Unfortunately, his Olympic medals were stripped from him in 1913 for playing semi-professional baseball in North Carolina (they were restored to his family in 1983). Thorpe had a successful seven-year baseball career playing for the Giants, Reds, and Braves. Thorpe was named the greatest athlete of the first half of the twentieth century by the Associated Press in 1950, and ranked third on the AP list of athletes of the century in 1999. After his professional sports career ended, Thorpe lived in abject poverty. He worked several odd jobs, struggled with alcoholism, and lived out the last years of his life in failing health.

South Dakota

Hubert Humphrey

1911–78
Wallace

Wallace, which as of the 2000 census had a population of just 86, is where Hubert Horatio Humphrey Jr. was born on May 27, 1911. Humphrey served as vice president under President Lyndon Johnson, starting in 1964. In 1968, Humphrey himself became the Democratic Presidential candidate and was narrowly beaten by Republican Richard Nixon. Humphrey's career in politics included many notable tenures, first as mayor of Minneapolis, Minnesota, in the mid-1940s, then as a U.S. senator from Minnesota until 1964, the year he was selected for the vice presidency. A noted proponent of civil rights and
social issues, Humphrey returned to the senate from 1971 until his death in 1978. He passed away from cancer while still in office, at which point his wife, Muriel Buck Humphrey, was appointed by Minnesota's governor to finish his term.

Rose Wilder Lane

1886–1968
Laura Ingalls Homestead
20812 Homestead Road
De Smet
(800) 776-3594
www.ingallshomestead.com

Rose Wilder Lane, daughter of Laura Ingalls Wilder (see page 198), was born here on December 5, 1886. She is best known as one of the founders of the American libertarian movement, along with Ayn Rand and Isabel Paterson. Lane was also a journalist, novelist, and travel writer. Rose was the only child of Laura Ingalls and Almanzo Wilder to survive to adulthood. Today, a state historical marker sits at the site of the cabin where she was born.

Texas

Dr Pepper

1885
Dr Pepper Museum
300 S. 5th Street
Waco
(254) 757-1025
www.drpeppermuseum.com

Was Dr Pepper really inspired by the sensitive nose of a pharmacist? In 1885, Charles Alderton, a young pharmacist working at Morrison's Old Corner Drug Store in Waco, is believed to have invented the drink, using his acute sense of smell. He spent most of his time mixing up medicine for customers, but in his spare time he enjoyed serving carbonated drinks at the soda fountain. But mostly, Alderton loved the smell of the drugstore, where the aromas of all the various fruit syrups mixed together in the air. He decided to try to capture it by creating a drink that tasted like that smell. Keeping a journal, he experimented repeatedly until he finally hit upon a mixture of fruit syrups that he liked. Morrison is also credited with naming the drink "Dr. Pepper" (the period was dropped in the 1950s). Unfortunately, the exact origin is unclear, though the Dr Pepper Museum has collected more than a dozen different stories on how the drink obtained its peculiar name. To this day, the Dr Pepper Company is the oldest major manufacturer of soft drink concentrates and syrups in the United States.

Morrison's Old Corner Drug Store, originally located in Waco at the corner of N. 4th Street and Austin Avenue, can now be seen here at the Dr Pepper

Museum. The exceptional museum tour includes many interesting smells and flavors in the Old Corner Drug Store, a tour of the bottling room, and the chance to crown a soft drink bottle and enjoy a Dr Pepper in the soda fountain.

PRESIDENTIAL BIRTHPLACE
Dwight D. Eisenhower

34TH

1890–1969
**Eisenhower Birthplace
State Historic Site
609 S. Lamar Avenue
Denison
(903) 465-8908
www.eisenhowerbirthplace.org**

Dwight David Eisenhower, thirty-fourth president of the Unites States and supreme commander of the Allied Forces in Europe during World War II, was born in this modest two-story house on October 14, 1890. He was the only one of David and Ida Eisenhower's seven children born in Texas. Eisenhower graduated from West Point in 1915. As president, "Ike" oversaw the cease-fire of the Korean War, engaged the USSR during the Cold War, launched the "space race," initiated the Interstate Highway System, and expanded Social Security. Visitors to his birthplace can see hundreds of items relating to Eisenhower and his role in American and world history, including a bronze bust of Eisenhower, historic photographs of the Denison native, and the "Ike Jacket," the brown short-waisted, tailored wood field jacket sported by the general.

Hilton Hotels

1919
**300 block of Conrad Hilton Avenue
Cisco**

Conrad Hilton, who grew up working in a family hotel in New Mexico, planned to open a bank there after he returned from serving in World War I. Having no luck, in 1919 he headed to Cisco, Texas to buy a bank—but when the owner raised the sale price, Hilton gave up the effort. Frustrated, he went looking for a place to sleep for the night and found that there were no rooms available. So Hilton gave up his dream of banking and bought the Mobley Hotel in Cisco. He had a real knack for the hotel business, and soon expanded his hotel concept throughout Texas, eventually purchasing other properties and forming the Hilton Hotels Corporation in 1946. As for the original Mobley, he sold it to his mother, Mary Hilton, in 1924, and it stayed in the family until 1931. It later became a boarding house, a nursing home, and even a private residence. It then remained vacant for years and was deteriorating until the Hilton Foundation donated $1.2 million dollars for its restoration. Today, the old hotel is used as the Cisco Chamber of Commerce, museum, and community center. The Mobley has also earned a place in the National Register of Historic Places. A state historical marker is located at 104 E. 4th Street.

Indoor Rodeo

1918
Cowtown Coliseum
121 E. Exchange Avenue
Fort Worth

The world's first indoor rodeo was held here at the Cowtown Coliseum in 1918. The venue played host to a number of firsts both before and after that. In 1908, the coliseum hosted the first exhibition roundup of cattle ever held under a roof in the United States, as well as the first nighttime horse show in the country. Five years after the first rodeo, the world's first live radio broadcast of a rodeo took place, and in 1934, bull riding first became a part of the world of rodeo.

The coliseum was originally constructed in 1908 to provide a permanent home for the booming Annual Fort Worth Fat Stock Show. The construction was funded by the Swift and Armour Packing Companies and by the Fort Worth Stock Yards Company, which owned the property. The coliseum has served as a hub of cultural, educational, religious, social, and civic events. In 1911, former President Theodore Roosevelt spoke here, and in the years that followed, performers included the Chicago Grand Opera, Enrico Caruso, Bob Wills, Bob Hope with Doris Day, and Elvis Presley. In 1936, the Stock Yards Company sold the coliseum to the city of Fort Worth.

PRESIDENTIAL BIRTHPLACE
Lyndon B. Johnson

36TH

1906–73
Lyndon B. Johnson National
   Historical Park
U.S. Route 290 E
Stonewall
(830) 644-2252
www.nps.gov/lyjo

Lyndon Baines Johnson, the thirty-sixth president of the United States, was born August 27, 1908, in a small structure on his grandfather's farm. "LBJ" is remembered as the man who became president after the assassination of John F. Kennedy in 1963; but he also helped enact civil rights laws, Medicare, and Medicaid, and escalated American involvement in the Vietnam War. The 1889 house where Johnson was born was demolished in 1930, but he supervised its reconstruction in 1965. It's the only presidential birthplace that was interpreted by an incumbent president. He and architect Roy White relied on old photographs of the original house as well as family members' memories to guide the project.

Visitors at the Lyndon B. Johnson National Historical Park can see a photo of the original birthplace hanging in the barn. The house was used between 1964 and 1966 as a guest cottage. Johnson loved to tell visitors that the kitchen had the only original piece of furniture—a rawhide bottom chair with a hole in the seat. Mrs. Johnson loaned the park her Roycrafter high chair; etched on the back is "Lady Bird," the nickname given to Claudia Alta Taylor at age two. Also preserved are the president's first school, the "Texas White House," and the Johnson Family Cemetery. The Lyndon B. Johnson Historical Park Visitors Center, boyhood home, and Johnson settlement are fourteen miles east in Johnson City.

Janis Joplin

1943–70
St. Mary's Hospital
3600 Gates Boulevard
Port Arthur

Blues singer-songwriter Janis Lyn Joplin was born here on January 19, 1943. The gravel-voiced chanteuse rose to prominence in the late 1960s as the lead singer of Big Brother and the Holding Company, and later as a solo artist. Among her best known recordings are "Me and Bobby McGee" and "Piece of My Heart." She performed at Woodstock in 1969. She died in Los Angeles on October 4, 1970, of a drug overdose at the age of twenty-seven. In 2004, *Rolling Stone* magazine ranked Joplin #46 on its list of the 100 Greatest Artists of All Time.

A plaque can be found in front of her childhood home at 4330 32nd Street in Port Arthur. There is also a Joplin exhibit on the second floor of the Museum of the Gulf Coast, at 700 Procter Street. It features her artwork, music, and a replica of her painted Porsche. Near a Joplin statue, her music is in rotation with that of several other Gulf Coast musicians, such as the Big Bopper and George Jones. For more information on the museum, phone (409) 982-7000, or visit their Web site at www.museumofthegulfcoast.org.

Military Aviation

1910
Fort Sam Houston
1212 Stanley Road, Building 124
Fort Sam Houston

Military aviation had a "bumpy" birth here in 1910, when Lieutenant Benjamin Foulois flew the first Army aircraft at MacArthur Field. In 1909, Foulois accompanied Orville Wright on the final trial flight of the new and improved Military Flyer from Fort Myer, Virginia, breaking three world records: speed, altitude, and duration cross-country. The 1909 Military Flyer was purchased by the War Department for $25,000 and became the first military airplane. Foulois, later a brigadier general, was ordered to Fort Sam Houston with Signal Corps Aeroplane No. 1 to teach himself to fly. He had his first solo flight—takeoff, landing, and crash—on that machine, thereafter receiving flight instruction from the Wright brothers by mail. He was the only pilot, navigator, instructor, observer, and commander in the heavier-than-air division of the U.S. Army from November 1909 to April 1911. From May to July 1911 Foulois designed the first radio ever used in a military airplane. He also broke the world cross-country record with a passenger, and carried out the first aerial reconnaissance flights. The original military plane remained in active service until 1911. The Flyer is on exhibit at the National Air and Space Museum in Washington.

Audie Murphy

1943–71
U.S. Route 69
Kingston

The most decorated U.S. combat soldier of World War II, Audie Murphy, was born near Kingston on June 20, 1924, as one of thirteen children of poor Texas sharecroppers Emmett and Josie K. Murphy. His thirty-three awards and decorations included the Medal of Honor, the highest U.S. military award. Murphy joined the U.S. Army paratroopers after the Marines turned him down for being underweight and too short. After the war, Murphy enjoyed a lucrative film career, starring in forty-four movies such as *To Hell and Back* and *The Red Badge of Courage*. Murphy died May 28, 1971, in a Virginia plane crash and was buried in Arlington National Cemetery. His birthplace home has long been demolished, but four hundred yards from the site is a state historical marker honoring him. The marker is located 1.5 miles south of Kingston.

Chester W. Nimitz

1885–1966
247 E. Main Street
Fredericksburg

Chester William Nimitz, perhaps the greatest naval commander in U.S. history, was born in this home on February 24, 1885. A historical marker indicates the site of his birthplace on East Main Street. Nimitz graduated from the U.S. Naval Academy in 1905. After the attack on Pearl Harbor in 1941, Nimitz was selected Commander in Chief Pacific Fleet; and in 1944, he was appointed Fleet Admiral. His career's most significant moment came when he signed the Japanese surrender documents aboard his flagship, USS *Missouri*, on September 2, 1945, in Tokyo Bay. Admiral Nimitz died in San Francisco on February 20, 1966.

Onion Rings

1929
Pig Stand
Corner of Chalk Hill Road and the Dallas–Fort Worth Turnpike
Dallas

French-fried onion rings were likely invented by accident at the first Pig Stand restaurant in 1929, when a careless cook accidentally dropped an onion slice in some batter, pulled it out and tossed it in the fryer, and found the result tasty.

However, as with many of the world's favorite foods, it may not be that simple. Some historians argue that the modern onion ring was developed in the 1950s, when Sam Quigley began the process of perfecting his recipes for hand-cut and hand-breaded onion rings.

Pig Stands were also pioneers in other areas, such as installing drive-thru windows in 1931 and fluorescent lighting in 1939. Former Pig Stand carhop-turned-company president Royce Hailey initiated another famous invention: Texas Toast. Around 1941, when he asked his bakery to slice his bread thicker, they discovered that the slabs of bread would not fit in the toaster, so a cook suggested that they butter and toast both sides on the grill. Unfortunately, Hailey failed to patent this invention.

Babe Didrikson Zaharias

1911–56
2232 7th Street
Port Arthur

Mildred "Babe" Didrikson Zaharias was born in this Texas town on June 26, 1911. She was the daughter of Norwegian immigrants who grew up in this frame house in Port Arthur; she eventually moved to Beaumont with her family. In 1938, she married former wrestler George Zaharias.

Babe is considered the greatest female athlete of all time. She won gold medals and set Olympic records in the javelin and the 80-meter hurdles at the 1932 Olympic Games in Los Angeles (she would have won the high jump too, if the judges hadn't objected to her headfirst style). She won every major professional women's golf championship at least one time, won seventeen amateur tournaments in a row, and was a pioneer in the formation of the Ladies Professional Golf Association (LPGA) in 1950. She was also a three-time All-American basketball player. She was voted the Associated Press's "World's Greatest Woman Athlete of the First Half of the Twentieth Century" and for six years was their "Woman Athlete of the Year" (unmatched by any other athlete, male or female). Zaharias died of cancer in 1956.

WEST

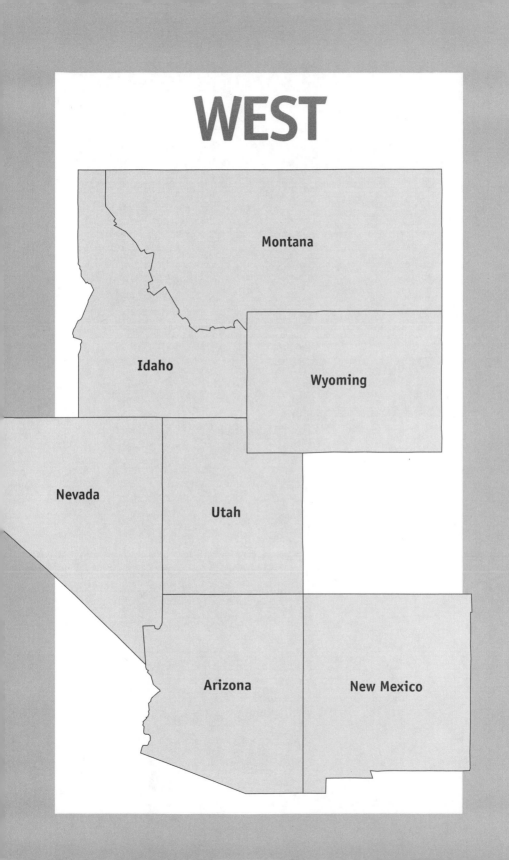

Arizona

Racing Innovations

1940s
Rillito Park Race Track
4502 N. 1st Avenue
Tucson

Rillito Park Race Track is a five-eighths mile-racing track in Tucson. This famous track on the banks of the Rillito River was the birthplace of many racing innovations still in use today. The Southern Arizona Horse Breeders Association (SAHBA), the organization that pioneered quarter horse racing in Tucson, had been hosting races at the Hacienda Moltacqua track since 1941. When Moltacqua was sold in 1943, J. Rukin Jelks volunteered the use of the training track on his ranch. Under the direction of Melville Haskell, an American Quarter Horse Hall of Fame inductee, and Van Smelker, who later became head of the American Quarter Horse Association Performance Department, SAHBA experimented with grading races, weighted handicaps, futurities, derbies and stake races, and photoelectric timers. World-famous sprinters such as Shue Fly, Joe Reed II, Piggin String, Hard Twist, Queenie, and Miss Panama all ran at Rillito.

Tequila Sunrise

Circa 1940
The Arizona Biltmore
2400 E. Missouri Avenue
Phoenix

The Tequila Sunrise is a cocktail made two different ways: the original (tequila, créme de cassis, lime juice, and club soda) and the more popular modern concoction (tequila, orange juice, and grenadine syrup). It was first served here at the Arizona Biltmore, and the cocktail is named for the way it looks after it has been poured into a glass. The grenadine and orange solids settle, creating variations in colors that mimic a sunrise. The history of the drink dates back to about 1940, when a bartender at the Biltmore named Gene Sulit created the drink. A regular guest at the hotel had asked Sulit to surprise him with a refreshing tequila beverage to drink poolside. Sulit blended soda and tequila with Créme de Cassis and fresh lime juice—and the original recipe was born for what would become a memorable cocktail. The drink's name was popularized in the 1973 Eagles single "Tequila Sunrise" and in the 1988 Mel Gibson/Michelle Pfeiffer film also titled *Tequila Sunrise*. Additionally, hip hop group Cypress Hill released a single entitled "Tequila Sunrise."

Idaho

Ezra Pound

1885–1972
314 2nd Avenue S
Hailey
(208)726-9491
www.sunvalleycenter.org

The birthplace of Ezra Pound, one of the twentieth century's greatest and most controversial poets, is now a cultural center. Pound was born in the house on October 30, 1885. He is best known for his poetic works including *Cathay* (1915), *Hugh Selwyn Mauberley* (1921) and *The Cantos* (1925). Many consider him to be the forefather of modern poetry, as he advocated a "freestyle" approach. Pound forever tarnished his reputation when he made anti-American radio broadcasts during World War II while living in Italy. He was arrested as a traitor in 1945 and held in a Washington, D.C., mental institution for more than a decade.

The family of Roberta McKercher had owned his birthplace since the 1930s. The terms of her bequest enabled the Ezra Pound Association to acquire the property in 1998. The house was gifted to the Sun Valley Center for the Arts in 2005. A small plaque near the door identifies it as the birthplace of Pound, who was likely born in an upstairs bedroom. The house, which is on the National Register of Historic Places, is open to the public.

Sacajawea

Circa 1788–circa 1812
Lemhi Valley
Lemhi County

Historians cannot agree on how to spell her name and nobody knows what she looked like—so you can understand why Sacajawea's (Sacagawea) birthplace is an educated (and controversial) guess. Most do agree, however, that Sacajawea was a Shoshone Indian born around 1788 who traveled with the Lewis and Clark expedition from 1804 to 1806. She was the slave wife of the expedition's French Canadian guide, Touissaint Charbonneau; the only woman in the party, she also carried with her an infant son, Jean Baptiste. Her native knowledge and her relations with her own tribe proved invaluable to the explorers. You can see the area believed to be Sacajawea's birthplace here in Lemhi County— some say she was born between Kenney Creek and Agency Creek along the banks of the Lemhi River.

Follow the trail of Sacajawea and Lewis and Clark by beginning at the junction of I-15 and Route 33 to Route 28 and on to Salmon. The Sacajawea Interpretive, Cultural, and Education Center, at 200 Main Street in Salmon, has a visitors center, an outdoor amphitheatre, a monument to Sacajawea, a mile-long interpretive trail, and recreational facilities. Contact them at (208) 756-1188, or visit their Web site at www.sacajaweacenter.org.

Montana

David Lynch

1946–
St. Patrick Hospital
902 N. Orange St.
Missoula

Writer/director David Lynch was born in Missoula on January 20, 1946. Lynch's dark, quirky films typically offer odd, twisting plots; some of his more well-known works include *Eraserhead* (1976), *The Elephant Man* (1980), *Dune* (1984), and *Blue Velvet* (1986). Lynch also found success on TV, most notably for the series *Twin Peaks* (1990). Some of his other more recent films include *Wild at Heart* (1990), *Lost Highway* (1997), and *The Straight Story* (1999). His 2001 film *Mulholland Drive* earned him another Oscar nomination for Best Director (his first had been for *Blue Velvet*).

The State of Montana

1846
Historic Old Fort Benton
Old Fort Park
Fort Benton
(406) 622-5316
www.fortbenton.com/museums/index.htm

Fort Benton, known as the "Birthplace of Montana," is located on the banks of the Missouri River in the "Golden Triangle" area of the state. Established in 1846 as an American Fur Company Trading Post, it is one of the oldest communities in Montana, and the fort one of the oldest buildings. After the discovery of gold in nearby territories, fortune seekers flocked to this riverside town, forging trails into Canada and making it a crucial link between the Missouri River and the Pacific Northwest. Steamboats chugged along the Missouri River to Fort Benton for thirty years until the railroad signaled an end to this town's prominence as the "World's Innermost Port."

This one-time critical outpost earned its place as a National Historic Landmark for its vital role in the expansion of the West. Today, Fort Benton is a haven for history buffs as well as adventurers seeking solitude and beauty along the Upper Missouri National Wild and Scenic River. Visitors to Fort Benton can also explore the Lewis and Clark National Historic Trail, the Nez Perce National Historic Trail, and the gateway to the Upper Missouri River Breaks National Monument.

Nevada

Las Vegas

1855
Old Las Vegas Mormon State Historic Park
500 E. Washington Ave
Las Vegas
(702) 486-3511
http://parks.nv.gov/olvmf.htm

It's a "loaded" question—when was Las Vegas born? It depends on your perspective, but it was probably around 1855. That year, William Bringhurst and twenty-nine fellow Mormon missionaries, the first permanent nonnative settlers in the Las Vegas Valley, built an adobe fort along Las Vegas Creek. They successfully farmed the area by diverting water from the creek. After the mission closed, the Old Las Vegas Mormon Fort served as a ranch, resort, and cement testing facility. Today, a small portion of the original fort wall, part of the bastion, the underground foundation of the ranch, and remnants of the testing lab remain to tell the story of the origins of Las Vegas.

New Mexico

Microsoft

1975
MITS Building
6328 Linn Avenue SE
Albuquerque

Perhaps you've heard of a little software company called Microsoft. In 1975, visionaries William H. "Bill" Gates and Paul Allen were sleeping many nights at the MITS (Micro Instrumentation and Telemetry Systems) building in Albuquerque, working around the clock to refine Altair BASIC. This innovative software would help the Altair 8800, the world's first personal computer, usher in the personal computing revolution. Gates and Allen had a passion for technology and a vision of a computer on every desk and in every home that resulted in the development of Microsoft's groundbreaking software. The original MITS site is now a parking lot—however, in 2006, the city dedicated a plaque at the site marking the birthplace of Microsoft. The company was located there from 1975 to 1979, when it moved to Bellevue, Washington. Visitors can also tour a permanent exhibit on Microsoft and micro-computing called "Startup" at the New Mexico Museum of Natural History and Science, located at 1801 Mountain Road NW. Telephone (505) 841-2800 or visit www.nmnaturalhistory.org.

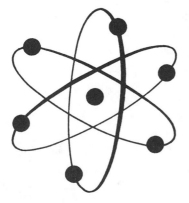

Nuclear Age

1945
Trinity Site
White Sands Missile Range
Almagordo
(575) 678-1134
www.wsmr.army.mil

The Nuclear Age was ushered in here at the Trinity Test Site on July 16, 1945, when the world's first atomic bomb was detonated at 5:29:45 A.M.

Mountain War Time. It is estimated that the 19-kiloton explosion vaporized 100–250 tons of sand, which went up in a massive cloud. A triangular-shaped monument at the Trinity Site on White Sands Missile Range marks Ground Zero, the exact spot of the detonation. The bomb not only led to a quick end to the war in the Pacific, but also opened up a path of technological and medical innovations that would benefit mankind for generations. The 51,500-acre area was declared a National Historic Landmark in 1975. The landmark includes the base camp, where the scientists and support group lived; Ground Zero, where the bomb was placed for the explosion; and the McDonald Ranch House, where scientists assembled the plutonium core to the bomb. Tours to the Trinity Site, conducted twice a year, include everything but the base camp.

Smokey Bear

1950–75
Smokey Bear Historical Park
118 Smokey Bear Boulevard (U.S. Route 380)
Capitan
(575) 354-2748
www.emnrd.state.nm.us/fd/SmokeyBear/SmokeyBearPark.htm

The living symbol of Smokey Bear was "born" in 1950, when a black bear cub was found alone, scared, and suffering with burnt paws and legs after a 17,000-acre forest fire in the Capitan Mountains. Soon, news about the little bear reached the national media, who broadcast the story and caused a nationwide outpouring of sympathy and interest in the little bear's progress. The state game warden, Ray Bell, approached the chief of the Forest Service about presenting the cub to the agency to serve in a publicity program for fire prevention and conservation. The bear got a new home in Washington, D.C.'s National Zoo, and became the living symbol of Smokey Bear. When Smokey died in 1976, he was brought home and buried in the park. Smokey Bear Historical Park was completed in 1979, and features exhibits about forest health, forest fires, wildland/urban interface issues, fire ecology, the history of the Cooperative Forest Fire Prevention Program, and a theatre. There is a plaque at the final resting place of the real Smokey Bear. The park also offers a playground, a picnic area, and the original train depot for the village of Capitan.

Utah

Butch Cassidy

1866–1908

North of Panguitch on Highway 89
Beaver

Born in Circleville (now Beaver) in April 1866, Robert Leroy (Butch Cassidy), went on to become one of the most infamous, legendary outlaws of the Old West. As the leader of Wyoming's "Wild Bunch," Cassidy and his gang robbed banks and trains throughout the west, usually retreating to their "Hole-in-the-Wall" hideout in central Wyoming.

In 1901 Butch fled to Argentina with his partner, the equally notorious Sundance Kid, and a woman named Etta Place. For several years they lived on a ranch there, but soon went back to robbing banks throughout South America. According to many reports, both men were shot to death in 1908 by Bolivian authorities. Cassidy's myth was brought to life by actor Paul Newman in the 1969 film, *Butch Cassidy and the Sundance Kid* (with Robert Redford in the role as the Sundance Kid).

Philo T. Farnsworth

1906–71
Indian Creek
Beaver County

Philo T. Farnsworth, the man who invented the first completely electronic television, was born in a log home in rural Beaver County in 1906. His family moved to Rigby, Idaho, when he was young; they later returned to Utah, and Philo studied at Brigham Young University in Provo from 1923 to 1925. Farnsworth then headed to California with funding from friends and associates to work on his vision of an electronic television system.

In 1927 at his lab in San Francisco, Farnsworth's "Image Dissector" transmitted the very first electronic television image to a charged screen (see page 258). Farnsworth spent the next ten years battling over patent rights with broadcasting pioneer David Sarnoff and renowned RCA engineer Vladimir Zworykin. In 1934, the U.S. Patent Office ruled in favor of Farnsworth, and in 1939 he sold his various patents to RCA. Although Farnsworth was awarded more than one hundred patents related to TV, he did not become famous as "the inventor of television." Today, scholars generally agree that the development of television involved many individuals, but it is also agreed that Farnsworth deserves the biggest slice of the credit.

Kentucky Fried Chicken

1952
3890 South State Street
Salt Lake City

Before his chicken was "finger lickin' good," Colonel Harland Sanders had to cross his fingers for a business deal. It happened here in Salt Lake City in 1952, the site of the world's first Kentucky Fried Chicken (KFC) franchise restaurant (then known as The Original Harman's Kentucky Fried Chicken). It all started when Sanders, fried chicken recipe in hand, traveled from Louisville, Kentucky, in search of a business partner. He approached local Pete Harman, owner of a hamburger place called the Do Drop Inn, who decided to take a chance on the 65-year-old's recipe. On August 4, 1952, they served their first bucket of chicken. The chicken dinner cost $3.50 and included fourteen pieces of chicken, mashed potatoes, rolls and gravy. The same meal would cost about $25 today. Today, KFC is a fast-food phenomenon with more than 11,000 restaurants in 80 countries. In 2004, KFC opened its largest restaurant, featuring a KFC museum, on this site.

Wyoming

Jackalope

1829
Douglas

Douglas has declared itself the jackalope capital of America because, according to legend, the first jackalope was spotted here around 1829. Just what is a jackalope? A fictitious antlered species of rabbit—though try telling the people in Douglas that he never really existed. The legend claims that the jackalope is an aggressive species, willing to use its antlers to fight. Thus, it is also sometimes called the "warrior rabbit." A large statue of a jackalope stands in the town center, and every year the town plays host to Jackalope Day. Jackalope hunting licenses can be obtained from the Douglas Chamber of Commerce, though jackalope season is restricted to the hours of midnight to 2 A.M. on June 31.

J. C. Penney Department Store

1902
722 J. C. Penney Drive
Kemmerer

James Cash Penney's very first retail store, called the "Golden Rule" (the predecessor to J. C. Penney), is affectionately known as the "Mother Store." His journey began in 1902, when twenty-seven-year-old Penney arrived by train here in Kemmerer to start a new business. The sprawling mining town had about one thousand residents, a company store that operated on credit, and twenty-one saloons where customers spent much of their spare cash. Penney based his new business venture on two breakthrough retail ideas: "cash only," and "do unto others as you would have them do unto you." He named his new store the Golden Rule, and by 1912, there were thirty-four Golden Rule stores with sales exceeding $2 million. In 1913, the chain incorporated as the J. C. Penney Company, Inc., and the Golden Rule name was phased out. By 1928, the J. C. Penney Company had 1,023 stores across the country.

PACIFIC

Washington

Oregon

California

Alaska

Hawaii

Alaska

Iditarod

1967
Knik Lake

The Iditarod Trail Sled Dog Race is an annual race in Alaska, where mushers and teams of typically sixteen dogs cover 1,049 miles from Willow to Nome in eight to fifteen days. The race was conceived in 1967 by the late Dorothy G. Page, who is considered the mother of the Iditarod. That year, a short race over the Iditarod Trail foreshadowed the first long-distance race. The full-length race started in 1973 as an event to test the best sled dog mushers and teams, evolving into the highly competitive race it is today. Teams frequently race through blizzards and whiteout conditions, and sub-zero weather and gale-force winds which can cause the wind chill to reach minus-100 degrees F (minus-75 C).

The ceremonial start in the city of Anchorage is followed by the official restart in Wasillia. The original starting point, Knik Lake, is still on the route of the race. However, this was discontinued because the weather frequently hovers around freezing, turning it into a muddy hazard. The race is the most popular sporting event in Alaska, and the top mushers and their teams of dogs are local celebrities; this popularity is credited with the resurgence of recreational mushing in the state since the 1970s. While the yearly field of close to one hundred teams is still largely Alaskan, competitors from fourteen countries have completed the event, including the Swiss Martin Buser, who became the first international winner in 1992.

California

Apple

1976
2066 Crist Drive
Los Altos

In 1975 the paths of two teenagers and former high-school classmates, Bay Area tech-heads Steve Jobs and Steve Wozniak, crossed once again. At the time, Wozniak was working on a primitive forerunner of the personal computer. Hewlett-Packard and Atari showed little interest in the Apple I, but Jobs thought there was something to the device and insisted that he and Wozniak start a company. In 1976, they wound up here in the Jobs family's garage, where Jobs' father removed his car-restoration gear and helped the boys by hauling home a huge wooden workbench that served as their first manufacturing base. The Apple I debuted at the Homebrew Computer Club in April of 1976, but few took it seriously. Little did they know how this computer would impact technology. The Apple Computer Company was incorporated on January 3, 1977, and has gone on to produce generations of user-friendly personal computers and software.

A&W

1919
13 Pine Street
Lodi

In the mood for some root beer? A&W Restaurants, which claims to be the first U.S. franchise restaurant chain, was founded here in the northern California town of Lodi. On a sweltering day in June of 1919, an entrepreneur named Roy Allen was passing through town on the day a homecoming parade was taking place to honor World War I veterans. Seizing the opportunity, he mixed up a batch of ice-cold creamy root beer and sold it from a beverage cart to the thirsty locals. Soon, on this spot, he opened his very first root beer stand—and the rest is history. After the huge success of this first root beer stand, Roy Allen would open a second stand in the nearby city of Sacramento. In 1922, Allen partnered up with Frank Wright, a worker from the first stand in Lodi. Combining their initials, the men officially formed what we know today as A&W Restaurants.

Boysenberry

Knott's Berry Farm
8039 Beach Boulevard
Buena Park
(714) 220-5200
www.knotts.com

Today it's a popular theme park, but Knott's Berry Farm really does have its roots planted in berries, as the name says. In fact, this is where the boysenberry was born. In 1923, a man named Rudolph Boysen crossed a loganberry, raspberry, and a blackberry and called the resulting hybrid the "boysenberry." Boysen never did anything with the boysenberry, and only a few vines languished at his old farm. Ten years later in 1933, a Buena Park farmer named Walter Knott rescued the vines and began cultivating boysenberries right here on what he called Knott's Berry Farm. When the Depression took hold, his wife fixed up a roadside stand and began hawking freshly baked pies, fresh preserves, and delicious home-cooked chicken dinners. So many people came around to visit the stand and buy her wares that Walter thought it would be a good idea to create an Old West Ghost Town so waiting customers would have something to do—and so Knott's Berry Farm was born. Today, Knott's Berry Farm features shows, attractions, rides, and, of course, boysenberry jam.

Cobb Salad

1937
The Brown Derby (former site)
1620–28 N. Vine Street
Hollywood

One night in 1937, Robert H. Cobb, the owner of The Brown Derby restaurant, prowled hungrily in his restaurant's kitchen for a snack. Opening the huge refrigerator, he pulled out a head of lettuce, an avocado, romaine, watercress, tomatoes, cold breast of chicken, a hard-boiled egg, chives, blue cheese, some old-fashioned French dressing—in short, a little of everything. He started chopping, added some bacon, and the Cobb salad was born. It was so good that Sid Grauman (of Grauman's Chinese Theatre), who was with Cobb that midnight, asked the next day for a "Cobb Salad." It was put on the menu and Cobb's midnight invention became an overnight sensation with Derby customers like movie mogul Jack Warner, who regularly dispatched his chauffeur to pick up the mouth-watering salad. The Vine Street landmark restaurant was demolished in 1994.

Disney Cartoons

1928
2725 Hyperion Avenue
Los Angeles

Though it seems now that Walt Disney's partner Ub Iwerks and not Disney himself actually created and animated Mickey Mouse, this is the spot where it all happened in 1928. Disney had opened his first studio here in 1926, and it was also here in the mid-1930s that Disney created the first feature-length cartoon, *Snow White and the Seven Dwarfs*. In fact, the Tudor-style cottages that inspired the look of the dwarfs' home can still be seen around the corner at 2906–12 Griffith Park Boulevard. Though the original studio site is now occupied by a market, a light pole on the sidewalk in the parking lot holds a sign that marks the site as the approximate entrance to the Disney studio.

Clint Eastwood

1930–
St. Francis Memorial Hospital
900 Hyde Street
San Francisco

Clint Eastwood Jr. was born May 31, 1930 at St. Francis Hospital in San Francisco. Eastwood was born the son of a steel worker named Clinton Eastwood Sr., and Margaret Ruth Runner. The Academy Award-winning actor, director, and producer won fame as the "Man With No Name" in Sergio Leone's spaghetti westerns, as well as "Dirty" Harry Callahan in the *Dirty Harry* films. Eastwood's 1992 movie, *Unforgiven*, won Academy Awards for Best Director and Best Picture. Eastwood's recent work as a director on films like *Million Dollar Baby* and *Letters From Iwo Jima* has also earned him worldwide acclaim. The building in which Eastwood was born was renovated in the late 1960s, and the hospital, today known as St. Francis Memorial Hospital, no longer has a maternity ward.

Egg McMuffin

1971
3940 State Street
Santa Barbara

In 1971, a McDonald's restaurant owner/operator named Herb Peterson heard that some other owner/operators had started serving pancakes and doughnuts during breakfast. Peterson believed that McDonald's needed to add breakfast to its menu. But he thought it needed to be something unique—and something that could be eaten by hand, like all other McDonald's products. Experimenting with his version of an eggs Benedict sandwich, Peterson discovered that when he added a piece of cheese it melted with the exact consistency he was looking for. The Egg McMuffin was born. Peterson invited the legendary Ray Kroc to try the product and Kroc gave it the thumbs up. So why did the Egg McMuffin take nearly four years to roll out? Because McDonald's wanted to first perfect pancakes and sausage and add scrambled eggs as a third option so they could offer an entire breakfast menu. A plaque at this McDonald's identifies it as the home of the Egg McMuffin.

French Dip

1918
Philippe the Original
1001 North Alameda Street
Los Angeles

Philippe the Original is one of the oldest and best-known restaurants in Southern California. It was established in 1908 by Philippe Mathieu, the man thought to have created the French dip sandwich. According to one version of the story, one day in 1918, while making a sandwich on a French roll, Mathieu inadvertently dropped it into the roasting pan filled with juice still hot from the oven. The patron, a policeman, said he would take the sandwich anyway and returned the next day with some friends asking for more dipped sandwiches. We don't know if it was dubbed a French dip because of Mathieu's French heritage or for the French roll the sandwich is made on.

Google

1998
Google Garage
232 Santa Margarita Avenue
Menlo Park

No need to search any further—this garage is the site of the first office and birthplace of Google following its conception at Stanford University. It all started in 1998, when Stanford graduate students Larry Page and Sergey Brin dreamed up the search engine concept in Page's dorm room and registered the domain name Google.com. After receiving $1 million in backing, they incorporated Google and moved the operation into this garage at the Menlo Park home of Intel employee Susan Wojcicki, who charged them $1,700 a month to help pay her mortgage. Google's explosive growth prompted the duo to move two more times—first to a small office in Palo Alto, then to their current Googleplex in Mountain View. Wojcicki remained an integral part of the company, eventually becoming Google's vice-president of product management. In fact, she even introduced Brin to her sister Anne, who became his wife. In October 2006, Google purchased the 1,900-sqare-foot home for an undisclosed sum to preserve it as part of their legacy.

Grateful Dead

1965
838 Santa Cruz Avenue
Menlo Park

Back in the early 1960s, a rambling old house stood here, sort of a hostel for various musicians, artists and beatniks. Banjo player Jerry Garcia resided here with lyricist Robert Hunter, and so for many fans, this is the Grateful Dead's spiritual birthplace. Once they started up as The Warlocks (they would change their name soon after), they would play a local pizza place, Magoo's Pizza Parlor, which was located at 639 Santa Cruz Avenue in Menlo Park. Today, that site is a furniture store.

Hewlett-Packard

1939
HP Garage
367 Addison Avenue
Palo Alto

The HP Garage played a large role in the development of Silicon Valley. It began here in Palo Alto, where Stanford University classmates Bill Hewlett and Dave Packard founded Hewlett-Packard (HP) in 1939. The company's first product, built in this Palo Alto garage, was an audio oscillator—an electronic test instrument used by sound engineers. One of HP's first customers was Walt Disney Studios, which bought eight oscillators to develop and test a sound system for their movie *Fantasia*. The home is now a private residence, and is not open to the public. In 2005, HP restored the garage to its 1939 appearance. There is a state historical marker at the site that details the history of the garage.

Hot Fudge Sundae

1906
7007 Hollywood Boulevard
Hollywood

Legend has it that the hot fudge sundae was invented here in 1906 by Clarence Clifton (C. C.) Brown. For many years, the most celebrated names in the entertainment business frequented C. C. Brown's Ice Cream Shop. Many years ago, on days of big movie premieres, fans lined up outside Brown's for hours while stars like Joan Crawford signed autographs. The location closed in 1996.

International House of Pancakes (IHOP)

1958
4301 Riverside Drive
Toluca Lake

The first International House of Pancakes (IHOP) restaurant was opened at this site in 1958 by a man named Al Lapin. The restaurant, whose menu was originally focused on pancakes, quickly grew in popularity and by 1962 there were fifty IHOP locations. Lapin chose the familiar blue roof and A-frame architectural style to distinguish his restaurant. Over the years, a number of items have been added to the menu, and today IHOP has a full lunch and dinner menu. This building, though no longer an IHOP, is the original structure, and still retains its distinctive A-frame style.

Internet

1969
University of California, Los Angeles (UCLA)
Henry Samueli School of Engineering and Applied Science
Boelter Hall
Los Angeles

The next time a Web site crashes, don't feel bad—online bugs have been a part of the Internet since its birth in 1969. It all started with a series of U.S. government computer networking efforts in the 1960s. The Advanced Research Projects Agency (ARPA), created in 1958, funded the creation of the Arpanet— the predecessor of the Internet—to network computer scientists around the country. In 1967, ARPA enlisted the help of Bolt, Beranek, and Newman (BBN) to design, implement and deploy the Arpanet. The first two "switching nodes" were installed at UCLA and Stanford Research Institute in August of 1969. The Internet (or Arpanet) was born on September 2, 1969, when researchers connected the first host computer to the network switch, known as an Interface Message Processor (IMP), and within hours, bits began moving between the UCLA computer and the IMP. The first host-to-host message was delivered over Arpanet on October 29, 1969 at 10:30 P.M. when UCLA engineering professor Leonard Kleinrock and graduate student Charlie Kline attempted to send a message from one computer to a similar unit hundreds of miles away at SRI. The first message was supposed to be the word "login," but the system crashed as they typed in the letter "g"—and so, the first message was "lo"—and the Internet was, prophetically, born with a glitch. By December, two more sites were connected (UC Santa Barbara and the University of Utah) and UCLA was already working to debug the network—a lofty aspiration.

Irish Coffee

1952
Buena Vista Café
2765 Hyde St
San Francisco

"Didn't Irish Coffee come from Ireland?" you may ask. Yes, it did—but the American version originated here in the Buena Vista Café. In 1952, the Buena Vista Café was a saloon where longshoremen and cannery workers sipped whiskey during their breaks. Owner Jack Koeppler decided to offer them something new, and enlisted the aid of international food critic Stanton Delaplane to recreate the Irish Coffee that Delaplane had enjoyed at the Shannon Airport in Ireland. The two worked hard mixing and experimenting, but could not get the taste right nor the cream to float. Koeppler even traveled to Ireland to research the beloved concoction. Eventually, the duo found the perfect Irish whiskey, and they solved the floating cream problem by using aged and frothed cream (suggested by the San Francisco mayor, who was also a prominent dairy owner). The Buena Vista Café, still on the corner of Beach and Hyde Streets, says they make about two thousand Irish Coffees a day. In 2002, they celebrated the 50th anniversary of their famous beverage. They estimate that they have served more than 32 million Irish Coffees over the years, which would make them the largest consumer of Irish whiskey in the U.S.

Jack in the Box

1951
6720 El Cajon Boulevard
San Diego

In 1951, businessman Robert O. Peterson opened the first Jack in the Box restaurant in San Diego on the main east–west thoroughfare leading into city. Equipped with an intercom system and drive-thru window, the tiny restaurant served up hamburgers for just 18 cents, while a large jack-in-the-box clown kept watch from the roof. In 1960, Peterson expanded his restaurants outside California, and today Jack in the Box has 2,100 restaurants in eighteen states. Unfortunately, the original restaurant is no longer there.

Bruce Lee

1940–73
Chinese Hospital
845 Jackson Street
San Francisco

Bruce Lee is the famed high-kicking, fist-fighting movie martial artist who got his start in America as Kato, the sidekick in the 1960s television series *The Green Hornet*. Later, Lee went to Hong Kong and more or less created the genre of kung fu movies. Charismatic and universally famous, Lee reached a pinnacle in 1973 with *Enter The Dragon*. His untimely death before the film's release helped make him an enduring cult figure. Other films featuring Lee include *Way of the Dragon* (1972), *The Big Boss* (1971) and *Marlowe* (1969). A plaque in the lobby identifies the hospital as Bruce Lee's birthplace.

Levi's Blue Jeans

1873
14–16 Battery Street
San Francisco

Blue jeans may be a fashion statement today, but they were born with a purpose at this location in 1873. Twenty years earlier, a young German immigrant named Levi Strauss had come from New York to San Francisco to open a West Coast branch of his brothers' dry goods business. One of his customers was Jacob Davis, a Reno-based tailor who regularly purchased cloth from the wholesale house of Levi Strauss & Co. Davis had a difficult customer who regularly ripped the pockets of the pants that Jacob made for him. Unable to find a way to strengthen the pants, Davis decided to put metal rivets at the points of strain on the pocket corners and the base of the button fly. The unique "riveted pants" were a huge success with many customers. Jacob, fearful that the idea could get stolen, wanted to apply for a patent—but he lacked the $68 required to file the papers. In need of a business partner, he teamed up with Levi Strauss. The two men received patent 139,121 from the U.S. Patent and Trademark Office on May 20, 1873, the official birthday of blue jeans. This is the site of the original Levi Strauss store where the pants were first sold.

Jack London

1876–1916
490 Brannan Street
San Francisco

One of the greatest American writers of the early twentieth century, Jack London was born here on January 12, 1876, as John Griffith Chaney (he adopted the name "London" from his stepfather). Known as America's first working-class writer, London achieved fame with his book *The Call of the Wild* (1903), the story of a family dog that is kidnapped and shipped to the wilds of Alaska where he becomes a sled dog. He also enjoyed success with *The Sea-Wolf* (1904), *White Fang* (1906), and *Martin Eden* (1909), among others. London was famous for his dashing lifestyle and true adventuring spirit—he spent years in the Klondike searching for gold, which inspired some of his best work. He even designed and built his own ship, the *Snark*, and sailed it to the South Pacific. *The Cruise of the Snark* chronicles his adventures. London later retired to his ranch near Sonoma, where he died at age forty. A simple plaque placed by the California Historic Society on the Wells Fargo building at 3rd and Brannan Streets in San Francisco marks his birthplace. London's original home on this site, then 615 Third Street, was destroyed in the fire that followed the earthquake of April 18, 1906.

Mai Tai

1944
Trader Vic's (formerly Hinky Dink's)
9 Anchor Drive
Emeryville

The Mai Tai's origins can be traced not to a lush island paradise, but rather to a small bar near Oakland, California. One afternoon in 1944 at a bar called Hinky Dink's—which would later become Trader Vic's—owner Victor J. Bergeron created a special treat for friends visiting from Tahiti. He mixed Jamaican rum, lime juice, a few dashes of orange curacao syrup, French orgeat, and rock candy syrup. Vic's guests promptly proclaimed "Maita'i roa!" which in Tahitian translates to "Out of this world!" However, another mixologist—Don the Beachcomber of Hollywood—also stakes a claim to the Mai Tai. He has said that in 1933 he created a cocktail based on rum and juice called the Original Beachcomber Rum Concoction—or, the original Mai Tai. In response to this and other competing claims to the origin of the Mai Tai, Victor Bergeron contacted the friends who first tried his concoction and had them sign an affidavit attesting to it origins. In fact, Bergeron's 1947 bartender's guide included the admonition, "Anybody who says I didn't create this drink is a dirty stinker."

Martini

Late 1800s
Amato's Restaurant (formerly Richelieu's Saloon)
414 Ferry St.
Martinez

Whether shaken or stirred, the martini was invented in the late 1800s in a Martinez saloon. A miner who had just struck gold stopped at Julio Richelieu's Saloon on Ferry Street (now the site of Amato's Restaurant) to rest his horse and wet his whistle. He plunked down a sack of gold nuggets and asked for champagne. Richelieu told him that champagne was not available, but that he would make something special instead. Richelieu whipped up an impromptu cocktail, dropped in an olive, and told the customer to enjoy a "Martinez Special." Some say that in its original form, it consisted of two ounces of sweet vermouth, one ounce Old Tom gin, two dashes of maraschino cherry juice, and a dash of bitters. It was shaken with ice, strained, and served with a twist of lemon. The "z" was later dropped, allegedly because it made the name of the drink too difficult to pronounce after actually drinking one. In 1992, a group of proud Martinez locals installed a brass plaque on the corner of Alhambra and Masonic streets to commemorate the birthplace of the martini.

McDonald's

1940
1398 N.E. Street
San Bernardino

Many claim to be the first, but this is where the McDonald's hamburger empire truly started in 1940. Brothers Maurice and Richard McDonald opened the original McDonald's restaurant on this site, serving ribs and pork sandwiches from a barbeque-heavy menu. Within eight years, they reopened as McDonald's Hamburgers, offering the famous paper-wrapped burgers for 15 cents and French fries for 10 cents. After opening eight more outlets, they sold the business to fast-food pioneer Ray Kroc. The original McDonald's is gone, but there is a fascinating museum there that's free to the public. Crammed with thousands of McDonald's items, it'll make you long for the days of the charming and simple original menu.

Today, the oldest functioning McDonald's is located in Downey, California, and it's the last one featuring a red-and-white striped tile exterior. After opening in 1953, it immediately became the national standard for the company's franchises. The building and its sixty-foot neon sign with "Speedee the Chef" are currently eligible for listing on the National Register of Historic Places. It is located at 10207 Lakewood Boulevard at Florence Avenue.

Marilyn Monroe

1926–62
Los Angeles County Hospital
 & USC Medical Center
1200 North State Street
Los Angeles

Norma Jean Mortenson, aka Marilyn Monroe, was born on June 1, 1926, in the charity ward of the Los Angeles County Hospital (now part of the University of Southern California Medical Center). Her grandmother, Della Monroe Grainger, had her baptized Norma Jeane Baker. When Norma Jean was seven years old, her mother, Gladys (Monroe) Baker Mortenson, was hospitalized with paranoid schizophrenia. Norma Jean spent much of her childhood in foster homes and the Los Angeles Orphans' Home Society. In 1944, while she was working at a defense plant, a United States Army photographer noticed her and put her image on posters for the troops. She was on her way to fulfilling her destiny—not just as a movie star, but also as the most famous international sex symbol of the twentieth century. Monroe's acting credits include roles in *Gentlemen Prefer Blondes* (1953), *Some Like It Hot* (1959), and her last film, *The Misfits* (1962). In later years, the hospital's notable Art Deco main building would be used as the exterior of the hospital in the opening titles of the soap opera *General Hospital*, and for the 1998 movie *City of Angels* starring Meg Ryan and Nicolas Cage.

Motel

1925
2223 Monterey Street
San Luis Obispo

Motels are so abundant that we take them for granted. But the first one arose in 1925 at this site about halfway between San Francisco and Los Angeles, and part of it remains standing. The word motel was coined here by architect Arthur Heinemen. Heinemen came up with the term "motel" by combining the words "motor" and "hotel." Construction started in 1925 at a cost of $80,000. When the Motel Inn opened, guests paid only $1.25 per night for a quaint, two-room bungalow with a kitchen and a private adjoining garage. All the units faced a central courtyard with a swimming pool and picnic tables for social gatherings. Though much of the original structure was recently razed, part of it still stands. A plaque on the building notes that the Motel Inn was the first motel.

Murphy's Law

1949
Edwards Air Force Base
Rosamond

Murphy's Law ("If anything can go wrong, it will.") seems to have been born here in 1949, named after Captain Edward A. Murphy. He worked as an engineer on Air Force project MX981 to test the human tolerance for g-forces in a crash. One day, after finding that a sensor had been incorrectly wired, he cursed the technician responsible and said, "If there is any way to do it wrong, he'll find it." Ironically, the project was a success, with the positive outcome indirectly attributed to the manager's commitment to overcoming "Murphy's Law."

PRESIDENTIAL BIRTHPLACE
Richard Nixon

37TH

1913–94
Richard Nixon Library and Birthplace
18001 Yorba Linda Boulevard
Yorba Linda
(714) 993-5075
www.nixonlibraryfoundation.org

Richard Milhous Nixon, the thirty-seventh president of the United States, was born in an upstairs bedroom of a small farmhouse in Yorba Linda on January 9, 1913. He became the first U.S. president to resign, doing so in 1974 after his involvement in the Watergate scandal was revealed.

Nixon served in the navy in World War II and went on to become a U.S. congressman, senator, and vice president under Dwight D. Eisenhower. After losing to John F. Kennedy in the 1960 presidential election, Nixon was elected president in 1968 and reelected in 1972. Nixon ended U.S. involvement in Vietnam and improved relations with the U.S.S.R and China.

Today at his birthplace, the Nixon Library features an extensive collection of memorabilia and photographs of Nixon and his family. The President's VH-3A "Sea King" helicopter is on permanent display outside the museum. The helicopter was in the presidential fleet from 1961 to 1976, and carried President Nixon on his final flight from the White House to Andrews Air Force Base on August 9, 1974. Next to the museum is the original house in which Nixon was born; it is fully preserved and contains many original furnishings. Nixon and his wife, Pat, are laid to rest next to the house.

Plutonium

1941
Gilman Hall
University of California at Berkeley

In February 1941, plutonium was discovered in the third-floor lab (Room 307) here at Gilman Hall by scientists Glenn T. Seaborg, Arthur C. Wahl, Joseph W. Kennedy, and Edwin McMillan. Plutonium was used in the first atomic bombs,

and is still used in bomb making. It has also been used as a compact energy source on space missions, including the Apollo lunar missions. Room 307 was declared a National Historic Landmark in 1966 on the twenty-fifth anniversary of the discovery of plutonium. Gilman Hall was designated a National Historic Chemical Landmark in 1997, and was listed on the National Register of Historic Places in 2003. Today, a plaque in the hall commemorates the historic discovery. Gilman Hall has been used continuously by UC Berkeley's College of Chemistry for eighty years, and today it is occupied by the Department of Chemical Engineering.

Popsicle

1905
Alameda Point
Alameda

In 1905, an eleven-year-old boy named Frank Epperson mixed flavored soda powder and water with a wooden stick and left it outside overnight. The next morning he realized he'd created something new. In 1923, Epperson was running a lemonade stand at Neptune Beach Amusement Park, and he applied for a patent for his unique frozen treat. (The patent documents call the creation "frozen ice on a stick.") First, he called it an Epsicle, which later became Popsicle, because his kids called it "Pop's 'sicle". Within five years, he had sold more than 60 million Popsicles. During the Great Depression, he created the twin Popsicle, which allowed kids to share one for a nickel. Epperson also invented the Fudgsicle and the Creamsicle. Today, Neptune Beach is the site of Alameda Point, formerly the Alameda Naval Air Station. No trace of the park remains.

Reality Television

1973
35 Woodale Lane
Santa Barbara

Reality television was born in this house, the setting for the 1973 public television cinema verité miniseries, *An American Family*. The groundbreaking PBS production, filmed in this house in Santa Barbara, followed the lives of Bill and Pat Loud and their five children. More than 10 million viewers played voyeur as this real-life middle-class drama documented marital tension, divorce, a son's gay lifestyle, and the changing values of American families—more shocking in the early 1970s than today.

Silicon Valley

1956
391 San Antonio Road
Mountain View

The Silicon Valley boom occurred long before the Internet and personal computers. Its birth can be traced to 1956, when William Shockley founded Shockley Semiconductor Laboratory, generally recognized as the birthplace of Silicon Valley. He founded the company to produce silicon-based semiconductors to replace unreliable vacuum tubes—and it is from here that virtually all the valley's dominant companies and technologies would emerge. Years before, Shockley had been the leader of the team that created the transistor, widely considered the most important invention of the century. While trying to found his new company, he was unable to lure his former Bell Labs coworkers to join him—so, he filled his ranks with the best and brightest engineering school grads, including Gordon Moore, Sherman Fairchild, and others who went on to form Silicon Valley companies such as Fairchild Semiconductor and Intel. This building in Mountain View is the original site of Shockley's company, but it has not been preserved. A marker notes the location as the birthplace of Silicon Valley.

John Steinbeck

1902–68
132 Central Avenue
Salinas

John Steinbeck, iconic American author, was born on February 27, 1902, in this beautiful Victorian house. Steinbeck wrote the Pulitzer Prize-winning novel *The Grapes of Wrath* (1939) and *Of Mice and Men* (1937). He was a prolific writer of fiction and nonfiction. Steinbeck received the 1962 Nobel Prize for literature.

The house is now a charming restaurant and a gift shop which features Steinbeck books, including first editions. You can tour the home and view family heirlooms, mementos and personal photographs. The National Steinbeck Center is located nearby at 1 Main Street. For more information, call (831) 796-3833, or visit their Web site at www.steinbeck.org.

Surf Music

1960s
312 Catalina Avenue
Redondo Beach

In the early 1960s, the Bel Air Club on this site became the birthplace of surf music and a hub of the burgeoning youth surf culture. A band called The Belairs often played here in 1961, whipping the beach crowd into a frenzy with their new sound. The band's catchy instrumentals caught on—especially the seminal surf tune, "Mr. Moto," which became a local hit and even inspired the Beach Boys. An office building is now at the former site of the club.

Taco Bell

1962
7112 Firestone Boulevard
Downey

Few people know that the Bell in the name Taco Bell comes from the last name of the founder. In 1962, Glen Bell opened the first Taco Bell restaurant here in Downey. Two years later, the first Taco Bell franchise was sold. After expanding Taco Bell around the world, Glen Bell would eventually sell the company for $130 million. The original building is still standing, but it's occupied by a local taco stand.

Television

1927
Farnsworth's Green Street Lab
202 Green Street
San Francisco

Philo Taylor Farnsworth (see page 235), the "Genius of Green Street," invented the television here in 1927. Farnsworth moved to San Francisco in 1926 to develop an electronic television. In his lab here on Green Street he invented and patented the first operational television system on September 7, 1927. The twenty-one-year-old inventor and several dedicated assistants successfully transmitted the first all-electronic television image, a major breakthrough that brought the practical form of this invention to mankind. A state historical marker at the site commemorates his invention.

Video Games

1972
157 W. El Camino Real
Sunnyvale
Rooster T. Feathers (formerly Andy Capp's Tavern)

Pacman, Mario Bros., Sonic . . . all your favorite video game heroes can trace their roots to a cozy bar in northern California called Andy Capp's Tavern (now the Rooster T. Feathers comedy club). It was here in 1972 that Atari founder Nolan Bushnell field-tested *Pong*, the first commercially successful video game.

Bushnell had been dabbling in video games since playing *Spacewar* on a DEC mainframe in the late 1960s. After the failure of his game *Computer Space*, he was inspired to craft a more consumer-friendly product after seeing a Magnavox Odyssey ping-pong video game at a consumer electronics show. Sensing its potential, he directed Atari engineer Al Alcorn to develop an improved version, called simply *Pong*. Bushnell installed it at the tavern and the game was an immediate hit, with lines running out the door to try the new 25-cent contraption. In fact, the tavern manager once thought the machine had broken, when it was actually just stuffed with quarters. Bushnell would go on to revolutionize home console systems with the introduction of the Atari 2600.

Wienerschnitzel

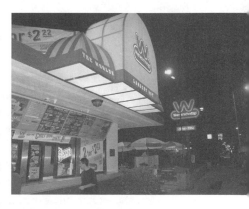

1961
900 W. Pacific Coast Highway
Wilmington

In 1961, amidst the fervor of the burgeoning fast-food industry dominated by hamburgers, entrepreneur John Galardi wanted to stand out. The twenty-three-year-old businessman had an idea: hot dogs! Soon after, the first der Wienerschnitzel opened along Pacific Coast Highway in Wilmington. A year later, Galardi opened a second restaurant, introducing the signature red A-frame roof—a breakthrough design that also helped pioneer the drive-thru concept in Southern California. Since then, the company has changed its name to simply Wienerschnitzel and has expanded to more than 300 stores in ten states and Guam. A plaque at the original restaurant details its history.

Hawaii

PRESIDENTIAL BIRTHPLACE
Barack Obama

1961–
Honolulu

44TH

Barack Hussein Obama, the forty-fourth president of the United States—and first African American president—was born in Honolulu on August 4, 1961. There has been some discrepancy about the actual site of Obama's birthplace however. A UPI article from November 4, 2008, says Obama was born at Queen's Medical Center: "Obama described his birth at Queen's Medical Center in Hawaii Aug. 4, 1961, to a young white woman from Kansas and a father of Luo ethnicity from Nyanza Province in Kenya, as an all-American story transcending orthodox racial stereotypes and experience." However, a December 3, 2008, article in the *Honolulu Advertiser* suggested Obama was born at Kapi'olani Medical Center. The article, which talked about tourists visiting Hawaii to view Obama's birthplace, stated: "His tours swing by Noelani Elementary School, where Obama went to kindergarten. And past his birthplace, Kapi'olani Medical Center for Women and Children." Obama's half sister also said that Obama was born at Kapi'olani Medical Center. So which place was it? Interestingly, the issue has yet to be officially resolved. Obama's birth certificate, at least the version that was released to the public, does not state the specific hospital in which he was born.

Surfing

1500s
Waikiki Beach
Oahu

Hundreds of years before the Beach Boys went "Surfin' USA," surfing (or "he'e nalu") was born in Hawaii. An integral part of Hawaiian culture, myth, and religion, some ancient Hawaiian chants tell of great surfing feats dating back to 1500, and ancient petroglyphs carved into lava rock depict surfers. But the earliest written record of surfing is from a 1779 journal entry of Captain James Cook, who related that "the natives, taking each a long narrow board . . . place themselves on the summit of the largest surge, by which they are driven along with amazing rapidity toward the shore." In the early 1800s, Christian missionaries outlawed surfing, but the sport experienced a revival in the early twentieth century. On Waikiki Beach, surfer George Freeth amazed tourists with his astonishing feats; author Jack London wrote about surfing and ignited worldwide interest; and Alexander Hume Ford helped found the Outrigger Canoe Club. But the beloved father of modern surfing was Duke Paoa Kahanamoku (1890–1968), a Waikiki native credited with ushering in modern surfing. Kahanamoku introduced surfing around the world through his travels as an Olympic gold-medal swimmer.

Oregon

Nike

1957
University of Oregon
Hayward Field
Eugene

On your marks, get set—just do it! The story of Nike, appropriately enough, starts on a running track. It all began in 1957 at the University of Oregon's Hayward Field. Future Nike co-founders Phil Knight and Bill Bowerman met when Knight became a runner on Coach Bowerman's team. Both shared a dissatisfaction with American running shoes, so in 1964 they formed Blue Ribbon Sports as a way distribute shoes from Japanese shoemaker Onitsuka Tiger—often selling products from the trunk of a car.

In 1968, Knight and Bowerman changed their company's name to Nike, and soon after began manufacturing their own shoes based on Bowerman's lightweight designs. His most famous innovation was the "waffle" soles he invented by shaping rubber on the waffle iron in his kitchen in 1972; that, in turn, led to the famous "moon shoe," named for the resemblance between the sole's imprint and astronaut footprints.

In 1973, University of Oregon star and American record holder Steve Prefontaine became the first runner to use Nike brand shoes. Nike's athlete endorsements and product tie-ins, most notably with basketball legend Michael Jordan and his "Air Jordan" shoes, helped the company become the top athletic shoe maker in the world.

Today, the headquarters for Nike is located near Beaverton on Bowerman Drive, named in homage to the company's co-founder.

U-Haul, Retail

1945
8816 SE Foster Road
Portland

While the actual birthplace of U-Haul is located in Ridgefield, Washington, (see page 267), the retail birthplace of U-Haul can be found in Portland. There's a marker at the U-Haul location recognizing it as the first U-Haul retail location. The history of U-Haul goes back to 1945, when twenty-nine-year-old Leonard Shoen co-founded the company with his wife, Anna Mary Carty.

Washington

Kurt Cobain

1967–94
Grays Harbor Community Hospital
915 Anderson Drive
Aberdeen

Grunge rocker Kurt Cobain was born to Don and Wendy Cobain at Grays Harbor Community Hospital on February 20, 1967. Cobain formed the band Nirvana in 1987 with another local musician, Krist Novoselic. Within two years, Nirvana had become a fixture of the burgeoning Seattle grunge scene. In 1991, the arrival of Nirvana's "Smells Like Teen Spirit" marked the beginning of a dramatic shift of popular rock music away from the dominant genres of the 1980s, which included big-hair glam metal, arena rock, and dance-pop. The industry eventually christened the song the "anthem of a generation," and, with it, Cobain was labeled a spokesman for Generation X. During the last years of his life, Cobain struggled with drug addiction and the media pressures surrounding him and his wife, Courtney Love. On April 8, 1994, Cobain was found dead in his home in Seattle, the victim of what was officially ruled a self-inflicted shotgun wound to the head. Cobain remains an iconic figure today, still influencing youth culture from beyond the grave.

Flying Saucers

1947
Mount Rainier

On June 24, 1947, above Mount Rainier, Seattle pilot Kenneth Arnold experienced what is considered to be the first modern sighting of UFOs, spurring the birth of the term, "flying saucer." Arnold was piloting a single-engine Cessna, and he was in search of a missing military transport plane. At about 3 P.M. he spotted objects zooming in and out of formation above Mount Rainier, later describing them as nine brilliant, boomerang-shaped "discs." (The term "flying saucer" was coined by a reporter writing about the sighting.) He claimed to have clocked them as they flew between Mount Rainier and Mount Adams, estimating their speed at 1,200 mph. Arnold described each object being as big as a DC-4 passenger plane, "flat like a pie pan," and so shiny that it reflected the sun like a mirror. The story enthralled the public, but was dismissed by the military. An Army spokesman in Washington, D.C., commented at the time: "As far as we know, nothing flies that fast except a V-2 rocket, which travels at about 3,500 miles an hour—and that's too fast to be seen." Despite this, accounts of Arnold's sighting spread around the world and spawned a new interest in the subject of "flying saucers." Of course, it didn't end there . . . on the afternoon of July 4, 1947, Frank Ryman, an off-duty U.S. Coast Guard yeoman, shot what is believed to be one of the first photographs purported to be of a flying saucer from the yard of his home in Lake City, north of Seattle.

Jimi Hendrix

1942–70
5801 Carson Avenue S
Seattle

Guitar great Jimi Hendrix was born on November 27, 1942, in Seattle while his father was in army camp in Oklahoma. His mother, seventeen-year-old Lucille Hendrix, named him Johnny Allen Hendrix at birth. Soon after his birth, his mother put him in the temporary care of friends of the family, a couple in California. On his release from the army his father, James Allen "Al" Hendrix, retrieved him and renamed him James Marshall Hendrix in memory of his deceased brother, Leon Marshall Hendrix.

Hendrix went on to become one of the most influential guitarists in rock history. After initial success in Europe, he achieved fame in the United States following his 1967 performance at the Monterey Pop Festival. Later, Hendrix headlined the iconic 1969 Woodstock Festival, where his era-defining rendition of "The Star-Spangled Banner" became an instant classic. Hendrix died on September 18, 1970, in London of a drug overdose. As far as visiting the hospital, it's a little too late for that. In March 1956, the health department closed the facility down; the Georgetown building was sold for $109,500, and demolished soon afterwards.

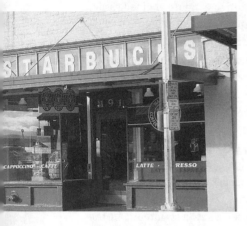

Starbucks

1971
Pike Place Market
1912 Pike Place
Seattle

Got your morning Starbucks fix? Good—then you'll have the energy to learn how Starbucks went from a slow-brewing notion to a percolating success. In 1971, English teacher Jerry Baldwin, history teacher Zev Siegel, and writer Gordon Bowker joined together to open the first Starbucks at Pike Place Market in downtown Seattle. They derived the name "Starbucks" from Herman Melville's classic novel *Moby Dick*.

The original Starbucks location, operating from 1971–76, was at 2000 Western Avenue. Drawing inspiration from Alfred Peet of Peet's Coffee and Tea, the founding trio originally opened the store to sell premium coffee beans and specialty coffee equipment. Siegel actually worked in Peet's Berkeley, California, store for a few months to learn the trade and even modeled the design of the first Starbucks after Peet's popular Berkeley coffee house (with his permission). Peet supplied the coffee beans for roasting in their new store, but Starbucks soon began buying its own beans directly from growers.

In the original logo—now only found in this original store—the siren was topless, which stirred up controversy when the company brought back the logo in 2006 to celebrate its 35th anniversary. Today, visitors can see the store and its sign in original form thanks to the Pike Place Market's strict historic design guidelines.

U-Haul

1945
5586 Pioneer St.
Ridgefield

The idea for U-Haul came in 1945, when co-founders L. S. "Sam" Shoen and his wife, Anna Mary Carty Shoen, tried to rent a trailer to move from Los Angeles to Portland. Nobody offered such a service, so they had to take only what they could fit in the car. The Shoens figured they weren't the only ones who needed to rent a trailer from one location to leave at another. So, the family made the drive to Portland, along the way dreaming up the concept of the U-Haul Trailer Rental System. They launched U-Haul that summer, buying the first trailers from welding shops and private owners. Soon, the first trailer was offered for rent from a service station. By the end of 1945, thirty were available in Portland, Vancouver, and Seattle. Their visionary business model sparked the mobility of the population across the U.S. and Canada. The orange U-Haul trailers were the covered wagons of the new pioneers, and an industry was born. In 2005, a commemorative sign was erected to mark the birthplace of U-Haul. The original building was moved to make way for the Ridgefield National Wildlife Refuge.

Acknowledgments

Thank you to Matthew Sjoquist for his invaluable help on this project, and also to my friends at Cohn & Wolfe in Los Angeles. I also would like to acknowledge Hampton Inn Hotels for allowing me to be a part of the award-winning Save-A-Landmark program, specifically Hidden Landmarks. To know that a corporation does so much in the way of preservation and historic education is impressive and to be a part of it is a privilege. At Hampton Inn, I thank Judy Christa-Cathey, Kendra Walker, Tori Roberson, Sheryl Shelton, Sharon Fells, Charmaine Easie-Samuel, and the rest of their fine team. It is such a pleasure to work with you. I encourage readers to visit www.hamptonlandmarks.com to experience all that Hampton Inn is doing.

I appreciate the work of my editor, Kyle Weaver, and everyone else at Stackpole who contributed to the production of this book, including editorial assistant Brett Keener, copyeditor Diane Reed, designer Beth Oberholtzer, paginator Kerry Handel, production manager Cathy Craley, and art directors Caroline Stover and Tessa Sweigert.

And to my family—Jean, Charlie, Claire, and Mom—words never seem enough, but I love you immeasureably.

Index

Picture Credits

Library of Congress

George W. Bush (4), Susan B. Anthony (10), George H. W. Bush (12), Nathaniel Hawthorne (15), John F. Kennedy (16), Edgar Allan Poe (18), Franklin Pierce (24), Daniel Webster (25), George M. Cohan (26), Chester A. Arthur (29), Calvin Coolidge (30), Joseph Smith (31), Brigham Young (32), John Philip Sousa (38), Grover Cleveland (44), Stephen Foster (46), Millard Fillmore (55), Franklin D. Roosevelt (66), Theodore Roosevelt (67), Walt Whitman (70), James Buchanan (73), Honus Wagner (84), Pearl S. Buck (85), Jimmy Carter (99), Ty Cobb (99), Martin Luther King (103), Andrew Johnson (108), Wright Brothers plane (107), James K. Polk (109), William Clark (114), Robert E. Lee (117), Zachary Taylor (122), John Tyler (123), George Washington (124), Woodrow Wilson (125), Bill Clinton (129), Jefferson Davis (131), Abraham Lincoln (134), George Washington Carver (144), Harry S. Truman (148), Mark Twain (149), Ronald Reagan (160), Herbert Hoover (168), George Custer (182), James A. Garfield (183), Ulysses S. Grant (184), Warren G. Harding (184), Benjamin Harrison (186), Rutherford B. Hayes (186), William T. Sherman (189), William H. Taft (190), Gerald Ford (206), Hubert Humphrey (213), Dwight D. Eisenhower (216), Lyndon B. Johnson (218), Butch Cassidy (234), Richard M. Nixon (255)

Library of Congress, Carl van Vechten Collection

Eugene O'Neill (63), Erskine Caldwell (98), Dizzy Gillespie (111), William Faulkner (138), F. Scott Fitzgerald (177), Orson Welles (197)

National Archives

Bob Dylan (176)

About the Author

C hris Epting, born at New York Hospital in New York City on December 22, 1961, lives in Huntington Beach, California, with his wife and two children. He is the author of sixteen books, including *James Dean Died Here*, *Road-side Baseball*, and *Led Zeppelin Crashed Here*. He travels the country extensively, appearing on TV and radio as the national spokesman for Hampton® Hotels' Save-A-Landmark® program, and is host of the syndicated radio program "The Pop Culture Road Trip."